African Migrations Research

AFRICAN MIGRATIONS RESEARCH
INNOVATIVE METHODS AND METHODOLOGIES

EDITED BY
Mohamed Berriane
and Hein de Haas

AFRICA WORLD PRESS
TRENTON | LONDON | CAPE TOWN | NAIROBI | ADDIS ABABA | ASMARA | IBADAN | NEW DELHI

AFRICA WORLD PRESS
541 West Ingham Avenue | Suite B
Trenton, New Jersey 08638

Copyright © 2012 Mohamed Berriane and Hein de Haas
First Printing 2012

Book design: Jacqueline Smith
Cover design: Saverance Publishing Services

Cover photograph by Alpha Abebe (http://www.alphaabebe.com/)
'In memory of Itaytay, a woman whose legacy continues to travel'.

Library of Congress Cataloging-in-Publication Data

African migrations research : innovative methods and methodologies / edited by Mohamed Berriane and Hein de Haas.
    p. cm.
    Includes bibliographical references and index.
    ISBN 978-1-59221-893-6 (hard cover) -- ISBN 978-1-59221-894-3 (pbk.) 1. Emigration and immigration--Research--Methodology. 2. Africans--Migrations. 3. Africa--Emigration and immigration. I. Berriane, Mohamed. II. Haas, Hein de, 1969-
    JV8790.A65 2012
    304.82096--dc23
                    2012007057

Table of Contents

Chapter 1

═══>◦◦◦═══

NEW QUESTIONS FOR INNOVATIVE MIGRATION RESEARCH

Mohamed Berriane *and* Hein de Haas

Over the past 15 years, African migration has become a hot topic for debate and research in Europe as well as in Africa. However, this interest has remained largely limited to the northbound migration flows originating from sub-Saharan Africa, either towards the Maghreb countries or, through them, towards Europe. This is striking in light of the fact that most African migrations are not directed towards the global North, but towards other African countries, while there is also substantial African migration to other world regions, such as the Gulf countries and the Americas (cf. Bakewell and de Haas 2007).

The excessive media coverage of supposedly Europe-bound African migration through the Sahara and Mediterranean is a key factor explaining the heavy over-representation of this migration flow in the mindsets of researchers and policy makers. It obscures numerically much more important forms of migration *within* the continent, and contributes to the 'myth of invasion' (de Haas 2007).

This myth is underpinned by perceptions of 'hordes' of 'hungry' sub-Saharan migrants trying 'desperately' to enter Ceuta and Melilla, two Spanish enclaves on the northern Moroccan coast; imagined 'mass' arrivals on the Italian island of Lampedusa; and images of numerous sub-Saharan migrants being intercepted off the coast of the Canary Islands.

The recurrence of this myth of invasion is commonly fuelled by electoral campaigns in Europe and the generally journalistic and, at best, anecdotal nature of the evidence. This has led to a situation in which even many academic researchers largely base their perceptions of African migration on media images and generally refrain from rigorously applying methods and methodologies which would allow for an improved understanding of the nature, volume and trends of African migration.

Yet, we have to acknowledge the many methodological challenges facing researchers of African migration based outside and, particularly, inside Africa. Because of financial and institutional constraints, and the lack of funding for independent academic research, much research on African migration is largely defined, steered and funded by the institutions and interests of wealthy, 'Northern' countries or international organisations. Hence, the research and output tends to reflect their largely short-term control- and security-focused agendas. African migration research has tended to reproduce and justify Northern preoccupations with regards to migration, as is exemplified in the one-sided focus on trafficking, smuggling and illegal migration to Europe in many scientific and most policy accounts of African migration.

The high dependency on commissioned research is a more general problem of migration research, which is often guided by the short-term policy interests to 'solve' what are perceived as 'migration problems' or 'migration challenges', rather than trying to achieve a more profound understanding of the nature, causes and consequences of migration. Because policy-focused funding tends to be limited and short-term, there is little room to explore alternative conceptualisations and methodologies which would allow a more fundamental critique of the way migration is conventionally conceived in policy and research.

The biased nature and the weak empirical basis of much African migration research is the original motivation to compile this volume. This aim of this book is to contribute to the development of independent reflections on research *methodologies* and, particularly, the relationship between methodologies and our conceptualisation of migration issues both inside and outside Africa. This should contribute to the elaboration of a migration research agenda which is driven by relevant empirical and theoretical questions rather than by policy concerns focused on immigration control, or by ill-founded hysteria around alleged 'mass' migration from Africa to Europe.

A major difficulty facing African migration research is the lack of appropriate official and social scientific data as well as the frequent absence of appropriate sampling frameworks in the form of census or survey data. Official migration statistics are either patchy or simply non-existent and generally fail to capture most flows. There is a general absence of systematic research on emigrants and, particularly, immigrants in African countries. Moreover, the undocumented and irregular nature of much African migration, as well as the often vulnerable position of migrants within Africa, makes it difficult to approach and interview migrants. This renders it even more problematic to identify and sample migrants for quantitative or qualitative research. For these reasons, migration in Africa (and, in fact, many other less-developed regions of the world) does not easily lend itself to traditional research methodologies, such as large-scale, representative sample surveys. This partly explains why Africa has remained a blank on most migration maps.

In order to begin to fill some of these gaps, the chapters in this book show how several less-conventional and often cost-effective methods can significantly contribute to mapping migration in Africa and other less-than-ideal research environments, and how these methods can help to obtain valuable empirical data in contexts where appropriate sampling frames are often absent, migrant populations are difficult to identify or approach, and resources are limited. The book also addresses the more fundamental methodological and epistemological questions underpinning the different methods of data collection. Although the chapters are based on research conducted in Africa, the methods presented in this volume are also applicable to migration research beyond the continent and in other fields of social scientific inquiry.

Preceding these empirical chapters, Chapter 2 lays out the general epistemological framework for this book. Its author, Stephen Castles, argues that we need to make a fundamental distinction between *methods* and *methodology* of research. These terms are commonly confused, but while they are closely connected, they are not the same thing. While research methods pertain to the specific techniques used to collect and analyse data, methodology refers to epistemological questions and the underlying logic of research. Castles argues that while most empirical studies specify the methods of data collection, migration researchers should also pay sufficient attention to methodological questions which address whether and how 'objective' or 'factual' knowledge can be generated.

Although methods and methodology are analytically distinct, the use of particular methods is intimately linked to methodological and epistemological assumptions or beliefs, though the latter are rarely made explicit in migration research. Methodology involves the systematic application of epistemology to research situations, and a particular methodological standpoint has fundamental consequences for the choice of methods. For instance, this becomes evident in disciplinary disputes about 'appropriate' ways of conducting research, such as the oft-contested need for representative sampling or the distinction between so-called 'quantitative' and 'qualitative' approaches. Castles suggests strategies to ensure that the choice of particular methods is better informed by the specific research questions at stake. While he insists that migration research should pay more attention to methodological questions, he also emphasises that the various research methods do not necessarily exclude one another and that combining and triangulating different methods can improve our knowledge and understanding of migration.

Following the general epistemological framework laid out in the second chapter, the eight empirical chapters highlight the distinctions and linkages between methodological considerations and the various methods that are used and often combined in the same study.

Most chapters are written by early-career scholars based in African universities whose studies – all based on original qualitative or quantitative empirical research – show how innovative methods of migration research help map new and fascinating dimensions of African migration. The chapters are based on a selection of papers that were originally presented at a workshop on African migrations organised by the International Migration Institute (IMI) of the University of Oxford, and the Mohammed V University (Morocco) in Rabat from 26–29 November 2008. This bilingual English/French workshop was attended by approximately fifty participants from across Africa, Europe and beyond, and twenty papers, selected on the basis of an open call, were presented.

In brief, the chapters in this volume offer fresh evidence on rapidly changing migration patterns on the African continent. They do this by presenting innovative methodologies and methods of migration research used in eight different case studies in a range of countries across the continent. This volume brings together work from both Anglophone and Francophone researchers, allowing for a synthesis and comparison of methods across a range of academic disciplines while bridging linguistic and concomitant methodological divides, which have traditionally obstructed African migration research.

In Chapter 3, Mohamed Berriane, Mohamed Aderghal and Lahoucine Amzil present their study of recent migration between Morocco and Andalusia (Spain). They used a mix of quantitative and qualitative methods and a multi-sited methodology comprising the simultaneous collection of data in origin and destination areas. The authors argue that such methods are necessary in order to capture the diversification and fluidity of contemporary mobility and the increasingly transnational nature of migrants' lives, in which movement no longer links one origin and destination country but involves networks straddling several countries. While international migration research has long been locked in a unidirectional spatial logic that has fixated movements in a single pairing of origin and destination, the multi-sited and multi-method approach used in this study is better able to capture migration empirically as a social process. By doing so, the study shows how Morocco and Spain have become articulating elements of a larger West-Mediterranean migratory sub-system which involves constant mobility between many places, challenging classic migration paradigms. The study also shows how school surveys can be used as an alternative sampling method in the absence of official sampling frameworks.

Although remittances sent back home by migrants abroad have recently attracted massive attention from governments and international institutions such as the World Bank as a potential development resource, most analyses are based on official, national statistics on remittances flows or, in some instances, on large-scale representative household surveys in origin countries. Such methods generally fail to capture the underlying motives for remitting as well as the transnational social and economic ties between remittance senders and receivers. In order to address some of these gaps, in Chapter 4, Una Okonkwo Osili aims to improve understanding of remittances sent from the US to Nigeria based on a matched sampling surveying technique. This study used a unique data set – the US–Nigeria Migration Survey – both to investigate the likelihood that migrants initiate community transfers ('collective remittances'), as well as to try to find out the total amount sent towards community development projects in hometowns.

A central research goal of the US–Nigeria Migration Survey was to illuminate the motivations for migrants' remittances using a matched sample of migrant and origin households. Previous empirical work has dealt with the transfer of resources between the migrant and the origin family, using data on the migrant or using data obtained solely from the household of origin. However, theory suggests that a complete understanding of remittances and other intra-family transfers requires another methodological approach, simultaneously collecting data on both sending and receiving households. The matched sampling involved a first-round survey in the US and a second-round survey in Nigeria with a sub-sample of households connected to US-based households. The results indicate that migrants tend to send community-related transfers to more developed hometowns, and not to less developed communities, which does not seem to support the predictions of the altruistic model of transfers. It would have been impossible to attain these insights using conventional surveying methods.

While there has recently been a surge in attention given to trans-Saharan migration, this focus has remained rather Eurocentric and focused on what is perceived as a massive rise in the number of sub-Saharan migrants heading towards Europe. However, Julien Brachet's study in Chapter 5 on (trans) Saharan migration in Niger demonstrates that migration researchers need to pay more attention to the place and importance of the 'journey' in migration. Brachet argues that the way in which the subject of 'migration' is approached empirically has a profound effect on the resulting data, but also that the choice of particular methods itself reflects the way migration is conceptualised. Whereas migration studies have long reduced migration to the fixed times and places of individuals' departure and arrival, this study reconceptualises transit as a significant part of, or moment in, the migratory process. It looks at the illegal taxations of migrants by Nigerian state officials along transit routes in the region of Agadez, and uses 'on-the-move' methods to allow for the production of valuable empirical knowledge. While acknowledging the importance of combining qualitative and quantitative methods, the study discusses the practical limits and ethical concerns involved in the oft-attempted quantification of transit flows. This also highlights that methodological choices cannot be discussed in isolation from the political dimension of research into migrations between sub-Saharan Africa, the Maghreb and Europe.

Based on fieldwork conducted in South Africa, in Chapter 6 Darshan Vigneswaran presents an innovative sampling and data collection strategy employed to study the use of corruption in the enforcement of immigration law in a context of predominantly irregular migration. The growing presence of large populations of undocumented and/or disenfranchised people in Africa exacerbates and complicates relationships between 'states' and 'citizens'. The author argues that governments do not simply struggle to define and limit informal migration, but that migration is also increasingly informalising African governance structures. While officials may feel less obligated to act within their official mandates, 'informal' migrants also possess strong incentives to disengage from formal governance structures, which may encourage corrupt behaviours. The chapter argues that these dynamics and the 'informalisation' of migration compel us to reorient the methodologies we use to study the relationships between governance, informality and migration.

The concealed nature of corrupt behaviour, and the disincentives potential respondents face to provide accurate accounts, confound conventional research methods. To address this need for appropriate methods, this chapter presents an experimental data collection technique dubbed as 'incident reporting'. This method combines a systematic spatio-temporal procedure for sampling observed instances of immigration enforcement with a process of using analytical benchmarks to categorise and code observations of informal behaviour by officials, using GIS (Geographic Information Systems) analysis. While paying attention to several safety and ethical issues, the chapter suggests that incident reporting could usefully be incorporated into the study of migration governance across multiple research sites in Africa.

As mentioned above, a lack of research funding and infrastructure is a formidable obstacle to implementing large-scale migration surveys in poor countries. However, as Agbada Mobhe Mangalu shows in Chapter 7, on the basis of his comparative analysis of the nature, direction and selectivity of Congolese migrations toward Africa, Europe, America and Asia, there is a potential to partly fill this gap with relatively modest means. He argues that the lack of nationwide studies on migration from the Democratic Republic of Congo (DRC) explains why knowledge about Congolese migration has remained piecemeal and fragmented. This study shows how relatively small-scale quantitative surveys can make a valuable contribution to understanding contemporary African migration dynamics even when criteria of national representativity are not met. This particularly applies when the primary aim is to compare groups. The study draws on a survey carried out in Kinshasa, covering a random sample of 945 households and 992 individual biographies. It suggests that most migrants move to other African countries rather than other continents. With regards to selectivity, the study shows that low-skilled single male migrants primarily moving for economic reasons tend to stay within Africa, whereas highly skilled, married female individuals and those migrating for educational purposes are more likely to migrate out of Africa.

Isaïe Dougnon's study in Chapter 8 on migration by Dogon and Songhai communities from Mali to Ghana highlights the added value of historical comparative research. The tendency, particularly in anthropological research on African migration, has been to study a single community, at a particular site and at a particular historical

8

moment. Instead, Dougnon compares migration dynamics as they have manifested over time and across ethnic groups. The historical perspective of his research allows Dougnon to show how and why the character of Dogon and Songhai migration changed from 'migration for prestige' to 'migration for survival'. Moreover, his comparative approach shows the diverging ways that the two ethnic groups have adapted to the Ghanaian context, each specialising in fields in which they felt they had the most talent and experience. The Dogon favoured colonial work over self-employment, and in the post-colonial period they found themselves in an unenviable economic situation, while the Songhai, who excelled in commerce, became key economic players in the fuel and building sectors, and the trade in foodstuffs. Dougnon's comparative approach thus elucidates the configuration of the ethnic division of labour within the immigrant community in colonial and post-colonial Ghana as a whole.

The limited availability of resources for conducting representative surveys has inspired Chapter 9 by Tara Polzer, in which she explores the potential value of non-random surveys. Based on an empirical study conducted in South Africa, which consisted of data collection on migrants through service-provider NGOs, Polzer discusses the added value and limitation of the use of non-random surveys in comparison with more conventional methods using random sampling. Conducting methodologically defensible, logistically feasible and affordable large-scale national surveys of migrants is a serious challenge particularly in many African countries. Based on the Migrant Rights Monitoring Project (MRMP) conducted in South Africa, this chapter outlines the pros and cons of working with and through NGOs which provide services to migrants in order to conduct a national survey on migrants' access to basic public services.

The chapter argues that although this method does not result in a sample which is representative, it can nevertheless generate useful knowledge. Some of the resulting limitations are outlined, including urban bias, nationality bias, documentation bias, gender bias and vulnerability bias. Polzer argues that these biases are problematic and we need to be aware of them, but that they are not necessarily much greater than is the case with more conventional methods. Furthermore, the chapter asserts that there are strong benefits of such NGO-linked methodology. Apart from being cost-effective, such benefits include the formation of active and collaborative networks among organisations in the migrant rights sector; research capacity building within this sector; and the direct use of empirical data in local and national advocacy work. This equally exemplifies the inherently normative and political nature of methodological choices.

While misconceptions about irregular migration are commonly linked to the practical difficulties involved in identifying and approaching irregular migrants as well as the informal sectors in which they often operate, the mobility of children in Africa is perhaps even less understood. In his anthropological study in Chapter 10 on the mobility of children in West Africa, Abdou Ndao presents innovative methods allowing the study of this important form of African migration. The author argues that despite frequent attention paid to the mobility of children in West Africa, there is a lack of pertinent empirical data which explains why dominant ideas about this migratory phenomenon are based more on supposition than empirical knowledge. The ethnographic study presented in this chapter aimed to fill part of this gap. The study involved several institutions including West African development NGOs, searching to understand how the mobility of children and young people is organised in West Africa, notably in Bénin, Togo, Ghana and Nigeria. More specifically, the study aimed to understand the decision making, motivations, itineraries and strategies used by child migrants as well as the (perceptions of) the difficulties they encountered.

The ethnographic data presented in this chapter is based on innovative, play-related methods better adapted to the anthropology of children in West Africa than conventional methods. The empirical data presented here illustrate that the mobility of children cannot simply be explained by economic push, or be reduced to the category of forced migration. There is a huge gap between the overall positive mobility experiences of children and the stigmatisation of this phenomenon which is still regarded by many as trafficking. Children have agency and actively develop many tactics in order to respond to the challenges facing them. This study demands that the phenomenon of child mobility in West Africa be viewed in a more open and constructive way rather than conceptualising child mobility as a problem *per se*. The methodological inference is that in order to understand child mobility, we need to develop specific research methods that take their experiences, perceptions and opinions into account. A synthesis of the findings of the studies compiled in this volume leads us to three central observations. First, the findings challenge existing perceptions of the nature, magnitude and causes of African migration, which compels us to *ask new research questions* in order to capture new or, rather, as yet under-rated dimensions of African migration. In particular, the studies exemplify the need to go beyond official state perspectives. For instance, they highlight that, rather than a temporary or permanent movement from one particular origin to one particular, fixed destination, migration is a phenomenon in constant flux, in which migrants continuously circulate and regularly change plans according to changing circumstances. This draws attention to the process of migration itself rather than the conventional focus on either receiving or sending societies. This compels migration researchers to conduct research in the spaces travelled by migrants, in between perceived 'origins' and 'destinations', which often turn out to be multiple and changing over time, depending on experiences in place and spaces 'in between'.

The studies also highlight the importance of irregular or undocumented migration by men, women and children as a 'normal' and socially licit rather than an exceptional and socially illicit phenomenon. Several chapters also point to the existence of close, intricate and reciprocal linkages between irregular migration and endemic corruption among state officials, and between irregular migration and the large size of informal economies in most African countries. This further questions states' real ability to steer migration. However, the studies also show that most migrants, although living in often very difficult situations and being confronted with exploitative work conditions and hostile state apparatuses, do have agency and actively attempt to improve their destiny. This refutes conventional accounts representing African migrants as (rather passive) victims of warfare, poverty and other sorts of human misery.

Second, in parallel with the elaboration of new methodological perspectives on migration research highlighted in the second chapter, the book aims to explore various new methods for data collection which have recently been developed within the African research context. In particular, the importance of fluidity, informality and irregularity in African migrations highlights the need for other methods which enable researchers to capture and better understand the magnitude, nature and causes of African migrations. Although we would endorse any call for better official statistics, it would be an illusion that official statistics will ever be able to capture the 'unofficial', informal and personal dimensions of African migrations. Several alternative methods are presented in this volume.

The chapters cover various key methodological issues including methods for random and non-random sampling drawing on a variety of data sources; single-sited, multi-sited, matched and 'on-the-move' methods for data collection; the use of spatial samples; and the use of non-conventional data sources such as information obtained through NGOs working with migrants. Several chapters present innovative methods based on studying vulnerable or difficult-to-approach migrant populations that traditional methods have difficulties capturing, such as undocumented migrants, child migrants, refugees and migrants who are 'in transit'. Two chapters focus on methods that allow us to measure the enforcement of migration policy and the role of officials' corruption in migration processes. Some chapters also critically consider the need for representativity and show different ways in which multi-method approaches and data triangulation can generate valuable knowledge on migration. The book also addresses crucial ethical and safety issues when conducting research among migrants in vulnerable positions, which makes it particularly important to consider the political economy of knowledge production on African migration.

Although the methods elaborated in this volume do not always correspond with the standard repertoire of social sciences and migration research, they testify to the creative and innovative ways in which researchers have started to overcome the manifold practical difficulties of African migration research while producing original information with reduced costs. It is important to emphasise that these methods are not only relevant for their capacity to overcome the practical difficulties of doing fieldwork in sub-optimal conditions; they also allow for answering research questions on migration phenomena, such as irregular migration, economic informality or the role of corruption, which conventional research methods largely fail to capture. In this sense, the merit and relevance of the methods explored in this volume go well beyond the specific African context, as they can be applied in any setting with sub-optimal research conditions.

Third, besides explaining and discussing new methodologies and innovative methods for migration research in Africa and beyond, this volume also has a broader theoretical merit: it highlights the fact that empirical research on African migrations can also improve general knowledge of human migration and may further challenge the epistemological basis of prior research. After all, as Julien Brachet argues in his chapter, not only does the way in which the subject of migration is approached empirically profoundly affect the resulting data, but also the choice of particular methodologies itself reflects the way migration is conceptualised.

On the one hand, this is important in the light of the relative absence of African migrations in wider theoretical debates on migration. The contributions in this volume from the predominantly young researchers from different national backgrounds in Africa, Europe and elsewhere can be seen as an encouraging sign and proof of the creativity and imagination that researchers have recently deployed to consolidate a place for Africa in international migration research.

On the other hand, the innovative approaches presented in this volume uncover dimensions of migration which are not unique to African migration. The inherent danger in presenting a volume on 'African migration' is to suggest that African migration is essentially different from migration elsewhere in the world. Rather, we would suggest that, although the levels of irregularity, informality and fluidity of migration might be higher in various African countries than in other parts of the world, these are also 'normal' and possibly increasingly important dimensions of migration elsewhere in the world. To paraphrase Hoerder (2002: 8), particular migratory phenomena in Africa (and elsewhere) are unique in character but certainly not unique in kind.

So, while based on an analysis of methodologies and methods of migration research in Africa, the empirical and epistemological lessons to be drawn from this volume are also relevant to the study of migration more generally. In general, this endorses the broader critique on 'methodological nationalism' (cf. Glick Schiller et al. 1992) in migration research, characterised by the dominance of state perspectives and the one-sided reliance on and belief in official statistics. This points to the need for a better understanding of migration as a complex social process rather than as a problem to be solved. We hope that the chapters presented in this volume will contribute to a shift in our perception of migration as well as improved creativity and imagination in applying methodological and methods of research in order to better understand the nature and magnitude of African and, in fact, global migration.

References

Bakewell, O. and H. de Haas (eds.) (2007) 'African migrations: continuities, discontinuities and recent transformations', in L. de Haan, U. Engel and P. Chabal, *African Alternatives*, Leiden: Brill.

de Haas, H. (2007) 'The Myth of Invasion: Irregular Migration from West Africa to the Maghreb and the European Union', Oxford: International Migration Institute, University of Oxford.

Glick Schiller, N., L. Basch, and C. Blanc-Szanton (1992) *Towards a Transnational Perspective on Migration: Race, Class, Ethnicity, and Nationalism Reconsidered*, New York: New York Academy of Sciences.

Hoerder, D. (2002) *Cultures in Contact: World Migrations in the Second Millennium*, Durham and London: Duke University Press.

Chapter 2

━━◆◆◆━━

METHODOLOGY
AND METHODS:
CONCEPTUAL ISSUES

Stephen Castles

THE TASKS OF SOCIAL SCIENCE

According to the US sociologist and social critic, C. Wright Mills, a feature of all classic work in social science is the distinction between 'the personal troubles of milieu' and 'the public issues of social structure'. *Troubles* have to do with the character of the individual and his immediate relations with others, while *issues* have to do with matters that transcend these local environments of the individual and the range of his inner life. Mills illustrates this point by looking at unemployment: if one man in a city of 100,000 is unemployed, that is his personal *trouble*, and the solutions lie in his own character, skills and opportunities. But if in a nation of 50 million employees, 15 million are unemployed, that is an *issue* that cannot be resolved by an individual, but requires action by the economic and political institutions of society (Mills 2000 [1959]: 8–9).[1] In his famous work on *The Sociological Imagination*, Mills argued for the need to link history and biography – that is to 'understand the larger historical scene in terms of its meaning for the inner life and the external career of a variety of individuals' (Mills 2000 [1959]: 5). This is a simple but profound statement of the tasks of social science: it needs to analyse the collective behaviour of human beings and how this is linked to social structures and institutions, the changing historical context of specific societies, and the character types prevailing in each society. No social action can be understood without an understanding of the broader context in which it takes place. Isolated studies of single issues (or 'social facts') do not help people to grasp the complex processes that are at work, nor do they lead to adequate strategies for public policy. Social inquiry should be relevant to the pressing issues facing individuals and groups in society, and should be grounded in historical understanding. This is particularly important for migration research: it is indeed important to carry out micro-level studies of specific migratory experiences, but they should always be embedded in an understanding of the macro-level structural factors that shape human mobility in a specific historical situation.

How can we understand social issues?

Such principles are convincing – although certainly not uncontroversial. But how can social researchers implement them in practice? In other words, what social scientific methodology and what specific research methods can be used to develop our understanding of social behaviour and issues within their historical context? The debate on this topic continues to play an important part in the social sciences as a whole and within each individual discipline. For example, the American Sociological Association publishes an influential journal entitled *Sociological Methodology*. University libraries contain shelves of books on the methodology of economics, political science, geography, demography, anthropology and indeed all the social science disciplines. Professional conferences include workshops and training sessions on how best to plan and implement research. Methodology is our chart to navigate the social world while methods are the tools of our trade.

Yet there are wide divergences between and within discipline in methodological approaches, ranging from the emphasis on quantitative analysis of large datasets (i.e. econometrics) and the relative absence of fieldwork in economics, to the reliance on in-depth case studies and ethnographic fieldwork in anthropology. Other disciplines are somewhere in-between, but all grapple with problems of knowing and understanding. In recent years, the rise of 'mixed methods' approaches within disciplines and the call for interdisciplinarity in addressing complex real-world issues (such as migration or development) have made things even more complicated. A key problem of interdisciplinarity is the very different definitions of knowledge and the assumptions on how to obtain it that social scientists absorb during their specific training in the various disciplines.

In the USA, quantitative methods were dominant until quite recently in such disciplines as sociology and political science, and a great deal of social research has been concerned with refining statistical techniques to improve analysis of large datasets. For many years, critical thinkers (such as C.W. Mills) have argued that such approaches may advance the description of social phenomena, but do very little to increase understanding of the processes which bring them about or indeed to find solutions to the pressing dilemmas of society. In recent times, recognition of the need for qualitative research and case-studies has grown, and professional bodies (such as the American Political Science Association) encourage training in such approaches. However, their advocates in the USA sometimes seem to be trying to justify why qualitative methods can be a useful 'second best', and some advocates of 'mixed methods' appear to have an almost patronising attitude to qualitative approaches, trying to introduce forms of analysis and automation (e.g. in textual analysis) that turn quality into quantity (see for instance King et al. 1994).

This emphasis on the quantitative has been driven by two factors: the availability of high-quality statistics in large datasets such as censuses and labour-force surveys, and the declining costs and growing power of computer analysis packages. These factors do not necessarily prevail everywhere in the world. In many developing regions, censuses and other official data collections may be absent, irregular or unreliable. Similarly, high-quality computer equipment is often not widely available to researchers. Reliance on official data can be especially problematic in migration research. Even in the most developed regions, migration statistics are based on differing definitions and categories, and are collected in different ways from country

to country, because they reflect national migration policies and ideologies. Even the OECD has taken some 30 years to work towards
comparability in the data published each year in its annual Migration Outlook reports (formerly known as the SOPEMI reports).
Many users of this data would argue that comparability, although
improved, is still far from perfect.

Migration researchers therefore need to be very cautious in
aggregating national data into regression models. This applies all the
more in Africa, where such data may not be available or reliable, and
where international comparisons therefore require great care. African
researchers need to develop methods of data collection and analysis
that reflect the realities of the continent. However, such approaches
should not be seen as a 'second best', made necessary by lack of 'real'
data. Rather researchers working in such contexts can draw on a range
of traditions in the social sciences, which emphasise the importance of
understanding social phenomena and the processes which bring them
about, rather than merely describing and counting superficial indicators. A precondition for innovation in migration research methods is
an examination of the epistemological basis of the varying approaches.

METHODOLOGY AND METHODS

Methodology and methods are often confused, or used as if they
meant the same thing. Many articles in the social sciences have a
section on 'methodology' that merely describes the methods used in a
study, but does not actually discuss methodology. Methodology and
methods are closely connected, but they are not the same thing.

Methods are specific techniques used to collect and analyse information or data. *Data collection methods* include for instance: literature
reviews, censuses or other large datasets, surveys, qualitative interviews,
household budget analysis, life histories, and participant observation.
Data analysis methods include for instance: literature analysis, content
(or textual) analysis, qualitative analysis, simple tabulations, cross-
tabulations, regression analysis, social mapping, network analysis and
socio-grams. It is important to specify the methods of data collection
and analysis in any report or publication describing a research study.[2]

Methodology, by contrast, is about the underlying logic of research.
It is closely linked to the branch of philosophy known as *epistemology*

– literally 'the theory of knowledge'. Epistemology asks such questions as: 'What is knowledge?' 'How is knowledge acquired?' 'How can we know something to be true?' A key dispute in epistemology is between *positivists* who claim that there is an objective world outside ourselves as observers, and *constructivists*, who believe that meanings are constructed, interpreted and constantly re-constructed by people in their perceptions and social interactions.

Methodology involves the systematic application of epistemology to research situations. It deals with the principles of the methods, concepts and procedural rules employed by a scientific discipline. Each discipline has its own methodology. Here we are concerned with the methodology of the social sciences and its application specifically to migration research.

OBJECTIVITY VERSUS SOCIAL CONSTRUCTION

In the social sciences the dispute between positivists and constructivists has been particularly important. Positivists believe that there is a single objective truth or *reality* that can be found in studying social institutions or practices. The influential early French sociologist Emile Durkheim spoke of *social facts*, which he characterised as 'ways of acting, thinking and feeling, external to the individual, and endowed with a power of coercion, by which they control him' (Durkheim and Catlin 1938 [1895]: 3). His 'first and most fundamental rule' of sociological method was to 'consider social facts as things' (Durkheim and Catlin 1938 [1895]: 14). The implication was that social practices and institutions take on an objective and hence measurable character, which is independent of human action and agency. Later US functionalist sociology followed this approach (see Parsons 1951).

By contrast early German sociologist Max Weber argued that the observer has to try to understand the *meaning* of social action and institutions for the people involved, leading to the idea of 'interpretative sociology'. He argued that 'an "objective" analysis of cultural events, which proceeds according to the thesis that the ideal of science is the reduction of empirical reality to "laws" is meaningless' (Weber et al. 1949: 80). An important reason for this was that social and cultural knowledge was always conditioned through 'evaluative ideas'. He therefore argued that value judgements – especially about the relevance of social matters – could not be banished from science. Rather, the principle of 'value freedom' meant that the researcher should strive to make a clear distinction between values and knowledge (Weber et al. 1949: 49–112).

Thus, Weber argues: 'both for sociology in the present sense, and for history, the object of cognition is the subjective-meaning complex of action' (Weber 1947: 101); (quoted here from Berger and Luckmann 1966: 16).

In an important work on the *sociology of knowledge*, Berger and Luckmann argue that this apparent gulf between the two great theorists actually reflects 'the dual character of society' leading to the central question for sociological theory: 'how is it possible that subjective meanings *become* objective facticities?' (Berger and Luckmann 1966: 17, emphasis in original). Berger and Luckmann make a strong argument for social constructivism – that is the principle that knowledge about social relationships and practices is constantly being created, modified and re-created through processes of social interaction. People in society perceive social phenomena as a reality that is independent of their own volition, even though these social phenomena are constructed by human beings and can therefore be changed by them. Judgements on reality are socially relative: 'what is "real" to a Tibetan monk may not be "real" to an American businessman'. 'Reality' and 'knowledge' pertain to specific social contexts – and these contexts must always be analysed before a social scientist can understand the meaning of these concepts for the people concerned (Berger and Luckmann 1966: 2–3). This concern for context harks back to Marx's recognition that 'man's consciousness is determined by his social being' (Berger and Luckmann 1966: 5).

THE CONSEQUENCES OF METHODOLOGY FOR CHOICE OF RESEARCH APPROACHES

For positivists, social science is a matter of improving research methods to the point at which they can accurately describe and measure social facts. For constructivists, social sciences have to interpret the social meanings that they find, and may actually influence these in the process. Positivists believe in objectivity, while constructivists believe that there is no single truth in social phenomena. Early positivists claimed to be bringing the certainty and objectivity of the natural sciences into social research. However, the questioning of the immutable laws of Newtonian physics by early twentieth-century quantum mechanics undermined this approach. Quantum mechanics works with probability rather than certainty and its 'uncertainty principle' (proposed by the physicist Heisenberg) states that by measuring something, the researcher actually changes it (Heisenberg et al. 1977). Nevertheless, many quantitative social researchers have come to believe that ever more sophisticated statistical packages and computer analysis can lead to objectivity.

Constructivists, by contrast, point to the complexity of social situations, and the impossibility of building models that can really include all possible factors. They argue that the dominant approach to social science (often imposed through the peer review process of influential US journals) is inherently reductionist: the researcher carries out a literature review and derives a research question from existing theoretical and descriptive material. The question has to be narrow or limited enough to be answered by linking a set of variables available in recognised datasets – fieldwork is rarely carried out by users of advanced statistical techniques. The researcher puts together a list of 'stylised facts' seen as the state of knowledge on the topic concerned. Then a hypothesis is tested by preparing a model of factors and interactions between them seen as relevant by the researcher. The data is fed through a regression analysis, and the researcher can then publish the results, which usually confirm his or her hypothesis. The reductionism is visible at various stages of the process: the existing understanding of the problem may be incomplete or flawed; the factors chosen for the model may not reflect the complexity of human decision-making so that important factors may have been left out; the people concerned are not asked about the meaning they attribute to practices or actions; the interactions of variables in the model may not reflect the importance of various factors in social processes, and there is a danger of detecting spurious correlations.

Emphasis on the social meanings constructed by people in diverse communities and societies, and on the relativity and context-dependence of these meanings implies quite different ways of doing research. The aim must be to understand the historical and current processes through which social meanings develop and change, and what they signify to people. The methods needed to understand processes and meanings include ethnographic study, qualitative interviews (using open-ended questions to allow people to explain their own meanings), case-studies and participant observation. But both positivist and constructivist approaches can be one-sided. The social scientist needs to find out both what actually happens in society – i.e. what are the forms of social behaviour, practices, customs and institutions – and why and how it happens. Thus there is a need both for big-number analysis using descriptive and analytical statistics and for micro-level studies using ethnographic and case-study methods. Mixed-method approaches seem the best way to develop greater understanding of social issues and of their relevance to individual and group life. Ideally, research teams should include people with knowledge of a range of approaches, and – hardest of all – with the ability to co-operate across methodological and disciplinary boundaries.

METHODOLOGY AND METHODS IN MIGRATION RESEARCH PRACTICE

Methodology asks such questions as:
- How can we obtain knowledge about a social practice or a relationship, such as about its frequency, its significance, the process through which it emerges and its links with other aspects of a social situation?
- What leads us to believe that the methods of data collection and analysis we want to use will actually provide valid and reliable data?
- How can we understand the significance and meaning of a social practice or institution for those involved?

For example, if we use the method of a sample survey in an African city to answer a research question about people's intentions to migrate to another country, how do we know:
- That our sample is representative of the population we want to study?
- That our respondents have the same understanding of the questions as we do?
- That they are willing and able to tell us what they really think?

- That their stated intentions provide an accurate guide to their actual behaviour?

Many further issues could be added. These are methodological questions that cast doubt on uncritical use of quantitative methods. They require us to ask if the methods we use will really provide accurate answers to our research questions. The use of increasingly sophisticated data-analysis software has led some people to think that if they feed quantitative data (numbers) into a regression analysis package, they will get scientifically valid results. However, if the quality of the data is poor (due to mistaken or narrow assumptions, lack of reliable statistics or inadequate survey techniques) then the results may be misleading. Of course this applies to use of qualitative methods too: if sampling techniques are biased or inadequate, or if the researcher's understanding of the factors involved in the process under investigation are wrong, then the findings are unlikely to be valid.

To address such problems, it is important that a migration study (just like any other social scientific study) should include reflection on methodology as well as a justification of the methods used. Ideally, a research paper or report should have a section on methodology and another one on methods. At the least, an author should always address both themes, even if in the same section. A migration research *proposal* should:

1. Outline the issue or problem to be studied, and explain why it is significant.
2. Discuss existing literature on the theme.
3. Outline migration theory and broader social scientific theory relevant to the theme.
4. Develop one or more hypotheses or research questions based on the previous steps. These should include both *descriptive questions* (what forms of migration are taking place and what are the motivations and decision-making processes of the people involved?) and *analytical questions* (how do the studied migratory behaviours and practices relate to each other, to other migratory patterns and to more general processes of social interaction and change?).
5. Discuss the methodological challenges to be faced in answering these questions in the research situation concerned.

6. Describe and justify the methods to be used for data collection and analysis.
7. Outline the type of outputs that are expected from the study.
8. Provide a research plan that shows how the work is to be carried out with the resources and time that are available.

A migration research *report* should cover the same themes, with the addition of a presentation of the information collected, a descriptive account of the data collection and analysis processes and any problems that arose during these, and a discussion of the findings. All publications arising from a migration research project should provide summaries of the methodology and methods used, and provide the reader with links or contacts to obtain fuller information on these matters if required (e.g. by reading the full report and accessing the archived research data).

A methodological discussion of how a social scientist can know something or answer the research questions will often highlight the limitations of any one method of data collection and analysis. The methodological conclusion will frequently be that there should be a *triangulation of methods* – that is a range of different methods should be used to collect and analyse data on any specific migratory process. If the answers are the same with a range of methods, this allows a much higher degree of confidence in their accuracy. If the answers are different, then it is likely that the methods are not actually answering the questions as the researcher had expected. In addition, use of multiple (or mixed) methods provides broader and more profound information on the topic.

Another important methodological point is that different types of methods can answer different types of question, e.g.:

- A cross-sectional survey (a study covering a representative sample of the individuals, families, groups, regions and countries that make up a specific population at any one time) can answer such questions as current levels of income or mobility, but it cannot tell us anything about how a phenomenon has changed or developed.
- A longitudinal study can show how such indicators have changed over time, but cannot explain the motivations or the social meanings attached to behaviours, practices and institutions.

- Use of qualitative methods (non-directive interviews, social biographies, asking about family mobility trajectories) can help us understand intentions and social meanings, but cannot give an accurate measurement of the frequency of certain attitudes or behaviours.
- Historical studies can help show the development and significance of social practices, but cannot show their current extent.

This list could be prolonged. The point is that it is usually necessary to use a range of methods. For instance, the Mexican Migration Project has used a mix of large surveys and qualitative studies to describe and explain patterns of migration from Mexico to the USA. Because the project has carried out several waves of research over a long period, it also has a longitudinal (or historical) dimension (Massey et al. 2003 [2002]).

A valuable collection of reports on migration research experiences argues that 'the validity of social science knowledge derives from making manifest, and exposing to critique, the process by which meaning is derived from research'. That means demonstrating the 'credibility of the procedures by which factual information and interpretations of its significance have been acquired and produced' (DeWind 2007: 9). This book – available as a free download from the website of the US Social Science Research Council – is highly recommended to migration researchers for the many useful lessons on research practice that it provides (DeSipio et al. 2007).

One of the most important lessons concerns the need for *flexibility* on the part of the researcher: repeatedly, unexpected issues and obstacles encountered in the actual research process caused researchers to question and modify their original assumptions and their research strategy. Indeed, one might conclude that anyone who starts research convinced that she or he already knows the best way of getting the answers may have a tacit belief in already knowing the answers, and will therefore probably find what he or she expects – whether it is accurate or not. In other words, the results will reflect mistaken or inadequate assumptions which have influenced the problem definition and the choice of methods.

Flexibility implies *adaptability*: the willingness of the researcher to respond to the lessons of the field and to hear what respondents are saying by changing the research strategy. This may well involve concluding that the original research question was not the best one, or that the starting hypothesis was mistaken.

GLOBAL SOCIAL TRANSFORMATION AND HUMAN MOBILITY

I will conclude this chapter by sketching briefly my own perspective on contemporary research on human mobility: this starts from the principle that migration researchers should always site their research in the context of broader processes of societal change, and link migration theory to general trends in contemporary social theory (see Castles and Miller 2009, especially Chapter 3).

That means, first, seeing migration not as something exceptional or problematic, but as a central part of processes of social change everywhere. Migration should be analysed therefore not primarily as a *result* of social transformation, nor a *cause* of social transformation, but as *an integral part* of most processes of social transformation (Castles, 2009). This means questioning the widespread understanding of 'migration as a problem to be solved' that is expressed in many official statements on migration policy as well as in official rationales for migration research (IMI 2006). The dominant role played in migration research by governments and intergovernmental bodies (especially in Africa) has led to a 'sedentary bias' (Bakewell 2008; Bakewell and de Haas 2007), which often blocks understanding of the significance of migration as a way of accessing opportunities, improving human rights and security, and developing sustainable livelihoods (UNDP 2009).

Second, it means reflecting on the nature of processes of contemporary social transformation, and including in our analytical models such key trends as neo-liberal globalisation (and the resulting growth in inequality); the increasing economic, political and cultural integration of local communities and national societies into cross-border interactions; and the growth of transnationalism as a form of human agency.

Contemporary trends to cross-border economic and political integration lead to processes of social transformation in all types of society. The idea of *transformation* implies a fundamental change in the way society is organised that goes beyond the continual processes of social change that are always at work.[3] This arises when there are major shifts in dominant power relationships. Massive shifts in economic, political and military affairs since the mid 1970s (and especially since the end of the Cold War in the 1990s) represent such a fundamental change. Globalisation has uneven effects. Indeed it can be seen as a process of inclusion of particular regions and social groups in world capitalist market relations, and of exclusion of others (Castells 1996).

Rural–urban migration in the global South is driven both by the erosion of older forms of rural production and the growth of new urban opportunities. Often social transformation starts in agriculture. The 'green revolution' of the 1980s involved the introduction of new strains of rice and other crops, which promised higher yields, but in return required big investments in fertilizers, insecticides and mechanisation. The result was higher productivity but also concentration of ownership in the hands of richer farmers. Many poorer farmers lost their livelihoods and had to leave the land. The process continues today with the introduction of genetically modified seed-stock. The pressure on farmers in poor regions is increased by farm subsidies in rich countries – especially US cotton subsidies and the EU Common Agricultural Policy (Oxfam 2002) – which depress world market prices.

At the same time urban employment opportunities have grown – albeit unevenly. In the early stages of urbanisation, most urban growth is the result of rural–urban migration. As cities grow, and rural labour reserves are used up, natural increase in cities outstrips new rural inflows, although that natural increase can also be seen in part as a consequence of earlier inflows of young adults. Cities also grow through the outward expansion of their boundaries, as formerly rural areas are absorbed (Skeldon 2009). Industrialisation in emerging economic powers such as China, India and Brazil has been linked to a rapid growth in inequality between urban and rural incomes (Milanovic 2007: 35–9). The cities of the South, like Sao Paolo, Shanghai, Calcutta or Jakarta, are growing at a rate of about 70 million a year. Labour market entrants with the skills, education or good fortune to find jobs in formal sector activities may do well, but formal employment growth cannot keep pace with labour market growth, so that large numbers of workers end up in precarious informal-sector jobs, or in cycles of sporadic work and unemployment. For these groups, standards of housing, health and education are low, while crime, violence and human rights violations are rife. Such conditions are powerful motivations to seek better livelihoods elsewhere, either in growth areas within the region or in the North.

Inequality has not been reduced by the global financial crisis of 2008–9 – indeed the overall effect may well prove to be even greater redistribution of wealth from poor and middle-income groups to the already wealthy. The social transformations inherent in globalisation do not just affect economic well-being – they also lead to increased violence and lack of human security in the global South. The great majority of those affected by violence are displaced within their own countries, or seek refuge in other – usually equally poor – countries in the region. But some try to obtain asylum in the richer states of the North, where they hope to find more security and freedom – as well as better livelihoods.

Social transformation drives emigration from poorer countries, but it is also a process that affects richer countries, shaping the conditions for immigration and incorporation. The increased export of capital to low-wage economies since the 1970s had a reciprocal effect in the global North: old 'rustbelt industries' declined, blue-collar workers lost their secure jobs, and often found their skills devalued. Factories were replaced by distribution depots, shopping malls and call centres, employing de-unionised and labour casualised. The neo-liberal turn in economic policy meant a decline in welfare states, trends towards privatisation and individualisation, and the erosion of community solidarity. At the same time, declining fertility, population ageing and changes in work locations and requirements created a strong demand for immigrants of all skill levels. Immigration and settlement thus took place in a situation of rapid change, uncertainty and insecurity for host populations. Immigrants became the visible symbol of globalisation – and were therefore often blamed for threatening and incomprehensible changes. This helps to explain the rise of extreme-right racist groups since the 1980s (Schierup et al. 2006).

CONSEQUENCES OF A SOCIAL TRANSFORMATION APPROACH
FOR MIGRATION STUDIES

The processes of social transformation that arise from globalisation are the crucial context for understanding twenty-first-century migration. The flows and networks that constitute globalisation take on specific forms at different spatial levels: the regional, the national and the local. These should be understood as elements of complex and dynamic relationships, in which *global forces* have varying impacts according to differing structural and cultural factors and responses at the other levels (see Held et al. 1999: 14–16). Historical experiences, cultural values, religious beliefs, institutions and social structures all channel and shape the effects of external forces, leading to forms of change and resistance that bring about very different outcomes in specific communities or societies.

For most people, the pre-eminent level for experiencing migration and its effects is *the local*. This applies especially where processes of social transformation create conditions which encourage people to leave their communities of origin to move elsewhere. Development processes may help people obtain the education, knowledge and financial resources needed to access opportunities for better livelihoods in other regions or countries. On the other hand, changes in agricultural practices or land tenure may drive farmers from the land, or development projects (such as dams, airports or factories) may physically displace people. Migration itself may become a force for further social transformation: the departure of young active people, gender imbalances, financial and social remittances can all transform conditions in the local community – in ways that may be either conducive to or detrimental to economic and social development. Similarly, the impact of immigration in migrant-destination areas is felt in the way it affects economic restructuring and social relations in local communities.

National-level impacts of global forces are also important. Nation-states remain the location for policies on cross-border movements, citizenship, public order, social welfare, health services and education. Nation-states retain considerable political significance and have important symbolic and cultural functions. But it is no longer possible to abstract from cross-border factors in decision-making and planning. One result of this is the growing importance of *regional* cooperation through bodies like the EU, NAFTA or ECOWAS.

Researchers therefore need to be aware of the way migration processes – like all forms of social transformation – work across socio-spatial levels. Whether we start from the level of global phenomena – like the overall expansion of international migration – or local phenomena – like changes in a specific village brought about by migrant remittances – we need to take account of multi-level linkages, and to examine the complex processes that shape these. Understanding migration as an integral part of social transformation has important consequences for the theory, methodology and organisational forms of migration studies.

THEORY

Migration theory is concerned with the social consequences of transnational or cross-border human movements. Migration studies should analyse movements of people in terms of their multi-layered links to other forms of global connectivity. Macro-trends in economic, political and military affairs are crucial in reshaping the global space in which people's movements take place. The closely related shifts in social and cultural patterns are also important in influencing the forms and volume of mobility.

Theorists of neo-liberal globalisation often argue that contemporary economic and political relationships imply shifts away from hierarchical power-structures towards network patterns, in which centralised power is being replaced by transnational functional cooperation. Multinational corporations or international organisations are seen as representing rational divisions of responsibilities, rather than top-down power hierarchies. Yet the differentiation of migrants between privileged possessors of human capital credentials and disadvantaged groups with weak legal status who can be easily exploited casts doubt on this positive view. By linking hierarchies of migration and citizenship to the power dynamics embedded in economic and political institutions, migration researchers can contribute to the analysis of new forms of social relationships.

As already pointed out, a key dimension of migration theory lies in conceptualising the way social transformation processes act at different spatial levels (local, regional, national and global) (compare Pries 2007). Analysing the mediation and transformation of global forces by local or national cultural and historical factors can help overcome the division between top-down and bottom-up approaches. This implies that attempts to create a 'general theory of migration' are unlikely to be helpful, because such a theory would be so abstract that it would give little guidance to understanding any real migratory processes (Portes 1999). Rather migration theory needs to be historically and culturally sited, and to relate structure and action.

METHODOLOGY

Migration researchers need to take an *holistic approach*, linking research on specific migration experiences to broader studies of the transformation of whole societies and how this is connected to global trends. This in turn implies the need for *interdisciplinarity*: migration processes affect all dimensions of social existence and cannot be reduced simply to the subject areas of specific disciplines like anthropology, law, sociology or economics. Migration researchers should work in interdisciplinary teams in larger projects, and make use of the published research findings of other disciplines in smaller ones.

Clearly, most forms of migration research are likely to require *mixed-methods approaches*. *Quantitative research* is important for obtaining comparative data to describe macro-social changes linked to migration. At the same time, *qualitative approaches* are needed to provide the understanding of the history and cultures of sending, transit and receiving societies that is vital in understanding any specific migration situation.

Migration studies can benefit a great deal from *comparative studies* of experiences in different societies, which can increase awareness of general trends and alternative approaches. Such studies can be linked to the growing interest in research on *transnationalism and transnational communities*, which are increasingly seen as an important social and cultural expression of globalisation. It is in any case vital to investigate the *human agency* of migrants and of sending and receiving communities, and the way this agency interacts with macro-social organisations and institutions. This requires *participatory research* to include the perspectives of the different actors, as well as qualitative research to understand processes and their social meanings.

ORGANISATION OF RESEARCH

Transnational networks of scholars should be a basic principle for organising migration research. By transcending the North-South division, such networks could play a particularly important role in overcoming the nationalist and colonialist legacy of the social sciences. Transnational research networks can also help surmount linguistic and cultural barriers, and counter the 'methodological nationalism' which has held back the development of migration research (Wimmer and Glick Schiller 2003).[4]

Transnational research networks can also help in the linking of socio-spatial levels: researchers from countries of origin, transit and destination of migrants can contribute their understanding of local social structures and cultural practices, while working together to analyse transnational relationships and global social forces. At the same time, it is important to remember that research is not a neutral activity: researchers can make conscious choices about goals. Working with civil society organisations (such as community groups or migrant associations) could be a counterweight to the power of government and funding bodies.

In fact international research cooperation in the migration field has grown in recent years, yet key concepts may have quite different meanings in different countries. Overcoming conceptual gaps is part of the research task, and building lasting international research part-nerships should be seen as an important long-term goal.

CONCLUSION

All migration researchers have to struggle with limitations of resources and time, and not every study can include detailed considerations of deep methodological questions. Nor can every specific piece of research engage with wider social forces at the various socio-spatial levels. What is being suggested here is more modest: that *all research-ers need to be aware of the broader implications of their research themes, and of the multi-levelled forces that condition social consciousness and action*. Specific studies need to be informed by a consciousness of how they fit together with other areas of social inquiry, and this in turn needs to be linked to a willingness to question both geographical and disciplinary boundaries – just because these are not 'social facts', but rather the product of layerings of past intellectual activity, which always takes place within specific societal contexts.

The authors of the following chapters on experiences of migration research in Africa demonstrate a willingness to innovate and question conventional wisdoms. This is crucial to the advancement of migration studies and to its emancipation from the methodological nationalism of the past. The contributions show that there are many strategies for developing understanding of the context and processes of human mobility in a region that is often ignored in debates on scientific methodology. There is a place for all these approaches, and combining them can lead to important insights.

ACKNOWLEDGEMENTS

This chapter owes much to discussions with and material provided by Ellie Vasta (University of Western Sydney) and Jenny Wuestenberg (University of Maryland). The author's thanks go to both of them. I also thank Mohamed Berriane (Université Mohammed V - Agdal Rabat) and Hein de Haas (University of Oxford) for their helpful comments on an earlier draft.

Notes

1. In keeping with the practice of earlier times, Mills and other social theorists tended to speak only of men when discussing society. Today we regard this practice as sexist, but it seems inappropriate to change their expressions when quoting or paraphrasing their work.
2. In this chapter, I will not go into detailed descriptions of the various methods, their uses and their problems, as there is a large number of handbooks and critical texts on this theme.
3. A crucial starting point for understanding the notion of social transformation is the work of Carl Polanyi (Polanyi 2001). Of particular interest is Joseph Stiglitz's Foreword to the 2001

edition of *The Great Transformation*. However, attempts to link transformation theory to globalisation can be found in greater detail in (Munck 2002; Stiglitz 1998, 2002).

4. 'Methodological nationalism' refers to national specificity in the social sciences, namely in their modes of organisation, theoretical and methodological approaches, research questions and findings. It originates in the role played by the social sciences of the nineteenth and early twentieth centuries in processes of constructing nation-states and national identities. See Beck 2007; Castles 2007.

References

Bakewell, O. (2008) 'Keeping them in their place: the ambivalent relationship between development and migration in Africa', *Third World Quarterly* 29(7): 1341–58.

Bakewell, O. and H. de Haas (2007) 'African migrations: continuities, discontinuities and recent transformations', in P. Chabal, U. Engel, and L. de Haan (eds.) *African Alternatives*, Leiden: Brill.

Beck, U. (2007) 'Beyond class and nation: reframing social inequalities in a globalizing world', *British Journal of Sociology* 58(4): 679–705.

Berger, P. L. and T. Luckmann (1966) *The Social Construction of Reality: a Treatise in the Sociology of Knowledge*, Garden City: Doubleday.

Castells, M. (1996) *The Rise of the Network Society*, Oxford: Blackwell.

Castles, S. (2007) 'Twenty-first century migration as a challenge to sociology', *Journal of Ethnic and Migration Studies* 33(3): 351–71.

Castles, S. (2009) 'Development and Migration – Migration and Development: What Comes First?', Migration and Development: Future Directions for Research and Policy, New York: Social Science Research Council, http://programs.ssrc.org/intmigration/2Castles.pdf, accessed 11 May 2009.

Castles, S. and Miller, M. J. (2009) *The Age of Migration: International Population Movements in the Modern World*, 4th edition, Basingstoke and New York: Palgrave-Macmillan and Guilford.

DeSipio, L., M. Garcia y Griego, and S. Kossoudji (eds.) (2007) 'Researching Migration: Stories from the Field', New York: Social Science Research Council, www.ssrc.org/publications/view/42451838-264A-DE11-AFAC-001CC477EC70/.

DeWind, J. (2007) 'Preface' in L. DeSipio, M. Garcia y Griego, and S. Kossoudji (eds.) 'Researching Migration: Stories from the Field', New York: Social Science Research Council, www.ssrc.org/publications/view/42451838-264A-DE11-AFAC-001CC477EC70/.

Durkheim, E. and G. E. G. Catlin (1938 [1895]) *The Rules of Sociological Method*, 8th edition, New York: Free Press of Glencoe.

Heisenberg, W., W. C. Price, and S. S. Chissick (1977) *The Uncertainty Principle and Foundations of Quantum Mechanics: A Fifty Years Survey*, New York: Wiley.

Held, D., A. McGrew, D. Goldblatt, and J. Perraton (1999) *Global Transformations: Politics, Economics and Culture*, Cambridge: Polity.

IMI (2006) 'Towards a New Agenda for International Migration Research', Oxford: International Migration Institute, University of Oxford, www.imi.ox.ac.uk/pdfs/a4-imi-research-agenda.pdf.

King, G., R. O. Keohane, and S. Verba (1994) *Designing Social Inquiry: Scientific Inference in Qualitative Research*, Princeton: Princeton University Press.

Massey, D. S., J. Durand, and N. J. Malone (2003 [2002]) *Beyond Smoke and Mirrors. Mexican Immigration in an Era of Economic Integration*, New York: Russell Sage Foundation.

Milanovic, B. (2007) 'Globalization and inequality', in D. Held and A. Kaya (eds.) *Global Inequality: Patterns and Explanations*, Cambridge and Malden MA: Polity.

Mills, C. W. (2000 [1959]) *The Sociological Imagination*, Oxford: Oxford University Press.

Munck, R. (2002) 'Globalization and Democracy: A New "Great Transformation"?', *Annals of the American Academy of Political and Social Science* 58: 110–21.

Oxfam (2002) 'Rigged Rules and Double Standards: Trade, Globalisation, and the Fight against Poverty', Oxford: Oxfam.

Parsons, T. (1951) *The Social System*, London: Routledge & K. Paul.

Polanyi, K. (2001) *The Great Transformation*, Boston: Beacon Press.

Portes, A. (1999) 'The hidden abode: sociology as analysis of the unexpected – 1999', Presidential Address to the American Sociological Association, *American Sociological Review* 65: 1–18.

Pries, L. (2007) *Die Transnationalisierung der sozialen Welt*, Frankfurt am Main: Suhrkamp.

Schierup, C.-U., P. Hansen, and S. Castles (2006) *Migration, Citizenship and the European Welfare State: A European Dilemma*, Oxford: Oxford University Press.

Skeldon, R. (2009) 'Migration, Urbanization and Development', New York: Social Science Research Council, http://essays.ssrc.org/developmentpapers/wp-content/uploads/2009/08/23Skeldon. pdf, accessed 1 December 2009.

Stiglitz, J. E. (1998) 'Towards a new paradigm for development: strategies, policies and processes', 1998 Prebisch Lecture UNCTAD, Geneva: World Bank.

Stiglitz, J. E. (2002) *Globalization and its Discontents*, London: Penguin.

UNDP (2009) 'Human Development Report 2009: Overcoming Barriers: Human mobility and Development', New York: United Nations Development Programme, http://hdr.undp. org/en/reports/global/hdr2009/.

Weber, M. (1947) *The Theory of Social and Economic Organization*, Oxford and New York: Oxford University Press.

Weber, M., E. Shils, and H. A. Finch (1949) *The Methodology of the Social Sciences*, New York: The Free Press.

Wimmer, A. and N. Glick Schiller (2003) 'Methodological nationalism, the social sciences and the study of migration', *International Migration Review* 37(3): 576–610.

Chapter 3

———⟫•◆•⟪———

MIGRATORY FLOWS AND MIGRANTS' PROFILES: MOROCCAN EMIGRATION TOWARDS SPAIN

Mohamed Berriane, Mohamed Aderghal,

and Lahoucine Amzil

INTRODUCTION

In the current context it is worth underlining the profound changes affecting mobility within the Mediterranean area. There has been a diversification in the forms of mobility and its implications. Certainly migration in its classic form exists, but there are also two-way movements linked to tourism, travel by businessmen and traders, be it official or informal, students, former migrants returning to their homeland, former military personnel, or smugglers. Then there is the tendency for this mobility to become transnationalised, in that movements do not link a country of origin and a country of destination, but are part of networks which straddle a number of countries. Now it is noticeable that the management of this mobility and the interest of the researchers have been focused on one single dimension of these various mobilities: migration, regular in the past and irregular now. Meanwhile, all other dimensions which remain unique to the Mediterranean region are brushed aside.

Starting from these various observations, the cases of Morocco and Spain (and Andalusia, in the heart of Spain) emerge as moving parts in a migratory mechanism which is specific to the Western Mediterranean, and which must be revisited in the light of these new dynamics.

Studies of international migration have long remained confined to a unidirectional spatial logic, locking movements into a single origin–destination pairing, whereas any understanding of migration as a social process must be based on the issue of trajectories in time and space. Besides, work on migration, which is often conducted on a large scale, lacks reliable numerical data, relying for the most part on official statistics, centring largely on a single branch of the flow, and resorting to explanatory models which are essentially demographically or socio-economically conceived.

The research project of which this chapter forms part hopes to move from the migratory paradigm to a mobility paradigm, focusing the research simultaneously on the two hubs of the movement (regions of origin and host regions), while cross-linking them to other hubs, by looking at the migration of Moroccans to Andalusia. To achieve this, this Hispano-Moroccan project has been developing a socio-geographic study of Moroccan immigration since 2006, in a series of locations in the Andalusian region, trying as much as possible to grasp its mobility within Andalusia and Spain as a whole, but also tracing the migrants' roots back to their social point of origin in Morocco, in order to get back to their original family environment and their 'migratory histories'. Overall, this will give us a composite view both of this migration and of how the equally complex mobility of the emigrant's family in the country of origin fits into the picture.

In this work, we have taken a 'transnational perspective', using an ethnographic methodology and working on the hypothesis of 'globalisation from the bottom up' (Portes 1997; Tarrius 2002). Within a single field of observation and analysis, our approach aims to include both the territories and societies which send out migratory flows and those which receive them, but also the social processes linked with these flows on both sides through various interactions, and any manifestations and forms of mobility which might be entailed in the 'circulation' of migrants.

Here we present part of the research findings, concentrating on three main areas: a presentation of the overall Moroccan-Andalusian project,[1] where special attention is paid to the questions asked and the methods used; and a consideration of the Moroccan sub-project, again dealing only with the questions asked and the methods used; a presentation of the results of the quantitative surveys carried out in Morocco.

MOROCCAN MIGRATION IN ANDALUSIA

The general objective of the project 'Moroccans in Andalusia: From immigration areas to mobility areas' is to conduct a quantitative and qualitative analysis of the immigrant population, of its spatial mobility and the economic and social causes which lie behind it. In order to pinpoint the issue at a territorial level appropriate to our approach, which aims to grasp the phenomenon both in its statistical entirety as well as through the detail of particular situations, the study is targeted at immigrant populations of Moroccan origin located in a sample of Andalusian municipalities which represent a series of distinct situations characteristic of the autonomous region of Andalusia. The novelty of this approach lies in the fact that the phenomenon is being observed simultaneously in the North and the South. This has necessitated the fine-tuning of an overall method applied in both Andalusia and Morocco. Due to a lack of space, in the following we have confined ourselves to the Moroccan aspect of the project and its quantitative part.

MOROCCAN MIGRATION TO SPAIN SEEN FROM THE SOUTH

Moroccan emigration to Spain

The emigration of Moroccans to Spain only began to occupy a central place on the migratory scene towards the early 1980s. Seen as a new destination, Spain offered an alternative as the traditional immigration countries began closing their borders. Its legislation

Box 1: Moroccans in Andalusia: from immigration areas to mobility areas

In Andalusia

The comparative study of geographical dynamics started with a survey in the municipalities of Granada, Almeria, Cordoba and Jaen. This survey is repeated over a minimum period of two years. Its aim is to assess the conditions for the integration of the immigrant population from Morocco, considering: the administrative situation, the demographic characteristics, the length of time since arrival and settling in Andalusia, the means of entering Spain, the socio-professional situation, the training, living accommodation and marital status, the migratory networks and other sociability networks in the areas where they have settled.

In Morocco

In Morocco, the project involves questions about the dynamics and workings of the networks, as well as the main branches of circulation which shape the fields of mobility. The migratory histories of the emigrants' families of origin need to be studied in detail to examine the flows which have opened the way to settlement in Spain and Andalusia against this background. Finally, the project aims to analyse the relational life which has been built up between Moroccan migrants in Andalusia and their families who have remained behind.

The study tries to reconstruct the migratory trajectories, tracing them back to their social point of origin and the family history, in an attempt to answer general questions such as: Who are they? When, how and where did they migrate in each case? What is the space-time trajectory followed by their mobility in Andalusia and Spain? What are the common features or what changes can be seen in relation to previous stages of Moroccan (and other) emigration to other European destinations? What roles do they play and what are the configurations of the migratory networks? What types of relationships may or may not be woven between immigrants and their families and territorial surroundings in Morocco? In short, the aim is to study the possible relationships between emigrating to Spain and settling in Andalusia, on the one hand, and, on the other, the family trajectory followed by the immigrants' mobility, evaluating the effectiveness of migratory networks and the roles they play in the immigrant's journey so that the possible and specific outlines of Andalusian immigration can be identified.

on the entry and exit of persons was less rigorous, and the Spanish state lacked experience in policy-making to regulate migratory flows. One should also take into account the economic renaissance of the period 1982–1992, which came about through joining the European Community and launching major public works projects occasioned, among other things, by the hosting of the Olympic Games in Barcelona and the Universal Exposition in Seville.

But the presence of Moroccans in Spain pre-dates this period by some considerable margin. In fact, there would seem to have been three emigration phases (Lopez Garcia 1993):

1. The first post-colonial phase, between 1956 and 1973, which was urban in nature, involved Jewish families from the main cities in the north and on the Atlantic coast (Tangiers, Tetouan, Larache, Ksar el Kebir, Casablanca, El Jadida and Essaouira). These people settled mostly in Madrid and Barcelona.

2. The second phase, after 1973, involved two categories of emigrants: irregular migrants, who chose to settle in Spain after France toughened up its entry controls; and agricultural workers who, in places such as Catalonia, filled in the gaps left by intense internal emigration by the Spanish people.

3. The third phase coincided with Spain's integration into the European Union, the main result of which was to change the economic, political and cultural profile of the country which became attractive and subject to increasingly large flows of migrants. To manage this new situation, and with a view to harmonising migratory laws with the European legislation, the Spanish state equipped itself with a legal arsenal allowing it to control the influx of immigrants and to take charge of the presence of foreigners on its soil. Throughout the whole period since 1985, the number of Moroccans in Spain was to increase considerably, and successive regularisations were to enable further stimulation of the irregular migration which is now the most striking aspect of the migratory phenomenon in Spain.

The nature of the problem posed by Moroccans' emigration to Spain cannot be separated from the twofold context of Morocco, on the one hand, and Spain, on the other. To understand the particular characteristics of this emigration, we start with the following premisses:

- Emigration to Spain has developed rapidly, contrasting with the traditional emigration of Moroccans to North European countries, which was rather slow to establish itself.
- This emigration involves the whole of the country, and there is a contrast between the long-established emigration regions, such as the Rif and the East, and the recent emigration areas, such as the Tadla, the Atlantic plains and plateaux, the Atlas Mountains and the oases south of the Atlas.
- This emigration has largely built up from a stock of irregular migrants belonging to both sexes and to different age groups.
- Spain now occupies a place in the emigration strategies of both rural and urban families from all social categories, and has caused the triggering of migratory processes which take a number of forms.
- It is a phenomenon which is becoming more and more selective, affecting socially well-integrated families in Morocco and people who have been educated to a very high level.

Seen from Morocco, emigration to Spain is part of the process of constructing migratory territories which, under the effect of the irregular immigrant problem, and the instability and precariousness of the emigrants' social situations, have become more volatile and have become organised into a network.

Two approaches

The types of approach which have been favoured in this work were determined right from the outset by the subject of the research, which requires information to be available which is both quantitative and qualitative. The work is built on two surveys focused on the emigrant's family. The first is directed towards the collection of quantifiable data about emigrants and their families, and the second more qualitative survey is also targeted at families, but concentrates on the route of a single emigrant, looking at the path taken by family mobility, with the objective of gaining a deeper understanding of the movements.

The quantitative approach

The main objective of the first survey is to reveal the broad lines of Moroccan emigration to foreign countries in general and to Spain in particular. This is a survey which was not rolled out across the whole Moroccan territory, but was limited to the migratory households which were identified as being most representative of the places of origin of emigrants questioned in Andalusia.

The results should enable us to achieve the following: i) a quantitative evaluation of the proportion of Moroccan emigration abroad accounted for by emigration to Spain; ii) the characterisation of the social context from which the emigrant has come, by profiling the family of origin; iii) the determination of the profiles of emigrants before departure according to a series of sociodemographic variables (age, gender, marital status and socioprofessional status); iv) the reconstruction of the routes followed by migrants across Morocco and an initial mapping of the territory covered by migration to Andalusia; v) the identification of the types of relationships maintained by the emigrants with their families which have remained behind.

The information collected in the course of this survey is intended first to establish the outline of new migratory forms driven by Spain as a destination, and to specify their new characteristics and what differentiates them from migrations to other destinations. This will then be of use in establishing a base of quantitative data on a reference population within which samples will be taken for future surveys which must look more deeply at an understanding of migratory movements and trajectories.

The qualitative approach

Attempting to understand the problems of migration from an exclusive consideration of the volume of the flows seems to us to be too simplistic to give an idea of the socio-economic and geographical determinants behind the phenomenon. There are aspects within the migratory phenomenon which are linked to the individuals' personal experiences, and which cannot be expressed through numbers. To see this dimension which is rather overshadowed by the general data, interviews were carried out in Morocco with the families of those emigrants who were surveyed in the Andalusian provinces. This was the case when those we surveyed agreed to give us contact details for their families at home. Here our scientific approach is similar to a multi-sited method.

The aim of these interviews was to reconstruct the migratory project, to re-establish its trajectory across Morocco, to identify the possible relationships between the person's emigration and any residential and social mobility within the emigrant's family, and to see how far a relational life is still being maintained with the emigrant's family and country of origin.

THE SURVEY IN THE HOUSEHOLD OF ORIGIN

Created with the intention of obtaining both quantitative and qualitative information on the people undertaking migration and their families remaining behind in the country, the questionnaire distinguishes between five categories of people: the survey subject himself or herself, their family, other migrant members of this same family, members of the extended family of the person surveyed who are involved in migration, and the survey subject's closest emigrant about whom they have more information.

Questions dealt with demographic aspects (numbers, age, gender), social aspects (marital status, relationship, level of education), professional aspects (type of activity, status in that activity, place of work) and aspects relating to the accommodation (type of accommodation, ownership status, year of construction, contribution to the construction).

Then, to obtain more detailed information about the lives of emigrants, we were more selective. First of all, we limited our questions to just eight emigrants out of all those emigrants declared by the survey subject; in other words, four emigrants belonging to his family, who could be his father, mother, brothers and/or sisters, and four in the collateral families of their aunts and uncles. The information collected about these eight emigrants looked at their demographic profile (age, gender, marital status before departure), their relationship to the survey subject, their professional status prior to emigration, their year of emigration, the form of this emigration (regular or irregular), the destination country, the country of first arrival and their current place of residence (country and town).

The qualitative side of the questionnaire looks at information relating to one case among all close family members or collaterals in a migratory situation. Here, it was a question of finding out the personal reasons behind migration, locating the migratory project both in time and geographically within Morocco, and identifying those factors which determined the choice of route and means used to travel.

Questions about the migratory experience and the number of migration attempts should help to reconstruct the itineraries from the point of departure, in other words the usual place of residence, until the crossing of the border, with a question to establish a distinction between regular and irregular emigration.

The final aspect tackled by the questionnaire concerns the relationship maintained by the emigrant with their family and country of origin. This relationship is assessed through the regular contact made possible by means of correspondence (letters, telephone, Internet); return visits whose frequency gives an indication of the stability of the emigrant in the host country; and the sending of money to the family to see whether it is to keep the family going materially or to finance projects.

The 'last place of residence' criterion

In order to achieve a greater understanding of the mobility of emigrants in a circulatory territory which has been marked by collective and individual experiences, and in accordance with the stipulations of the terms of our study, we were keen to base our determination of which households would be targeted by the study on a suitable criterion derived from the results of the survey conducted in Andalusia.

The results which came to us from the Andalusian surveys looked first at the origin of the emigrants, which corresponded to their place of birth. This criterion seemed to us to be inadequate for tracing the spatial outlines of the regions supplying flows of emigrants to Spain, especially since this emigration relies on the high mobility of persons even within Morocco itself, and we had actually chosen to integrate this internal mobility into our field of observation. This is why we tried to use the criterion of last place of residence as declared by the survey subject, based on the hypothesis that internal migration often precedes or prepares the way for international migration.

The comparison of numbers involved according to the two criteria makes it possible to reveal the importance of places like Tangiers, Casablanca, Tetouan and Kenitra in relation to the number of persons who declare that they resided there prior to emigration. In addition, those provinces which occur most frequently do not always correspond to regions which lead directly to Spain. The importance of Beni Mellal and the Casablanca-Kenitra belt expresses a tendency adopted by emigration towards Spain which has already been noted in previous studies which highlighted four main foci corresponding to the Eastern Rif around the city of Nador, the Atlantic urban belt between Casablanca and Kenitra, the internal plains around Beni Mellal, and the Tangiers and Tetouan region (Lopez Garcia and Berriane 2004) (see Figure 1). Either as a place of destination, or simply as a region of transit, Andalusia is now a part of the migratory project of Moroccans from all regions of the country.

But beyond the complexity of the routes taken and the diversity of means used, it could be said that for a large proportion of people, their last place of residence does not always match their place of birth. The last phase of the journey is often preceded by a long journey within the country. The last place of residence of an immigrant in Morocco is therefore an appropriate criterion for selecting the regions where the survey should take place.

Selection of provinces

In principle, the results of the survey in Andalusia retain information about the municipalities and rural communes for each province from which the Moroccan emigrants have originated. But a sweep of the numbers shows that the provincial capitals are generally most represented. This is why we judged it important in our first exploratory survey to stick to the provincial level, which encompasses both urban and rural populations. The total numbers are allocated by province, which is considered to be the most appropriate spatial unit for this stage of the study. Classification on the basis of the last place of residence criterion has enabled us to sort the provinces into five groups according to the proportion of the number of people surveyed in Andalusia: those provinces with less than 1 per cent of the numbers; those whose percentage lies between 1 and 3; those between 3 and 9; those between 9 and 12; and finally, those with more than 12 per cent of the numbers.

Those cities chosen for conducting the survey were the regional hubs located in the main areas sending emigrants to Spain: Nador in the Eastern Rif, Beni Mellal and Khouribga in the Tadla Plain and phosphate plateau, Tangiers and Tetouan in the Northwest, Oujda in the East, Larache in the Low Loukkos, Kenitra, Rabat, Sale and Casablanca on the North-Mid Atlantic coast.

Population targeted

To pinpoint the categories to be surveyed, in the absence of a stock population which could be used as a reference when choosing a sample, we targeted the category of young people educated to the final year of secondary school or the first year of university. Our preference for this category in a survey on emigration which tries to trace the broad lines determining migratory routes can be justified by the following facts:

- Studies on emigration to Spain have generally shown the significance of the youngest categories. Pupils and students follow information on this subject very closely and will seek information from their relatives and friends who have already left about the possibility of following their example. They are therefore generally well informed, and sometimes better informed than adults, on matters such as this.

- This is a category which it is easy to approach and is not reticent when responding to questionnaires, especially to questions touching on the legal or illegal aspects of migration.

- This is a category which it is easy to approach within a setting which does not impose major constraints, administratively speaking, on those conducting the survey.

Surveys took place in high schools and/or university faculties in the cities concerned, and were supervised by research lecturer colleagues from various Moroccan universities, in accordance with the research links that they each have with a particular region. Establishments were chosen in such a manner as to be representative of the different city districts. It is clear that this methodology, like others, presents a certain number of drawbacks. The choice of young people attending school or university is quite selective, and was based on the hypothesis that these young people are representative of the populations of the cities being surveyed. But a wise choice of school establishments according to their locations within the cities should improve representativeness. Similarly, while the interest in emigration exhibited by young people is an advantage, it may also result in bias, in that the perception of migration among these young people will be coloured by this interest. The fact remains that this is still one of the best quick and effective approaches for reaching the families of emigrants and non-emigrants.

Numbers surveyed

When choosing the number of people to survey, we based our approach on the proportions recorded for each province according to the results from the survey in Andalusia. Given that this survey was conducted among a sample of 487 people, and since we do not know how that corresponds in proportional terms to the city of origin, and given that we are trying to have a reference population available for future surveys, we have therefore proceeded empirically by multiplying the numbers deduced from the survey in Andalusia for each city by ten.

Table 1 shows the distribution of the proportions recorded in the survey in Andalusia, and the numbers of the population adopted for survey in the different cities selected. These numbers are therefore proportional to the city's representation in the sample surveyed in Andalusia. But some last-minute difficulties in the field were not always conducive to the full coverage of the numbers.[2] This was particularly the case in the city of Nador where, out of a planned 600, we only managed to complete 220 surveys.

Table 1: Proportions for each city (provincial capital or centre of prefecture) in the total survey population

City (Province)	Size of original sample		Numbers adopted to be surveyed	
	Numbers	%	Numbers*	%
Beni Mellal-Khouribga	76	15.6	760	18.9
Nador	60	12.3	600	14.9
Casablanca	51	10.5	510	12.7
Tangiers	49	10	490	12.2
Larache	34	7	340	8.5
Tetouan	33	6.7	330	8.2
Rabat Sale	27	5.5	270	6.7
Kenitra	27	5.5	270	6.7
Oujda	24	5	240	6
Al Hoceima	17	3.5	210	5.2
Total	381	78	3810	100

* proportion in original sample multiplied by ten

CHARACTERISATION OF A NEW EMIGRATION BY MOROCCANS

In this presentation of results, we concentrate on four points which to us seem to be of greatest value in showing the advantages and methodological limitations of studying the phenomenon of emigration by way of a large-scale survey. We shall deal in order with the numbers of emigrants going to all destinations and the proportion of these going to Spain, the demographic profiles of emigrants and their families of origin, emigrants' socio-economic profiles and their routes and mobility.

MAGNITUDE OF EMIGRATION AND RELATIVE IMPORTANCE OF SPAIN

Our working hypothesis takes as its starting point the huge change in Moroccan migration in the 1990s, namely the extension of the migratory phenomenon – initially limited to the outlying districts experiencing difficulties and the rural areas – to the whole of the Moroccan territory, and particularly the cities. Alongside this extension of the area of origin nationally, we also saw a broadening of the destination areas, with the appearance of new countries such as Spain and Italy. It might therefore be supposed that these migratory flows establishing new departure hubs in Morocco and new destinations in Europe will be different from the flows arising from the old migratory system which linked Morocco to long-established destinations such as France or Belgium.

Proportion of emigrants

In the cities where the survey was conducted, the total number of emigrants accounted for was as many as 10,541 people. To calculate the proportion of emigrants from the total family population, we restricted ourselves in this first analysis to the data corresponding to emigrants from what we refer to as the survey subject's close family. Out of a total population of 23,105 persons, emigrants represented 8.2 per cent, i.e. 1,894 persons. This value is close to the proportion identified nationally in 2005, i.e. 8.6 per cent emigrants.

The proportion of the emigrant population appears even higher at family level. Out of all families surveyed, 27.9 per cent count one emigrant abroad among their number, with an average of 1.8 emigrants per family.

Looking at the place of residence of the relatives, it is noted that 69.9 per cent are of urban origin, compared to 10.1 per cent of rural origin.[3] It is certain that this high proportion of urban dwellers can be explained by the fact that the survey was conducted in town, but it is still true that the major centres are now characterised by the amount of emigration. This is due not only to the urban dwellers' taste for emigration, but also to the fact that, in a context where emigration is the result of an individual strategy, the town has also become a mandatory stopover which punctuates the migratory route for emigrants of rural origin. Depending on the individual case, the stay in town may be longer or shorter for the rural emigration candidate, but long enough to be able to declare one's residence in the host town.

To appreciate the proportion of emigrants in each city, we compared the total number of migrants to the total numbers of people in the families of the people we surveyed. To do this, we only looked at emigrants from the close family.

Table 2. Proportion of emigrants in the total population of families surveyed

City	Number of emigrants	Number of emigrants in Spain	Number of total population	% of emigrant pop.	% emigrated to Spain
Al Hoceima	230	104	1671	13.7	6.2
Beni Mellal	210	119	3957	5.3	3.0
Casablanca	154	37	3077	5	1.2
Kenitra	114	37	1579	7.2	2.3
Khouribga	171	21	1228	13.9	1.7
Larache	115	78	1494	7.7	5.2
Nador	137	49	1359	10.1	3.6
Oujda	233	136	2454	9.5	5.5
Rabat -- Sale	29	7	1030	5.4	1.2
Tangiers	230	113	2615	8.8	4.3
Tetouan	271	173	2641	10.3	6.6
Total	1894	874	23105	8.2	3.8c

Source: E3R survey - Morocco

Distribution by town of the proportion of emigrants in the total population shows a considerable variability in the frequency of mobility. From this point of view, there are three distinct categories of cities:

- Cities with a high proportion of emigrants, i.e. >10%: Khouribga, Al Hoceima, Tetouan, Nador, Oujda.
- Cities with an average proportion of between 7% and 10%: Kenitra, Larache, Oujda, Tangiers.
- Cities with a below-average proportion, <8%: Casablanca, Beni Mellal, Rabat and Sale.

The results we have obtained therefore confirm the general picture of the distribution of the major hubs in the generation of Moroccan emigrants covered by these cities: the east of the Moroccan Rif region, along a strip joining Al Hoceima to Oujda, passing through Nador, with 30 per cent of emigrants; the Tingitane Peninsula, Tetouan, Tangiers, Larache, with 26.8 per cent; the Tadla-phosphate plateau hub made up of Khouribga-Beni Mellal, with 19 per cent; the hub within the Atlantic axis including Kenitra, Rabat, Sale, Casablanca, with 17.5 per cent. But they also illustrate the fact that the recent emigration to Europe has spread to new regions which were previously largely untouched, such as Beni Mellal and the surrounding region, Khouribga or the cities along the Atlantic axis (see Figure 1).

Spain as a prime country of destination

A distribution of the emigrants by place of residence confirms the direction taken by Moroccan emigration, which affects several countries. Despite this diversity in places of residence, Europe's domination of the Moroccan migratory flow structure is still evident, accounting for 87.8 per cent of the emigrants included in the present survey.

Table 3. Emigrants by current country of residence[4]

Current country of residence	Total	%
Spain	3496	43.2
France	1308	16.1
Italy	1009	12.5
Belgium	548	6.8
Netherlands	496	6.1
Germany	254	3.1
USA	164	2.1
Canada	64	0.7
The Gulf	73	0.9
Maghreb	21	0.3
Other	217	2.7
Not known	442	5.5
Total	**8092***	**100**

*Aspects relating to socio-demographic characteristics only covered a proportion, with four emigrants in the close family and four in the extended family, making a total of 8092, which is 76.8% of the total emigrants counted.

Source: E3R survey - Morocco

Out of the whole of Western Europe, Spain seems to be the favoured hub for migrants: it comes top of the list of emigrants' countries of residence (43.2 per cent). For a new destination for Moroccan migration, these figures are quite remarkable. This choice of Spain as the favoured destination for Moroccan migration is no coincidence, and is the result of a change in migratory strategies in response to the rigour of restrictions imposed by the traditional immigration countries. According to declarations from migrants' family members, the reasons for the choice of destination can be summarised as follows:

- The economic cost of regular or irregular migration is lower, given Spain's geographical proximity.

- The opportunities available for work do not require high levels of qualifications for a category of migrants who are generally educated to a low level. Those who spoke to us stressed the existence of greater tolerance towards irregular migrants in Spain and in Andalusia in particular. These migrants easily find work in the agricultural, building and service sectors, even if it is under difficult circumstances, as they are waiting to regularise their situation with the authorities.

- The prospect of obtaining residence permits during the collective regularisation campaigns favoured by the state is one positive factor placing Spain (and Andalusia in this case) at the top of the planned destinations included in the migratory projects of irregular migrants.

- Spain is also seen by a large number of emigrants as being the doorway into a larger economic and mobility area, namely the European Union and the Schengen area.

- Finally, Andalusia is one of those regions of Spain where the economic renaissance has gone hand in hand with a metamorphosis of the labour market. The development of the industrial agriculture and service sectors has largely relied on an immigrant workforce which has few demands in terms of pay and social rights.

But the possibilities offered by this development for the new arrivals to settle down do not match the facilities for social and economic integration. And this aspect is certainly present in the view of Spain and Andalusia that is held by family members. This is why the decision to stay over the shorter or longer term may equally well be the outcome of a migratory project which was clearly planned from the start or it may be a solution imposed by circumstances.

The distribution of emigrants living in Spain by city helps us to establish three separate categories of city (Table 4 and Figure 1):

Figure 1. Representation of Spain among destinations declared in surveyed cities

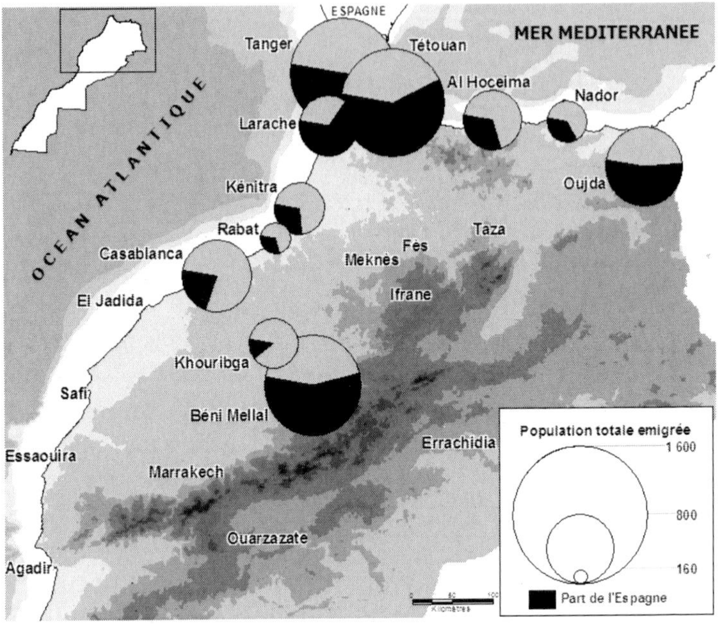

Source: E3R survey – Morocco

- Cities which have more than 50% of their emigrants in Spain: Larache, Tetouan, Oujda, Beni Mellal, Tangiers.
- Cities which have between 30% and 50% of their emigrants in Spain: Rabat, Sale, Nador, Al Hoceima.
- Cities with fewer than 30% of their emigrants in Spain: Casablanca, Kenitra, Khouribga.

The migratory hubs with a connection to Spain fall outside the traditional links connecting the Rif and the North of Morocco with this destination. Thus Beni Mellal and Oujda are ahead of Al Hoceima and Nador, which rank alongside Rabat and Sale. Are these sufficient grounds to talk of a change in the configuration of the main hubs sending emigrants to Spain?

Figure 2. Year of emigration

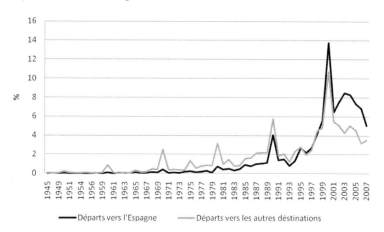

Source: E3R survey - Morocco

Looking at these emigration hubs at the country level, it is difficult at present, given the current state of our knowledge, to establish any kind of direct correlation between the socio-economic and demographic factors of a city and the extent of emigration to Spain. At most, we can talk of a relationship between internal mobility and external emigration, insofar as cities, from which the main flows of current emigration originate, have played the role of recipients for the rural exodus for several decades.

The most recent transformations to affect the direction of rural exodus flows, which were long polarised along the Atlantic coast, can be seen in the new geographical distribution arising from the economic dynamism experienced in regions such as the North West, around the port of Tangiers-Med, the North East between Nador and Oujda, as a border region, and the South West between Agadir and the Laayoune Dakhla coast (see Figure 1), in connection with the economic renaissance linked to agriculture, fishing and tourism.

But Khouribga's importance in the overall picture of emigration, and Beni Mellal's importance in emigration to Spain, comes from the fact that these are two cases which provide some variation from the picture which is relatively dominated by the coastal dimension. The cities of Beni Mellal and Khouribga are considered to be two great hubs sending out migrants which emerged during the 1980s.

The flows were fed first of all by the rural populations from the irrigated plain of Tadla and the countryside which was in crisis in the Khouribga phosphate region, before extending to take in urban dwellers in addition to the population of the mountainous regions of the coastal Middle Atlas and High Central Atlas.

Mostly recent migration

Spain is one of those new destinations which only started to attract a flow of migrants in recent times. The results of the survey conducted in Morocco show that it was at the start of the millennium, i.e. after 2000, that flows became large.

Of the total number of immigrants who have settled in Spain, 69 per cent arrived after this date, compared with 44 per cent of those who settled in the traditional immigration countries. This reflects a reversal of usual trends, because between the years prior to 1980 and the year 2000, the volume of flows heading towards Spain was low, and grew irregularly, with 11.2 per cent arriving before 1980, 5.9 per cent between 1980 and 1990, and 10.8 per cent between 1990 and 2000. Unlike Spain as a whole, Andalusia stands out because of the continuity of the growth in the flows that it has received. After a period of growth – 1.7 per cent before 1980, 10.8 per cent between 1980 and 1990 – there was a stagnation phase – 10.8 per cent between 1990 and 2000 – before the region saw a steep rise in flows, with 76 per cent after the year 2000.

Considerable irregular migration

These figures, which unquestionably bear witness to the increase in the volume of migration since 2000, contradict all talk of a slow-down, or even a halt, in emigration after the closure of Europe and controls on flows at this continent's southern boundary.

This is confirmed by the significance of irregular emigration in the accounts given by the survey subjects. The development of emigration practices, including those which are irregular in nature, is largely determined by the perception of the act of emigration against the background of Europe's withdrawal as a traditional destination for Moroccan emigrants, and of social change which sometimes proves difficult for a population feeling pressured to assert itself at the economic and socio-cultural level.

Table 4. Regular and irregular emigrants by city

City	Regular Number	%	Irregular Number	%	Total
Al Hoceima	284	80.7	68	19.3	352
Beni Mellal	516	62.5	310	37.5	826
Casablanca	540	76.5	166	23.5	706
Kenitra	423	90.4	45	9.6	468
Khouribga	376	74	132	26	508
Larache	367	72.1	142	27.9	509
Nador	416	90	46	10	462
Oujda	546	76.8	165	23.2	711
Rabat -- Sale	180	88.2	24	11.7	204
Sale	103	88.8	13	11.2	116
Tangiers	827	84.8	148	5.2	975
Tetouan	748	77.2	221	22.8	969
Total	4475	78.1	1467	21.9	6690

In the group of emigrants contacted in the survey, emigration is seen as irregular for 1,467 emigrants, which is 21.9 per cent of the total number of emigrants, of which 6.8 per cent are women. Here, the irregularity concerns what is entered into the entry status in the country of immigration.

The distribution by city shows the size of three hubs of irregular immigration: the hub of Beni Mellal-Khouribga-Casablanca, the hub of Larache-Tetouan, and the Eastern hub. The two main hubs centred on Beni Mellal and the East are known as two of the places where migratory practices emerged in relation to the new destinations, particularly Spain and Italy.

The distribution of irregular migrants by the first country of emigration shows a predominance of irregular migrants among emigrants for whom Spain was the first country of emigration, i.e. 32.8 per cent, with Italy at 28.9 per cent. Spain's importance in terms of irregular emigration is all the more evident in its contribution to the total number of emigrants who left the country in an irregular manner, i.e. 69.5 per cent.

Figure 3. Proportion of irregular migration in total declarations by immigration country

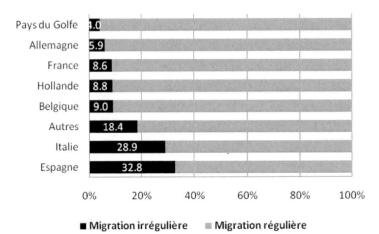

Source: E3R survey – Morocco - 2008

It can therefore be deduced from this distribution that regular emigration has continued to operate through allowed or recognised channels, and has coexisted to some extent with irregular emigration. This is because irregular emigration, beyond its increased frequency in certain cities, is relatively widespread across all cities and towards all destinations. However, it should be stated that in many cases, what was declared to be regular migration has later become irregular migration. This is the case for all Moroccan visitors returning to Spain with a tourist visa or who are registered for a course of study, who then become irregular migrants once their visa runs out.

A NEW DEMOGRAPHIC PROFILE[5]

As described by classic literature on migration (Berrada 1993; Bonnet and Bossard 1973; Bossard 1979; GERA 1992; Hamdouch et al. 1981), the profile of the Moroccan emigrants in the first phases of this migration was dominated by illiterate adult males of rural origin. Recent research has shown that this profile has changed considerably, becoming more complex at the same time, following various alterations including those to the socio-demographic parameters of emigration candidates. Apart from the effects of the family reunification phenomenon, and the birth of new generations of Moroccans in a migratory situation, there is the contribution made by new forms of emigration, including irregular ones. The results of our investigations have come together to create a migrant profile which bears the hallmarks of these new migratory forms.

Young, predominantly male emigration

From Morocco, the declarations from households give a glimpse of an age structure among migrants, who are predominantly young. This youth is even more marked in Spain compared with the total emigrants to Europe. The 18–29-year-old age group is remarkably high, since it represents 59.1 per cent of the average population settled in Spain, compared with 47.8 per cent for other destinations. The 30–49-year-old group is 36 per cent in Spain compared with 39.8% for the average across other countries hosting declared emigrants. The 60-plus age group works out at just 0.1 per cent in Spain compared with 3.4 per cent for emigrants in other European countries.

Figure 4. Age pyramid for the sample of declared emigrants

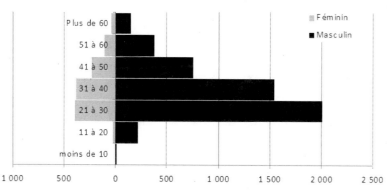

Source: E3R survey – Morocco - 2008

With the extreme youth of that group of Moroccan migrants settled in Spain compared with the average across all migrants, the demographic profile of emigrants residing in this country is similar to the situation in the Mediterranean countries of recent immigration, in that the category of young people of working age is larger than those who have retired. It also illustrates the highly selective nature of the migration.

The majority of emigrants leaving Morocco were men, with women making up just 22.7 per cent of those settled in Spain, and here too there was a difference compared with the average across other countries, which was 34 per cent. The presence of women allows one to suggest that this migration, although relatively recent, is currently undergoing demographic change, evidenced by a tendency to reconstitute families through family reunification, the ageing of the earliest emigrants, and the rise of a new generation born in situ. But qualitative interviews conducted in Morocco also bear witness to flows of women migrants on an individual basis, who are often single, divorced or widowed. The acceptance of mobility among women in a society which has until now been conformist is the result of a socio-cultural transformation imposed not only by greater openness to others, but also by the pressure of material needs, which weigh heavily on family life.

A preponderance of single people leaving

A breakdown by marital status on leaving shows the emigrant population is broadly dominated by single people, who make up 64.6 per cent of the total, but there is a difference between men (70 per cent) and women (42.8 per cent), the latter being better represented among married people. Thus, while for men emigration tends to involve young, particularly single people; among women, the proportion of married women would suggest that the migratory project continues to depend upon marriage and that migration retains its family-based characteristics.

This picture changes noticeably when the *current* status of immigrants is the focus. The percentage of single people drops by nearly a half. Marriage after migration has affected 28 per cent of the sample, and nearly one-third of the men.

THE SOCIO-ECONOMIC CHARACTERISTICS OF THE
EMIGRANT POPULATION

Emigration as a solution to the socio-economic problems experienced within the country of origin has long been the lot of the most underprivileged levels of society. In the current context of emigration, the social profile of prospective leavers has tended to diversify, and the search for a life elsewhere is a choice which is no longer subject simply to material constraints. To get closer to the new realities of migration, we looked at aspects relating to the emigrant's level of education, the social group of their family in Morocco and their socio-professional status prior to leaving.

Less and less illiterate on leaving

The level of education is a criterion which reveals much about the trends being followed by emigration, which is no longer a survival strategy restricted to the illiterate and less educated. The issue of education in fact goes beyond simple questions about the state of a community in terms of literacy and levels of skill in reading and writing, but instead there is a need to consider issues such as social success, the ability to adapt to changing situations in the labour market and the capacity to compete in an open market which is subject to the forces of globalisation. Moreover, the intellectual profile of a Moroccan emigrant has developed following the general provision of education and the cultural openness of society, particularly in towns and cities.

This development may be seen through the growing numbers of emigrants who have been through school. In the case concerning us here, 85.5 per cent know how to read and write, of whom 41.8 per cent have been educated at secondary level and 20 per cent at a higher level, compared with 17.7 per cent educated to primary level and 6 per cent who have never got beyond Qur'anic schooling. The prevalence of each category across the various countries where emigrants live shows a relative variation. In general, emigrants tending to have been educated to higher levels head towards North America, while more migrants educated to secondary level can be found in the Gulf States, and those who have not gone beyond primary level are more frequently found in the Maghreb countries.

Less and less extreme vulnerability on leaving

Vulnerability is a difficult aspect to judge in quantitative terms without recourse to the notion of income. The target survey population – young people – are ignorant of this kind of information, which remains the secret preserve of their parents, and questioning to find out the level of their income, quite apart from its lack of clarity, is not always welcome. Information about people's material standing must normally lead to a categorisation of families in terms of wealth and social position, and for these purposes the notion of income as indicated by salaries or allowances seems to us to be inadequate and has therefore been avoided.

The father's socio-professional status

Table 5. Father's profession in families with or without emigrants

Status	Families without emigrants	%	Families with emigrants	%
Business owner	704	30.7	280	33.5
Manager	361	15.8	128	15.3
State employee / employee	683	29.8	230	27.5
Day labourer	235	10.3	74	8.9
Other	306	13.4	124	14.8
Total	2289	100	836	100

According to the father's socio-professional status, emigrants generally come from families where the father is either a business owner (26.9 per cent), or an employee in the private or state sector (22.1 per cent), with day labourers and managers making up 20 per cent of the total.

When broken down by sectors of activity, the picture tends to be dominated by the service sector, which also includes public administration in the case of those who specified the father's profession, i.e. 10.8 per cent of all families having at least one emigrant.

Housing conditions

To measure housing conditions, we categorised emigrants identified in the survey of the subject's family according to the type of housing used by the parents. Out of the 1,040 families with at least one emigrant, the predominant housing type was the family house (69.6 per cent), while other types broke down into flats (11.2 per cent), detached houses (5.1 per cent), housing under construction (5.9 per cent) and shacks (0.9 per cent). When housing is broken down by ownership status, it can be seen that in the case of families with emigrants, 88.5% are owners, compared with 8 per cent who rent. The proportions noted among families with emigrants in Spain are similar.

If one considers that family houses, which are taken to mean family homes constructed in developments and consisting of one to three floors with a garage, are a form of dwelling which Moroccan families generally come to acquire on the basis of collective self-finance, it can be said that emigrants have generally come from families which are socially unremarkable, being neither poor nor rich.

To summarise, neither the type of housing nor the ownership status show any differentiation between families with no emigrants and those whose members have emigrated. Finally, the hypothesis according to which migration primarily affects families experiencing great socio-economic difficulties does not hold today.

The emigrant's socio-professional status prior to departure

Among those reasons used to explain the causes of emigration, reference is often made to unemployment, under-employment and vulnerability in a more general sense. Looking at this parameter for emigrants included in our survey, it can be seen that out of all emigrants 26.7 per cent were declared to be unemployed prior to departure and 45.6 per cent were employed, while just 18.6 per cent were considered to be students.

In comparison with these average values, it emerges that in the case of emigrants residing in Spain, more of them were employed

(48.5 per cent) than unemployed (28.9 per cent). This means that the motives driving emigration do not always arise from the desire to satisfy material needs.

Reference to the social categories from which the emigrants in the survey have come is conditioned by the level of accuracy of the available information. Through the parameters of housing and the father's professional status, we have been able to see that general traits can be sketched out, enabling us to put forward the idea that emigration is one social trait of the average Moroccan family, and it has tended to become the preserve of all upper middle classes.

HIGH INTERNAL MOBILITY PRIOR TO EXTERNAL MIGRATION

Looking at a single emigrant per household, namely the one about whom the survey subject has the most information, it is possible to reconstruct the migratory route within Morocco prior to emigration. In the case of regular emigration, departure is via a city which is linked to a foreign country through the presence of a port and/or airport. For unofficial emigration, the crossing points are more difficult to determine not only because the survey subject maintained a certain reticence about activities which are judged to be illegal, but also because the route followed by this type of emigration is sometimes only known to the emigrant, who himself is often kept in ignorance of the place which will be the crossing point.

Where the town or city of departure is concerned, out of 2,334 emigrants, 33 per cent crossed the border from a town or city which is not their usual place of residence. This town or city is just as likely to be the first or the last stage of a migratory route within the country which has passed through a number of locations.

To illustrate the types of routes followed by the emigrant, we shall cite the cases of Oujda and Beni Mellal as examples. Routes identified in Oujda bear witness to a refocusing on the East. The circulatory routes followed by emigrants interviewed in this city and leaving the city or the Eastern region are restricted to a territory based around the Mediterranean ports. Flows are centred on the region and rarely pass through the South West or the East. However, the routes identified in Beni Mellal reveal an almost nationwide spread. They are more dispersed, whether in terms of the points of departure or the final destinations, and they cover different parts of the national territory. This implies greater mobility and probably indicates a situation where Beni Mellal is becoming more and more an obligatory stopping place for departures and returns, and a central hub in the Moroccan migratory system.

CONCLUSION

Initially, the methods adopted in this project to analyse recent Moroccan migrations to Spain and Andalusia were meant essentially to rely on investigations of a qualitative type since, in co-ordination with the teams in Andalusia, we were to focus our efforts on interviews with emigrants' families who had remained in Morocco. However, we were unable to embark upon these interviews without having an idea of the overall characteristics of this migration, and particularly the amount of the total volume of migration accounted for by these two destinations (Spain and Andalusia). The quantitative survey presented here was seen as a quick and effective method to produce information intended to provide answers to these two questions.

The other strength of our methodological approach is the simultaneous observation of migrants in Andalusia and their families in Morocco. The survey was certainly guided from the outset by the results obtained from the survey conducted in Andalusia, whether it be the choice of towns and cities, or the selection of the people to be surveyed. The data collected in Morocco by means of this survey from emigrants' families could be compared with those gathered in Andalusia from these emigrants. This co-ordinated approach to a single phenomenon from two different observatories, each placed at one end of the socio-spatial field covered by this phenomenon, is both an innovation in the study of Moroccan migration and a challenge. Indeed, by virtue of the different characteristics and contexts of the two surveys, one could not expect always to come up with similar findings. However, this is already a meaningful result of the method, which illustrates the limits and the sometimes one-sided character of approaches which only observe the phenomenon from one end, whether it be the point of departure or the point of arrival. But we have also seen a considerable convergence in the results obtained, enabling us satisfactorily to describe these migrations.

Finally, the combination of this survey of a quantitative nature with the project's second methodological aspect, which is more qualitative, is also an innovation where Morocco is concerned. While there is not space to deal with this second aspect here, it must be stressed that the generation of knowledge about Moroccans who have settled in Andalusia is not limited to the simple quantification of the numbers involved and of their socio-demographic characteristics; it goes beyond this to understand the emigrant as a person caught between two territories and two lives.

For this reason, the qualitative approach using interviews was favoured as a second step. It was conducted in accordance with a procedure based on the co-ordination and simultaneity of interviews which took place in Andalusia. The people targeted for interviews in Morocco have a family relationship with the emigrant interviewed in Andalusia, whose consent was a necessary precondition. The details obtained from the interviews in Morocco helped, on the one hand, to throw light on the family context prior to and following the emigrant's departure, and on the other hand, made it possible to throw further light on the results of the first survey.

Thanks to the data collected through the quantitative survey, we have been able to describe this migration and pinpoint what sets it apart. We have only been able to discuss a few aspects of this description here, including the distribution of those involved in this migration and its timing, their demographic profiles, their socio-economic characteristics, and the first routes taken in Morocco by these emigrants.

Notes

1. This project involves two teams: a Spanish team from the Universities of Granada, Malaga and Almeria, coordinated by A. Cohen, and a Moroccan team comprising researchers from E3R, coordinated by M. Berriane. It has received finance under the Excellence Project initiated by the Consejeria de Inovacion, Cienca y empresa de La Junta Andalucia, with reference number SEJ-1390.

2. The timing of the survey clashed with periods of strike action or examinations.

3. The rest (20 per cent) did not give any response to this question.
4. A maximum of eight emigrants only is included in each questionnaire.
5. Aspects relating to socio-demographic characteristics only covered a proportion, with four emigrants in the close family and four in the extended family, making a total of 8092, which is 76.8% of the total emigrants counted.

References

Berrada, A. (1993) 'Migration et développement économique au Maroc', in *Migrations et Coopération Internationale*, Les enjeux pour les pays de l'OCDE, GD (93) 52, Paris: OCDE.

Bonnet, J. and R. Bossard (1973) 'Aspects géographiques de l'émigration marocaine vers l'Europe', *Revue de Géographie du Maroc* 23–24: 5–50.

Bossard, R. (1979) 'Un espace de migration. Les travailleurs du Rif oriental (Province du Nador) et l'Europe', Espace rural N° 1(CNRS-ERA 506): 213.

GERA (1992) 'Etude des mouvements migratoires du Maroc vers la Communauté Européenne', Etude pour le compte de la délégation de la CE au Maroc, Faculté des Lettres et des Sciences Humaines Rabat.

Hamdouch, B. et al. (1981) 'Migrations internationale au Maroc. Une enquête sur ses caractères et ses effets en milieu urbain', Rabat: INSEA.

Lopez Garcia, B. (1993) 'Espana y la inmigration magrebi: de pais de transito a pais de destino', RGM 15(1–2): 23–47.

Lopez Garcia, B. and M. Berriane (eds.) (2004) *Atlas de la inmigracion marroqui en Espana*, Madrid: Taller de Estudios Internationales Mediterraneos.

Portes, A. (1997) 'Globalization from Below: The Rise of Transnational Communities', Working Paper, Princeton, p.27, www. transcomm.ox.ac.uk/working%20papers/portes.pdf.

Tarrius, A. (2002) *La mondialisation par le bas*, Paris: Balland.

Chapter 4

<hr/>

UNDERSTANDING MIGRANTS' REMITTANCES: EVIDENCE FROM THE US–NIGERIA MIGRATION SURVEY

Una Okonkwo Osili

INTRODUCTION

Remittances to sub-Saharan Africa make up a central yet poorly understood outcome of the migration process. According to official estimates, remittances from overseas residents and non-resident workers to developing countries amounted to over $300 billion in 2008. Although there is considerable interest in understanding remittances, very few data sources provide a comprehensive picture of the economic ties between African migrants and their origin households.[1] Official macro statistics on remittances often underestimate remittance flows in Africa, particularly because a large share of transfers occurs through informal channels.

This chapter is based on an original data set – the US–Nigeria Migration Survey – a year-long programme of field research that provides a matched sample of migrants and their origin households. The survey was designed to better understand migrants and their economic linkages in their origin communities. The matched sampling involved a first-round survey in the US and a second-round survey in Nigeria, which yielded a sub-sample of Nigerian households connected to their US-based households. The methodology provides insights into the motives for migrants' remittances, relying on a formal survey instrument as well as in-depth interviews with migrant and origin households. Previous work has dealt with the transfer of resources between the migrant and the origin family, using either data on the migrant or data obtained solely from the household of origin. However, theoretical models of remittances and other intra-family transfers often emphasise the importance of collecting data on both sending and receiving households.

This chapter focuses on remittances from Nigeria–US migration. Nigeria is the only country in sub-Saharan Africa to rank among the top 25 remittance-receiving countries globally, and it accounts for 60 per cent of all the recorded remittance flows to sub-Saharan Africa. However, within the context of Nigeria, the study of remittances from international migration presents significant data challenges. There are high costs associated with collecting data on both migrants and their home families; thus, few existing data sets contain this type of information. Networks and contacts in both the host country and the country of origin are often needed to facilitate this type of data collection.

This chapter makes two important contributions. First, it represents a first attempt to use a matched sample of international migrants and their origin households to investigate the remittance decision. The sample is based on a year-long programme of research in 1997 conducted by the author in the US and Nigeria. An important goal was to provide a comprehensive picture of senders and recipients that could be used to investigate transfers between migrants and their families. By using independent measures of the economic circumstances of both the migrant and the home household, we can improve upon studies that rely on data obtained from only one side of the migrant–home family transaction. Although migrants reside in a distant geographical location, they continue to participate in family decision-making and the familial pooling of resources with their family members in the country of origin.

Second, this chapter aims to disaggregate remittances in order to better understand their overall impact in the origin country. Remittances are often treated in aggregate terms; however, considerable evidence shows that remittances are sent towards various end uses (Adams 1991; Banarjee 1984; Mexican Migration Project 2000). In particular, remittances may be sent towards the consumption needs of the home family, as well as channelled towards investments in the country of origin or even community development projects.[2] Much of the existing work tends to measure remittances in aggregate terms. However, to better understand their overall impact, we must distinguish between classes of remittances – migrants' transfers to family members versus their savings in the origin country as well as migrant contributions to community development projects in their origin communities. The matching methodology used in this study provides an opportunity to understand different types of remittances that are sent from both the migrant and origin household perspectives.

FIELD RESEARCH IN TWO CONNECTED WORLDS

The main research questions in this chapter involve disaggregating remittances – 'unpacking' the forms of economic exchanges that take place between international migrants and their families in origin countries. The research questions also involve illuminating migrants' motives for remittances. From the outset, I recognised that networks and contacts in both the origin (Nigeria) and host (US) countries would facilitate collecting data on both migrants and their home families. To collect data on international migrants and their home families, a multi-site approach would be required. In order to investigate sensitive topics such as money transfers and investment decisions, I would also need to gain the confidence of my survey respondents in the US and Nigeria.

I began the process by examining extant structured questionnaires on private transfers in the US and Nigeria and acquired training in less formal research methods. I also realised the limitations of formal questionnaires. Conventional survey instruments, while useful in documenting remittance flows, may be limited in their ability to illuminate the motives and beliefs of migrants and their origin households. In contrast, less formal research methods provide a unique opportunity to learn about migrants' beliefs, motives and attitudes. Informal conversations during field research can also provide a unique opportunity to study the ties that persist across transnational locations and the process of sending transfers to family members in the country of origin.

Table 1. Remittances from international migration

US–Nigeria Migration Survey 1997

Variable	US Migrants (Migrant Sample)		US Migrants & Origin Households (Matched Sample)	
	Mean	Standard Deviation	Mean	Standard Deviation
Migrant sent remittance in past year	0.93		0.93	
Origin household received remittance in past year			0.87	
Migrant sent transfer to origin family	0.85		0.86	
Migrant sent transfer towards savings in origin	0.35		0.40	
Total amount sent in past year (US$)	5807.43	10653.92	6018.52	7961.14
Transfers sent to origin family	3018.60	3797.58	3489.72	4317.56
Transfers received by origin family			2220.25	3970.48
Savings-related transfers	2706.95	8737.84	2400.07	5352.08
Community-related transfers	277.69	1216.65	128.73	467.28

Note: For the survey period $1=86 naira. Transfers sent refer to total remittances sent by a migrant to ALL family members in the origin country and is based on the migrant's report. Transfers received by the origin family refer to remittances received by a specific origin family member from a given US migrant and is based on the origin family's report. Savings-related transfers refer to migrant transfers sent towards investment and asset acquisition in the origin country. Other transfers refer to other transfers including transfers to origin community institutions.

DATA COLLECTION

The survey instrument was designed to explicitly link migrants and their origin households.[3] Given the extensive and fairly comprehensive nature of the data requirements, I kept my US sample size relatively small. Table 1 provides an overview of the economic ties that migrants maintain with their origin communities. The small sample size allowed for the collection of an unusually detailed set of survey instruments. It also permitted one-to-one interviews with each migrant household, including the opportunity for informal discussions. The survey design resulted in a very high rate of participation; only two migrant households declined to participate in the survey.

The first part of my field research involved the selection of a random sample of immigrant households. To obtain a random sample of Nigerian emigrants, I searched the Chicago-area telephone listings by surnames and first names, selecting distinctly Ibo names.[4] Each respondent in the US sample completed a required information sheet identifying the head of their origin household and two other adult family members who would be available for interviews in Nigeria. To facilitate eventual location and interviews with the home families of the initial survey respondents, I restricted my US sample to the Ibo of south-eastern Nigeria.[5] I chose this sub-sample of the Nigerian population to ensure relative ease in locating home families in Nigeria. Using the migrant survey instrument, I obtained information on the various methods that migrants use to transfer income to their home families and the types of remittances that they sent during the survey period. I also collected detailed information on the migrants' asset holdings in the country of origin and in the host country. Discussions of asset holdings emerged as a highlight of many interviews; several migrants retrieved documents and photos of their houses and landholdings in Nigeria.

In the second stage, using the contact information provided by the migrant households, interviews were conducted in Nigeria among home households. From these interviews, the following data sources emerge: (i) a sample of Nigerian emigrant households in Chicago, Illinois, and (ii) a matched sample of home households in Nigeria.

The home household information was obtained from interviews conducted in Nigeria during the summer of 1997. The home household sample is non-random by design, as the selection of home household respondents relied on information provided by the Chicago migrant sample. In the first stage of the survey, I asked each migrant household to identify the head of its home household as well as two other adult family members who would be available for interviews in Nigeria,[6] emphasising that my research questions involved studying both sides of remittances – the senders as well as the recipients.

The second component of my field research took place in Nigeria, which provided a unique opportunity to investigate the impact of both sides of the migrant–home family relationship in the migrant's investment decision. During the summer of 1997, I conducted interviews among migrants' home families in Nigeria. The home household sample consists of 61 families. The home household sample offers only a sub-sample of the initial sample of migrant households (112 households). A complete set of home households would include all the home families of the initial US migrant sample (N=112). Sixty-one of those 112 comprise matched migrant-origin household observations.

In general, I encountered a high response rate on all parts of the questionnaire while conducting field work in the US and Nigeria. The survey design was advantageous. In many cases, the migrant in Chicago had already informed the origin family in advance that I would be contacting them upon my arrival in Nigeria. This eliminated the need for extensive personal introduction during the origin household surveys in Nigeria.

One key question is whether this matched sample can be considered representative of the initial US sample. In order to address this issue, I discuss the yield rate from the initial US sample. The yield from the initial US sample can be explained by the difficulties associated with locating addresses and interviewing origin households. The yield rate varied considerably, depending on whether the origin family resided in an urban or rural area. In rural areas, where it was easier to find the respondents at home at the time of the interview and to locate the origin household identified by the migrant household, the yield rate was higher.[7]

In urban areas, it was often more difficult to establish contact with the origin household. In most cases, it was impossible to schedule an interview in advance, and, because in many urban areas in Nigeria, streets are unmarked, locating the origin household identified by the migrant household was less straightforward in urban areas than in rural areas. However, inquiries within the general vicinity proved useful in locating the residence of the origin household to be interviewed.

During my fieldwork, I caught glimpses of many houses in south-eastern Nigeria and was warmly received by nearly all the people that I visited. Some houses belonged to migrants who lived in Nigerian cities such as Lagos, Kano, Abuja, Port Harcourt and Enugu. But many houses belonged to migrants who lived in cities and towns in the US, the United Kingdom, Saudi Arabia, Italy and other destination countries. Migrants' houses could be distinguished by their imposing two- or three-storey red-brick structure, which were unusual in villages of small cement-block and mud bungalows.

By the end of the Nigerian component of my field research, I had surveyed migrants and their origin families in Nigeria using the names and addresses supplied by the Chicago sample. I had also visited many origin communities. Migrants' transfers and investments occur in diverse environments, and the home-town sample attempts to capture some of this variation. Seventy-one home towns, varying in terms of land area, population, urbanisation, and level of development, were included in the home-town sample.

DEVELOPING FORMAL MODELS

After reviewing my field notes and reflecting on my conversations on both sides of the Atlantic, I initially concluded that remittances were more complex than mere monetary transfers that migrants sent to their families for food and consumption needs. My interviews and data analysis from the US–Nigeria Migration Study suggested at least three main classes of migrant remittances: family transfers, investment-related transfers, and community transfers. I was particularly interested in developing theoretical and empirical models of investment-related transfers, or remittances that are sent to finance the migrants' own investments in the country of origin, as well as community transfers, or remittances that are sent to support community development projects in the migrants' origin communities.

MIXING METHODS: MIGRANTS AND HOUSING INVESTMENTS

A key observation from my initial field research was that nearly half of my sample of Nigerian immigrants in Chicago had initiated substantial housing investments in their communities of origin in south-eastern Nigeria. To uncover the importance of migrants' housing investments, I developed additional questions focused on housing, such as: why did Nigerian migrants invest in housing in their origin communities while they lived and worked in the US? Why were housing and real estate the dominant investments that migrants initiated in their origin communities?

My field research experience provided some clear directions towards understanding migrants' housing investments in their country of origin. To illuminate the motivations for migrants' housing investments, I developed theoretical models informed by insights from field research. The models suggest that migrants' investment decisions can be studied as an interaction of migrant and origin family characteristics as well as origin community variables.

My goal was to uncover the primary factors that formed the migrants' decision to invest in housing. Field research provided a unique opportunity to learn about the motivations behind housing investment decisions through direct observations and informal discussions with migrants and their home families. I recognised that home ownership is a near-universal symbol of economic achievement among Nigerian migrants. Housing has several desirable properties including durability, low monitoring costs, and visibility. In the Nigerian context, housing also represents a less risky class of investment. However, I could not rule out the possibility that the dominance of housing could also reflect limitations in the investment choices available to migrants in the country of origin. The lessons obtained from field research reinforce the need to consider extensions to the standard framework of investment behaviour.

First, the community of origin plays an important role in the migrants' decision to invest. Migrants view their housing investments as a contribution to their home towns. Direct fieldwork observations in several villages in south-eastern Nigeria also reveal the importance of migrants' housing investments to residents in the community of origin, who can benefit from the employment opportunities and increased demand for local construction materials created by these housing investments. In addition, housing investments modernise the existing housing stock and improve the outward appearance of the home town.

Second, during informal discussions with Nigerian migrants in the US, the relationship between membership in the home community and housing was emphasised. Fieldwork in Nigeria confirmed this relationship. In many villages, there is relatively good information about migrants who were residents outside Nigeria, particularly when these migrants owned houses in the home town. Within the home-town environment, home ownership served as a means of identification. Migrants could be distinguished within the home-town according to whether they owned a house(s) or whether they were currently building a house in the home town. Thus, a house in the home town helps to establish the migrants' membership in the community.

Finally, discussions with migrants highlight the role of the home family in the decision to invest in housing in the home town. In some cases, migrants undertake housing investments in order to provide a flow of housing services to their home families. However, migrants' houses may also lie vacant or under-occupied over long time periods. In this setting, it is likely that housing investments play an important role in providing information about the migrants' resources abroad and the home families' access to these resources. Less-formal interviews during the course of my fieldwork confirm the information role of migrants' housing investments. According to one village member:

> A house is a highly visible sign of accomplishment and wealth. Few people in the home town can observe the migrant's income level or the social status that a migrant has achieved in the United States, but the entire community can observe the size and quality of houses [that] that migrant has built in the home town.

The flow of information about the migrant's resources, as well as the migrant's resource connection to the home family, can confer benefits for the home family within the home-town environment.

Table 2. Nigerians in the US, 1990 Census

Comparing the US Census microdata sample to the Chicago Field research sample

	Chicago Sample Field Research 1997 N=112		Microdata Sample 1990 Census: Nigerians in US N=2262	
VARIABLE	Mean	Std Deviation	Mean	Std Deviation
Head of Household Characteristics				
Head's age	38.94	7.32	34.41	6.68
Male=1	0.92		0.88	
Citizenship (citizen=1)	0.44		0.22	
Marital status (married=1)	0.60		0.61	
Years of schooling	14.70	4.96	13.64	2.02
Bachelor's degree	0.85		0.70	

Year of Immigration	Percent	Percent
>=1990	22.30	
1985-1990	10.70	15.70
1980-1984	36.60	44.60
1975-1979	22.10	22.70
<=1974	0.90	17.00

Occupational Categories (using census categories)

Variable	Percent	Mean
Managerial & professional	0.46	0.39
Technical, sales & admin support	0.22	0.24
Service	0.06	0.16
Farming, forestry & fishing	0.04	0.00
Precision product, craft & repair	0.02	0.03

Operators, fabricators & labourers	0.19		0.14	
Household Characteristics				
Household size	3.42	2.03	3.60	1.97
Own at least one car	0.84		0.87	
Owner-occupied US house	0.36		0.24	
Rented for cash	0.63		0.74	
HH resides in a house	0.35		0.31	
HH resides in apartment	0.63		0.65	
HH resides in other residence	0.02		0.04	

Table 3. Migrant sample: characteristics by housing status in Nigeria

VARIABLE	ALL	Home Owners	Non Home Owners	Difference (Owners minus Non-owners)	
		(completed houses only)			
	N=112	N=44	N=68		
Migrant Household's Characteristics					
Male	0.92	0.95	0.89	0.06 (0.05)	
Age at first migration to the US	25.42 (7.40)	25.65 (5.59)	25.28 (7.43)	0.37 (1.32)	
Age (at the time of survey)	38.78 (7.33)	41.75 (7.10)	37.32 (5.56)	5.19 (1.34)	***
Years of schooling	16.46 (1.49)	16.77 (2.00)	16.25 (1.51)	0.51 (0.29)	*
Occupation (skilled=1)	0.51	0.60	0.46	0.15 (0.10)	
Per capita annual kousehold income (US$)	25470.18 (32045.32)	33055.26 (45538.85)	20452.35 (35082.90)	12602.91 (6209.34)	**
Cumulative US exp (in weeks)	732.72 (371.42)	858.00 (418.34)	667.33 (338.79)	172.91 (70.99)	**

| Inherited farmland in home town=1 | 0.13 . | 0.23 | 0.07 | 0.14 (0.06) | ** |
| No. of Nigerian trips since arrival in US | 4.64 (5.02) | 6.59 (6.08) | 3.38 (3.66) | 3.31 (0.93) | *** |

Remittances

| Total transfer sent in past year (US$) | 6003.25 (11300.26) | 9180.07 (16725.16) | 3994.38 (4870.65) | 5185.69 (16725.16) | ** |
| Non-housing transfer sent in past year (US$) | 3937.18 (5259.45) | 5679.04 (6817.20) | 2835.71 (3619.85) | 2843.33 ((992.75) | ** |

Home Family Characteristics

Migrant head's father alive(=1)	0.40	0.27	0.49	-0.21 (0.09)	**
No of buildings owned by migrant's father	2.53 (3.30)	2.63 (3.95)	2.55 (2.83)	0.11 (0.66)	
Head's father's occupation (farmer=1)	0.23	0.25	0.21	0.04 (0.08)	

Home-town Characteristics

Population (1991 census estimates)	75928.15 (104803.6)	87369.00 (126075.00)	66266.47 (84805.53)	17141.46 (20631.31)	
Distance from state capital (km)	21.56 (15.01)	21.16 (13.40)	22.06 (15.89)	-0.42 (2.96)	
Home town has access to a major road	0.79	0.84	0.75	0.09 (0.08)	
No. of higher education institutions in home town	0.44 (0.83)	0.41 (0.76)	0.47 (0.87)	0.05 (0.16)	

Standard errors are shown in parentheses * denotes significant at 10% level, ** at the 5% level, *** at the 1% level. The term OWNERS refers to migrants with completed houses in the home town.

Summary statistics

The field research in the US and Nigeria also yielded a rich data set on migrants and their origin families. I discuss the empirical findings in this section. Table 2 compares the Chicago sample with the census microdata sample on Nigerians. Table 3 presents summary statistics from the migrant sample by the migrants' housing status. Owners of residential houses within origin communities appear to be slightly older upon arrival in the US than non-owners. Migrants who own houses in origin communities are also more likely to have worked in Nigeria before migrating to the US. The percentage of migrants who own inherited farmland in the origin community is higher for homeowners relative to non-homeowners. I also find that migrant household income and educational attainment are higher among migrants who own completed houses in their community of origin. However, owners have been in the US longer than non-owners have. The mean year of migration to the US for owners is about 1980, compared to the mean year for non-owners, which is 1984.

The picture that emerges here is that families of homeowners are likely to have strong ties to the origin family. I find that owners report larger and more frequent transfers to the origin family. The matched sample allows the characteristics of the migrants to be examined along with independent information obtained from the origin family. One of the most significant differences by housing status relates to observed transfer patterns. Where migrants are homeowners, origin families receive larger remittances (excluding housing-related transfers). The mean non-housing transfer received by home households with migrant homeowners is about $4400 (nearly 3.5 times larger than the transfer amount received by home households whose migrants do not own homes).

I formalised these initial observations into three theoretical models. The first model, which I term the 'community-investment model', centres on the observation that migrants care about the communities they left behind and invest in order to contribute directly to the development of the housing stock in their home towns. In the second model, migrants invest in housing during their period of residence abroad in order to secure their membership rights in their communities of origin. Within this model, migrants must choose the optimal time to undertake housing investments. The third model expands the framework within which investment decisions are made to include the migrant's home family in the country of origin. In this third model, I develop the hypothesis that a migrant's housing investment signals the migrant's resource commitment to the home family, and this may improve the home family's access to informal markets in the home community environment.

One of the central questions is how migrant characteristics affect the decision to invest in housing in the origin community. Several of the theoretical approaches above suggest that migrants' current and future resources play an important role in determining investment decisions in their origin communities.

The empirical results from Nigeria provide support for two of these theoretical models: membership rights and signalling. Within the membership rights framework, migrants' investments are responsive to exogenous shocks that alter the benefits to membership in the community of origin. The signalling model suggests that migrants' housing investments can provide a signal of the home family's access to the migrant's resources. I find that migrants' remittances are more responsive to home family shocks in the presence of housing investments. There is less support for the community-investment model. Empirical results provide evidence that migrants tend to invest in *more-developed* communities, not in *less-developed* communities as predicted by the community-investment model.

The results presented in this section draw on the strength of the migrant/origin-family data in order to control directly for the economic position of the migrant and origin households and their impact on housing investments and community development projects in the community of origin. I also investigate the impact of migrant characteristics on origin-family characteristics.

Table 4. Determinants of migrants' housing investments

Probit and Tobit Maximum Likelihood Estimates

VARIABLE	PROBIT MODEL		TOBIT MODEL
	Marginal Effect	Coefficient	
		(1)	(2)
Migrant's Characteristics			
Age at the time of survey	0.029	0.074 *** (0.030)	0.058 ** (0.027)
Per capita annual household income (US$) (X 10³)	0.003	0.008 *** (0.004)	0.068 ** (0.026)
Years of schooling	-0.001	-0.003 (0.084)	0.214 (0.126)
No of Nigerian trips	0.040	0.104 *** (0.037)	0.068 *** (0.026)
Cumulative US exp (in wks)	0.000	-0.0002 ** (0.001)	0.001 (0.001)
Own inherited farm land=1	0.209	0.529 (0.419)	1.039 *** 0.358)
Home Family Characteristics			
Head's father farmer (=1)	0.103	0.266 (0.403)	0.024 (0.330)
No of buildings owned by head's father	0.013	0.035 (0.034)	0.065 ** (0.035)
Home-town Characteristics			
Log population (1991 census)	0.085	0.218 * (0.117)	0.200 (1.250)
Distance from state capital (km)	-0.002	-0.004 (0.009)	-0.019 ** (0.009)
Constant		-1.995 (2.54)	-5.888 *** (2.28)
No. of observations		103	103
Pseudo R²		0.35	0.16
Log likelihood		-46.2589	-105.071

Dependent variables are ownership of completed house in home town (Column 1), and the share of annual household income that is devoted to housing (Column 2). Standard errors are shown in parentheses. Marginal Effects are evaluated at the sample means for continuous variables. * denotes significance at the 10 per cent level,** at the 5 per cent level and, *** at the 1 per cent level

Table 4 presents the first set of empirical results. The probit specification (column 1) captures the likelihood that the migrant has undertaken housing investments in the community of origin. In the Tobit specification (column 2), the dependent variable is the share of migrants' income that is devoted to housing investments in the home town.

The coefficient on the age of the migrant at the time of the survey is positive in both the probit and Tobit estimates. In particular, a one-year increase in age at migration increases the likelihood of undertaking housing investments by about 3 per cent. The coefficient on the income of the migrant household is positive, and statistically significant in the probit and Tobit specifications.

The inclusion of home family variables adds some important insights. In particular, the coefficient of the dummy variable on the occupation of the migrant's father (farmer=1) has a positive, but statistically insignificant effect on the probability of investing. In addition, the coefficient on the number of buildings owned by the migrant's father is positive and statistically significant in both probit and Tobit specifications.

It is important to note that home-town characteristics have the opposite sign from the sign predicted by the community-investment model. The results presented in Table 4 suggest that migrants tend to invest in *more-developed* home towns, not in *less-developed* communities. First, migrants are more likely to invest in more populated origin communities. Second, migrants are more likely to invest where the origin community is located closer to the state capital.

Beyond migrants' housing investments

By studying migrants' housing investments, I gained insights into other aspects of migrants' remittance behaviour. In more recent work, I have returned to my original set of questions with the goal of unpacking remittances. Using my data, I constructed detailed measures of migrants' family, investment, and community transfers. 'Family transfers' are defined as the total remittances sent to the origin family. In contrast, 'investment transfers' are defined as the sum of all investment-related remittances sent by the migrant to finance their own investments in origin-country assets in the survey year (Osili 2004). Finally, community transfers refer to the total remittances that are sent towards community development projects in the origin community.

My results from Nigeria suggest that investment-related flows differ in important ways from family transfers. Family transfers appear to be motivated by concerns for origin-family members, with poorer origin family members in Nigeria receiving larger transfers, other things being equal. A different picture emerges from investment-related flows. Migrants' investment transfers tend to flow towards wealthier origin households. Many of these insights were made possible because matched data on migrants and origin households were available.

The US–Nigeria Migration Survey also provided a unique opportunity to investigate remittances to community development projects in the origin community by using a matched sample of migrants and their origin families.

Descriptive evidence shows that migrants maintain direct economic ties with their communities of origin.[8] The unique data from the US–Nigeria Migration Survey allowed me to investigate the likelihood that the migrant has initiated a community transfer as well as the total amount sent towards community development projects in the home town. About 13 per cent of the migrant sample sent a transfer towards a community development project. The main prediction of an altruistic model of community transfers is that less-developed home towns should receive more community-related transfers, other things being equal.

The findings from the US–Nigeria Migration Survey suggest that home town characteristics play an important role in the migrant's decision to send a community transfer. However, migrants tend to send community-related transfers in *more-developed* home towns, not in *less-developed* communities.[9] In Table 5, I measure origin community development by constructing an index of origin community that captures important amenities including population and distance from urban centres and the state capital, as both measures capture important aspects of home-town development. I also examine the impact of additional indicators of home-town development, including the number of higher education institutions, access to a major road, electrification, and access to potable water.[10] These results also do not lend support for the community investment model of community transfers in that migrants appear less likely to send community transfers in less-developed villages.

Table 5. Determinants of migrants' community transfers

Probit and Tobit Maximum Likelihood Estimates

VARIABLE	PROBIT MODEL			TOBIT MODEL	
	Marginal Effect	Coefficient			
		(1)		(2)	
Migrant's Characteristics					
Age at the time of survey	0.042	-0.065 (0.031)	**	-0.054 (0.039)	
Per Capita Annual Household income (US$) (X 10³)	0.0004	-0.005 (0.005)		-0.006 (0.006)	
Years of schooling	0.028	0.285 (0.218)		0.243 (0.181)	
No. of Nigerian trips	0.005	0.048 (0.037)		0.029 (0.028)	
Cumulative US exp (in weeks)	-0.0002	-0.002 (0.001)	***	-0.002 (0.001)	***
Own inherited farm land=1	0.178	0.810 (0.479)	*	0.977 (0.378)	**
Home Family Characteristics					
Head's father farmer (=1)	0.003	0.025 (0.517)		0.046 (0.427)	
No of buildings owned by head's father	-0.014	-0.135 (0.066)	**	-0.074 (0.062)	
Origin Community Characteristics					
Origin community amenities	0.062	0.484 (0.179)	***	0.616 (0.197)	***
No of higher educational institutions	-0.002	-0.004 (0.009)		-0.180 (0.206)	
Constant		-1.995 (2.54)		-4.001 (2.69)	***

No. of observations	99	99
Pseudo R^2	0.35	0.33

Dependent variables are community related transfer (Column 1), and the share of annual household income that is devoted to community transfers (Column 2). Standard errors are shown in parentheses. Marginal Effects are evaluated at the sample means for continuous variables.

* denotes significance at the 10 per cent level, ** at the 5 per cent level, and *** at the 1 per cent level

CONCLUSION

Policy makers and researchers have shown a growing interest in understanding the remittances from African migrants and their impact on the origin countries. However, household-level evidence on African migrants is unavailable for many sending and receiving countries, and very little is known about the impact of remittances on migrants and their origin communities. To better understand the nature of the economic ties between migrants and their countries of origin, new data sources are often needed.

This chapter investigated remittances from migration, using an original sample that simultaneously matches migrants and their origin families. One of the central research questions is how and why African migrants maintain economic ties with their origin communities. By collecting data on migrants, origin households and communities of origin, new insights emerge. The US–Nigeria Migration Survey sheds light on how and why economic ties between international migrants and their families in origin countries are maintained over time and across large geographical distances. Of considerable interest is the extent to which migrants invest their savings in their country of origin and contribute to community development projects in their origin communities. The matched sample allows us to disaggregate remittances and understand the extent to which remittances are sent to support the consumption needs of the origin household or migrants' investments in the origin community. The matched sampling approach also allows us to study migrants' transfers to community development projects.

The evidence from the US –Nigeria Migration Survey points to the significant economic potential of remittances when they are invested in the origin environment or sent to finance development projects in origin communities. The results presented in this chapter draw on the strength of the migrant/origin family data in order to control directly for the economic position of the migrant and origin households and their impact on transfers and savings in the origin and host countries. With the rising economic profile of remittances in Africa, new data collection methods are required to study migrants and their economic ties with their origin countries.

Notes

1. Mazzuccato's (2009) work on Ghanaian migrants and their transnational economic ties is an exception in the literature.
2. Okonkwo 1999 and Osili 2004 investigates the migrant's decision to acquire housing investments in the community of origin.
3. A copy of the survey instrument is available on request.
4. To draw a simple random sample from a telephone book, I identified 500 Nigerian family names from the Chicago phonebook. These family names were numbered sequentially. A computer generated 120 numbers randomly from 1 to 500.
5. The Ibo are the third largest ethnic group in Nigeria.
6. During the questionnaire revision stage, I received assistance from the Survey Design Laboratory at the University of Illinois at Chicago and Professor Greg Duncan at the Institute for Policy Research at Northwestern University.
7. Villages in south-eastern Nigeria usually lack street numbers or other identifiers; to locate families one must rely on inquiries within the village to identify the residence of a particular origin family.
8. Within the African setting, home-town associations formed by migrants play a prominent role (Attah-Poku 1996; Egboh 1987; Smock 1971). These home-town associations are of considerable importance in mobilising migrants' contributions towards the construction of schools, hospitals and roads, and the provision of other amenities in the community of origin.

9. Other measures (electrification, potable water, literacy rates) of village development deliver similar results. In general, urbanised home towns had a higher likelihood of receiving migrants' community-related transfers, other things being equal.

10. Unobserved heterogeneity across home towns (such as the size and strength of migrant networks, investment technology, and construction costs) may also influence the migrant's community transfer decision.

References

Adams, R. H. (1991) 'The Economic Uses and Impact of International Remittances in Rural Egypt', *Economic Development and Cultural Change* 39(4): 695–722.

Attah-Poku, A. (1996) *The Socio-Cultural Adjustment Question: The Role of Ghanaian Immigrant Ethnic Associations in America*, Brookfield, Vermont: Avebury.

Egboh, E. O. (1987) *Community Development Efforts in Igboland*, Onitsha, Nigeria: Etukokwu Press.

Mazuccato, V. (2009) 'Informal Insurance Arrangements in Ghanaian Migrants' Transnational Networks: The Role of Reverse Remittances and Geographic Proximity', *World Development* 37(6): 1105–15.

Okonkwo, U. M. (1999) 'Migrants and Housing Investments: Theory and Evidence from Nigeria', Northwestern University PhD Dissertation.

Osili, U. O. (2004) 'Migrants and Housing Investments: Theory and Evidence from Nigeria', *Economic Development and Cultural Change* 52(4): 821–49.

Smock, A. C. (1971) *Ibo Politics: The Role of Ethnic Unions in Eastern Nigeria*, Cambridge: Harvard University Press.

Chapter 5

———⟫◆⟪———

FROM ONE STAGE TO THE NEXT: TRANSIT AND TRANSPORT IN (TRANS) SAHARAN MIGRATIONS

Julien Brachet

INTRODUCTION

At the start of the 1990s, various economic and political factors led to an increase and diversification in migratory flows towards and across the Sahara. Since that time, some tens of thousands of migrants originating in West and Central Africa have been travelling over land to North Africa, whence a small proportion of them continue their journey as far as Europe. The extent of Saharan migration, which until that time had been cross-border in nature, covering relatively small distances, was thus transformed into a more complex international migratory system, forging relationships between distant areas and peoples in a way that had never been seen before. However, it was only from the early 2000s that these migrations gradually began to move to the forefront of the political scene in southern and western

Europe, and then in North Africa, and finally in various countries in West Africa. The media on both continents concentrated initially on covering the deaths of sub-Saharan migrants in the Mediterranean, while the European authorities concerned themselves with the new arrival of these illegal immigrants on Europe's southern shores. By focusing their attention in this way just on migrants heading for Europe, the media and the authorities in the countries concerned failed to consider the diversity and complexity of these migrations in north-west Africa.

Where academic research is concerned, (trans) Saharan migrations have mainly been studied by looking at countries in North Africa, and the regions where migrants have settled – either voluntarily or by default – but much less frequently by looking at those transit areas in the Sahel-Saharan states. While from the theoretical point of view current scientific work no longer reduces migration to fixed times and places for individuals' 'departures' and 'arrivals', empirical studies of migratory phenomena, by contrast, continue for the most part to work from these fixed locations in time and space, rather than the more volatile 'transit' locations. And when one looks at transit migration, it appears that *residency situations* are almost always given a higher priority in empirical data production methods than *travel situations*. Now, *where* 'migration' as the object of study is approached empirically, the way in which the fields of study are determined and exploited will have an influence on the data produced, thus raising questions of prime importance concerning methods and methodology (Clifford 1997; Spittler 1996).

In order to look again at the place of the journey within migratory processes, we would suggest that an understanding of contemporary migration in the Sahara, which is 'migration in stages', cannot be achieved without sufficient research centred on the Saharan transit regions. How do crossings of the Sahara take place, and what do they cost the migrants? What social relationships develop during the journey, on the transport? What does what happens between the stages of migration reveal about the relationship between states, their officials and these migratory movements? What are the effects of migratory transit on the areas crossed? Based on experience from research into (trans) Saharan migrations in Niger,[1] we see transit as a significant moment in the migratory process. We shall ponder the value and ways of working on this particular *moment* in migration, and the possibilities and prospects of involving the observer in this mobility. Through the study of illegal migrant taxation practices used by Niger state officials along the main routes in the Agadez region, we shall see that work in the transit areas, particularly in transport, can produce empirical knowledge which will add to that produced in other areas of migration.

TRANSIT AND TRANSPORT AS A WAY IN TO
UNDERSTANDING THE MOVEMENT

Transit: a moment in mobility between intention and action

The notion of transit is frequently used in the study of migrations between sub-Saharan Africa, North Africa and Europe, and refers to a number of different situations.[2] This notion, which has been kept in the foreground over the past decade by international institutions, can assume a strong ideological aspect according to the targets to which it applies and the field of discussion in which it is used, particularly when it is a question of legitimising the control or restriction of migrations which are seen by the public authorities as potential offences (Perrin 2008; Streiff-Fénart and Poutignat 2008). The diversity of uses of the notion of transit and its adoption as a political tool suggest that we should explain our understanding of the term as used in this work.

Derived from the Latin word *transitus*, meaning 'the action of crossing', 'passing through', transit refers to a process of movement. While the temporal aspect originally lay at the heart of the notion, whether applied to transit areas in international airports or the transit of goods across a national territory, where transit implies the virtual lack of any interruption to the movement, the issue of the time taken has little relevance in the field of migration studies. In this field, we consider that it is the thinking of the migrants which gives sociological meaning to the notion of transit migration, and which makes it useful in understanding certain aspects of the migratory flows currently crossing the Nigerien Sahara. In fact, the act of transiting – a town, for example – inevitably requires a certain amount of time, from a few hours to a few months, and a physical halt of movement. What distinguishes the transit town from the temporary destination town is the conscious change in the migrant's plan and not specifically the length of their stay, the physical circumstances of where they live, or their activities.

It seems that in North Africa and Mauritania, transit areas are all destination areas too, sometimes chosen deliberately, sometimes by default due to the inability of some migrants to continue along their route. The description of migration from south of the Sahara as being solely transit migration has therefore taken on a strong political connotation, since it has enabled states – Maghrebian ones, in this case – not to see or think of themselves as countries where there is immigration. This is why we use 'transit area' to mean any area where migrants arrive with the intention of continuing their journey *as soon as possible* to a further destination, holding on to this intention throughout their stay in the area, however long it may actually last. The transit function of a place or territory asserts itself once a number of migratory flows come together there, and the mobility of the migrants takes on a prominent role in movements there as a whole. Therefore, not all areas crossed by migrants are transit areas in any significant way. Defined in these terms, the notion of transit enables us to single out the Nigerien Sahara in comparison to numerous other regions of this desert which are also crossed by migratory flows. What actually sets the Nigerien Sahara apart is that it has never been a destination for international migrants but only ever a space which they cross, be it quickly or slowly. And even when their stay is prolonged, with very few exceptions, they never have plans to settle there voluntarily, which throws some light on the nature of the relationships forged by migrants in the Saharan regions of Niger, both among themselves and with the native populations.

The notion of transit is therefore valuable when characterising and analysing certain social situations. Nevertheless, when one knows that the future Algerian law on 'the conditions for entry, residence and circulation of foreigners' plans to distinguish between migrants who want to settle in the country and those who start out with the intention of continuing their journey further (Perrin 2008), talk of migrants' thinking, or even intentions, remains particularly delicate. Especially as this way of designating a section of those sub-Saharan migrants who are present on their soil as being simply in transit, and condemning them on the basis of the sole presumption that their intention is to get into Europe illegally, is common to the Maghreb countries as a whole. This use of the notion of transit, linked to the policy of externalising the control and management of migratory flows which has been introduced by the European Union (Rodier 2009), forces us to remember that there is clearly no link between being in a state of transit and involvement in illegal activities. While the notion of transit – such as it has been defined by us – may be of use in the field of social analysis and particularly in micro-social analysis, it should not, however, be used in any way as a tool in the political or legal spheres.

THE VALUE OF CONDUCTING RESEARCH IN TRANSIT AREAS

Migration is a movement, a moving of people. The observer's position along the migrants' route, on the one hand, and the categories of individuals prioritised in the survey, on the other, are two elements which will determine the view that can be formed of a migratory system. Nowadays, the majority of the research work on international migration is carried out in two categories of specific points along the route: 'departure' places and 'arrival' places. However, the status of such places may be either permanent or temporary, as is increasingly the case with migration taking place in stages. One of the great advantages of choosing these locations for surveys, quite apart from being able to study the effects of migration on the areas and the societies living there, is that one can work alongside migrants at length. If one is really to deepen the relationship with the individuals in the survey, to work in their language, to understand the workings of the networks enabling migrants to become a part of the towns where they settle, or again to get to the heart of the inter-ethnic relationships within migrant communities and between foreign migrants and natives, it may even be necessary to focus the research on one particular community of migrants caught up in the migratory process.[3] This kind of approach perfectly meets the needs of some lines of inquiry. But when one wants to pin down the organisation of a migratory system in its entirety, and it is used by migrants with a multiplicity of geographical points of origin and destinations (Figure 1), then how is one to proceed without basing one's analysis on too restrictive and specific a section of these migrants, which would give an excessively fragmented and partial view of the migration studied? Having dismissed the idea of a research team with sufficient human and physical resources to survey all migrant communities in their regions of origin and destination, the best way of obtaining the most complete view possible of these migratory movements as a whole seems to be to position oneself in the transit areas, where the flows are concentrated.

Figure 1. Origins and destinations of the principal migratory flows crossing Niger

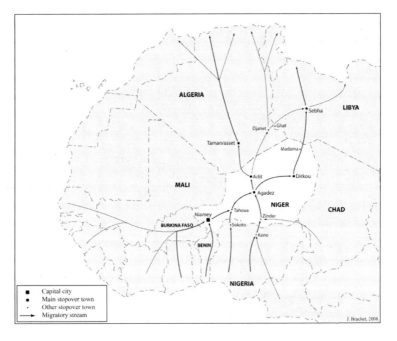

While the Sahara taken as a whole is a transit area, it is noticeable that there are relatively few places which operate as transit locations without operating as destination locations at the same time. The north of Niger is the area with the greatest share of the overland migratory flows, firstly in one town, Agadez, and then along two main routes heading for Algeria and Libya. Most 'categories' of (trans) Saharan migrants are likely to pass through here, regardless of their origin or destination. And those who are returning from North Africa also pass through here, finding it easier to talk about their migratory experiences here than in Algeria or Libya. While imposing particular methodological constraints, these transit areas, which are quite unique among those places affected by staged migrations, can provide some original empirical material, offering opportunities for further research to add to the research carried out at the migrants' places of departure and arrival. Alongside this, when we consider that migration cannot be reduced to a succession of fixed stages, and that transit areas are quintessentially areas of movement, we then have to consider, at the methodological level, how we can incorporate the notion of *movement*, which is the cornerstone of migration, into our work. How can one study the physical displacement caused by migration and the transitory and unstable social structures which are generated by it? To what extent is it possible to share this experience of mobility with those involved in order to grasp its implications?

TRANSPORT AND THE ISSUE OF THE OBSERVER'S MOBILITY

As movement, migration over land implies constant change of the surroundings in which migrants find themselves. Therefore, any study of it must assume the instability of the social structures it generates and concentrate on the adaptation of behaviour, on the ongoing (re)negotiation of relationships between the individuals, or the redefinition of their plans. If one is to understand the complexity of migratory routes, taken as a combination of steps and transfers, one needs to consider this variability in the surroundings, which also form the background to any observations and statements from the players involved. From the methodological point of view, this can result in the mobility of the observer, which itself can take two forms. The first of these is to travel in the field, in other words, to work in a succession of different migrant transit locations. The other is to see 'mobility' itself as a field for research, integrating the times and space of physical mobility into the analysis, i.e. by seeing the transport as a field for research.

Mobility *across* the field enables one to contextualise each survey location, each observed phenomenon, and to tackle them in a slightly different way every time one returns to or re-crosses a place where one has already worked; every time one runs into a person whom one has already met, following some time away from them. This kind of large-scale multiple-location ethnography makes it easier to control the output from the research subject, because with travel between different sites, the field is of necessity perceived through its relationship with the surrounding locations, through the networks which connect it to the regional or world areas into which it fits (Hannerz 2003; Marcus 1995, 1998). At the same time, it is possible to establish 'mobility' in the field. Working from the hypothesis that movement modifies the perception of individuals (Merleau-Ponty 1999 [1945]), and modifies migrants' perceptions of the people and places that they approach, move alongside or meet, and also modifies what they say (Clifford 1997; Lussault 2005), it becomes worthwhile, or even necessary, to start moving oneself and to observe the flows from within.

To summarise, it is a question of seeing circulation, the journey, as a particular survey and observation situation which grants access to certain aspects of the migratory process which cannot be observed from a fixed point. Working on the transport allows one, for example, to observe emerging sociability within the immediate vicinity of the meetings offered by and involved in movement, or the fleeting moments when mobile individuals come into contact with state officials. These discrete contacts, whether formal or informal, can only be studied from alongside those travelling, because state officials may be control officers (police officers, soldiers, customs officers) who operate in isolated places along the routes or at location entries or exits (checkpoints), where it is not easy to observe events as an outsider. By combining these two complementary forms of mobility in the field, it becomes possible to tackle migratory phenomena really like continua, like fluid processes and no longer as a succession of independent stages.

Figure 2. Mobile research fields: the lorries which transport migrants across the Nigerien Sahara (Brachet 2009a)

CORRUPTION AND VIOLENCE ALONG
THE MIGRATION ROUTES

Fleeting events and changing aspects of migratory movements towards and across the Central Sahara reveal themselves when one works in the transit areas, both in the successive stages of the journey, but also between these stages. This practical experience of the field highlights the importance of the ongoing variety of situations in which the migrants find themselves during their journey, which is an inherent characteristic of 'stage migration'. Among these aspects concerning the dynamics, the organisation and effects of (trans) Saharan migrations in Niger, which the methodological approaches mentioned above help to illuminate, here we shall concentrate specifically on the control and taxation practices employed by state officials along the route from the town of Agadez to Fezzan in Libya.

THE INSTITUTIONALISATION OF CORRUPTION IN TRANSPORT

In Africa, the transport sector is known to be one of the areas of activity most affected by small-scale corruption. Many roads are affected by roadblocks, at the very least where they enter or leave towns, where control points are seen by state officials as an opportunity for often illegal taxation, as is also sometimes the case at border crossings or bus stations. While corruption is widespread across this sector and across the continent, it seems however that the Saharan itineraries are affected in quite specific ways. This echoes the work of Giorgio Blundo and Jean-Pierre Olivier de Sardan (2001), who draw a distinction between corruption in Africa and corruption in Europe, not in terms of the 'presence or absence of acts', but in terms of size ('the difference lies in the amount'); it also seems that the special nature of corruption along the Saharan routes in Niger resides in the scale and spread of the problem, and even sometimes in the forms it takes.

> When a Nigerien comes to Nigeria, he has no problems, no-one asks him for his passport, he can travel freely, he has no problems. But when you travel to Niger, everyone asks for your passport, all the time. You have your passport, or you don't have your passport; either way, you have to hand over money....
> (Nigerian migrant, Blima, 9 December 2004)

It is not easy to distinguish between what is due to corruption, due to the simple dysfunction of the state apparatus, or due to organised crime. So, in order to account for the overlapping of different corrupt practices within state services and the operational peculiarities of the Saharan transport sector, we have decided to adopt a broad definition of the term 'corruption', including what, in legal terms, would fall under the heading of extortion.[4]

Over the field as a whole, transport operators find themselves obliged to pay illegal taxes or to pay commission to control officials in order to be able to continue their business. Nigerien travellers may circulate freely in the country, while foreign migrants, whether or not they are in a regular situation under Nigerien law, may not cross the country unless they pay these arbitrary taxes, sometimes as soon as they set foot on Nigerien soil. But when carriers and travellers journey along Saharan routes leading to Algeria and more particularly to Libya, they are confronted by state officials whose illegal practices dwarf those of officials working in the rest of the country. Yet despite this general absence of recognition and legitimisation through a legal institutional framework, which could also be explained by socio-cultural and economic factors (Dahou 2002; Olivier de Sardan 1999), this does not lead to a state of anarchy within the goods and passenger transport sector, because the informal regulatory bodies are produced by the players themselves (control officers and transport operators). Within these informal frameworks, the application of the (formal and informal) rules is variable, which involves and allows their regular redefinition, by negotiation, encouraging the development and endurance of corrupt practices. In this sense, corruption has become institutionalised in the transport sector in Niger, inasmuch as it is more the rule – statistically speaking – than the exception, and it has echoes of both a cultural and an organisational dimension (Médard 2006).

FROM AGADEZ TO THE LIBYAN BORDER:
A CONTROLLED ROUTE

The journey from Agadez to Dirkou (650km), much of which is taken up by crossing the Erg of Ténéré, takes between two and four days depending on the season and the type of vehicle used, and sometimes longer because of the frequent breakdowns affecting vehicles on this route. Migrants, of whom you might see 30 piled into the back of a pick-up truck, and even 150 on tipper trucks, are checked for the first time just a few kilometres out of the town of Agadez. Local police officers will then take an arbitrary tax ranging from 500 to a few thousand CFA francs. The next checkpoint, which is run by the state police, is located 80km further on, near the Toureyet wells.[5] Here, migrants pay a toll of around 1,000 CFA francs. Then comes the long crossing of the Ténéré, to Dirkou.

Figure 3. Locations of checkpoints between Agadez and Libya

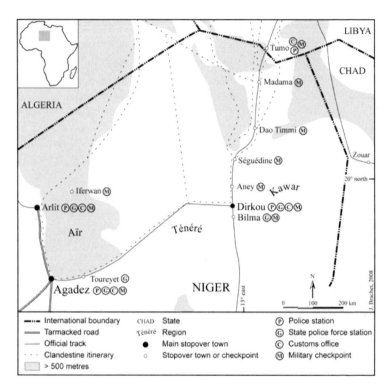

Arrival in Dirkou is always by day, because it is forbidden to enter and leave the oasis at night. As soon as the migrants arrive within the military compound at the entrance to the village, the first mandatory staging post for lorries carrying passengers, they are immediately hemmed in by armed soldiers, who make them get down from the vehicle and who demand a lump sum from the driver (which works out at between 500 and 2,000 CFA francs per migrant). Then they are driven to the state police post where they are taxed once more (1,000 to 3,000 CFA francs per person), sometimes violently, and where their identity papers are seized by an officer. They must then go and collect them from the police station in return for the payment of a few more thousand CFA francs. Here again, there is no relation between the amount of tax they need to pay and the legality of their situation. These arbitrary taxes imposed by the forces of law and order place a heavy burden on the migrants' budget, and they may then have difficulty in continuing their journey.

> When we arrived in Dirkou, there were more checkpoints... at the police station, they took our passports and searched our bags, and we paid 2,000 CFA francs... then we had to see the local police next door. We told them we didn't have any money, and they held us until evening. They were saying that they'd release us and give our passports back if we paid 5,000 CFA francs. Everyone paid 5,000 CFA francs. And that's how we arrived in the town; we didn't have any money left, we had our international passport from Nigeria, but we didn't know what to do or where to go any more.
> (Nigerian migrant, Bilma, 9 December 2004)

> It's because they'd taken all our money. When we arrived here in Dirkou, we paid 2,000 CFA francs. Then they told us to go to the state police station, there we were asked for 5,000. I said I didn't have 5,000. That was at four o'clock in the afternoon. By seven o'clock I was still there. They told us 5,000 was their last offer. I slept there. It was the first time I'd spent the night in a police station, the first time. In the morning another one came to see us. He said to hand over 1,000 francs. We gave him 1,000 francs and we got out. [...] It was my first time in Niger, there in the middle of the desert, and it was also the last... the first time and, I swear to you, it will be the last. Even when I return from Libya, I'm going to fly if I can.... I never want to come back here.
> (Migrant from Benin, Dirkou, 20 December 2004)

Many migrants find themselves stuck like this at some stage on the Nigerien migratory routes, lacking sufficient funds to continue on their way. These are generally individuals who have planned to work in Libya and who, having set off on their migration with capital ranging from one to several hundred thousand CFA francs, cannot keep up with the many expenses incurred while crossing Niger. Unable to go further or to return home, these migrants may stay for several weeks, or even several months, there where their journey has momentarily ground to a halt (Brachet 2009b).

Leaving the Dirkou oasis, and passing through the military checkpoints at Aney, Séguédine, Dao Timmi and Madama, the migrants are systematically relieved of several thousand CFA francs in a similarly authoritarian manner. If they refuse to pay, or cannot pay, Nigerien soldiers will not hesitate to use force to achieve the desired result.

In this country, everyone's poor, the people from this country are suffering, so when they see foreigners with a bit of money, they think of every possible way of taking it from them... when they see foreigners here, they know we're going to Libya, they know we've got money on us, and not just a little money. They do all they can to take it from us, they even beat us in Dirkou because we didn't want to pay... They took our Ecowas[6] passports, they said that we were breaking the law because we didn't have a visa... that's why they asked us for money, but with Ecowas passports you can come to Niger legally.

(Nigerian migrant, Bilma, 8 December 2004)

So, from Agadez to the Libyan border, every control situation has become an opportunity to squeeze more money out of travelling individuals. And there are no fewer than seven checkpoints on this route, leading to around ten checks. In total, the amounts which have to be paid frequently add up to several tens of thousands of CFA francs per migrant. On the basis of direct observation of these taxation practices (observations made possible by travelling alongside the migrants on a number of occasions), and working from interviews on this subject in a number of Saharan locations, it appears that the specific nature of the corruption and illegal taxation problems facing migrants in the north of Niger derives from three main characteristics. First, it is their systematic nature, regardless of the migrants' situation in respect of the law; second, it is the size of the amounts to be paid, regardless of the individual's nationality and resources; and third, at times, the violence they occasion.

Observing this little-known side of migratory movements in Niger enables us to shed light on other aspects of their own organisation and their effect on the transit areas. For example, the money extorted by state officials from the individuals travelling the tracks across the Sahara represents a considerable proportion of their own earnings and is an injection of currency which can revitalise the economies of the towns and villages which serve as stop-overs for the migrants (particularly Agadez and Dirkou). This partly explains why state officials do not try to apply the official legislation concerning the circulation of people in these regions and, similarly, why the Nigerien state, which pays its officers very little, does not watch their work more closely. Nevertheless, talking about the amount of resources drawn from corrupt practices and migratory circulations more generally suggests that the approximate amount is known, and therefore raises the issue of how to arrive at a quantitative evaluation of the volumes of migratory flows concerned.

WHY, HOW AND HOW FAR SHOULD WE QUANTIFY (TRANS) SAHARAN MIGRATIONS?

This research relies on an approach whose dominant characteristic is qualitative because of the themes studied and the conditions under which the empirical data are produced. Working in the north of Niger, in the absence of precise pre-existing data about the phenomena studied, it proved very difficult to find and determine a sample of individuals for inclusion in the survey who would be statistically representative, and to apply one or more questionnaire-based study protocols which would enable us to obtain well-delimited and quantitatively representative information on the official part of the migratory flows studied. The favoured approach should therefore allow us to be as close as possible to the situations in which the people lived, in order to be able to reveal highly personal points of view, hidden, illegal or clandestine practices, as well as the public statements and official actions of the players. Alongside what amounted to a slow immersion within the heart of the migratory networks and groups of migrants, an 'active impregnation' with a clear sense of direction, we also used classic data production techniques in a combined way (participant study, interviews, reviews). These two more or less structured sides of empirical data production clearly cover a great diversity of variants which are linked to one another in practice. Indeed, the work on the ground takes place in a space which is not controlled and requires the constant employment of *tactics* in order to be able to launch into suitable openings at the slightest opportunity, at the slightest indication, while employing pre-established techniques (De Certeau 1990; Ginzburg 1980). However, the effect of the migratory flows in the Saharan transit regions, for example at the economic level via the corrupt practices of control officials, cannot be appreciated without, as the very minimum, evaluating the volume of these flows.

The quantification of transit migrations implies that one should be preoccupied with flows of migrants, rather than stocks. Talking of 'stocks' or 'flows' does not mean there are just two types of quantitative data concerning migrations, but that there are two ways of looking at them, the one being static, the other dynamic. In general terms, migratory studies rely on the analysis of stocks of migrants, i.e. on the number of individuals living outside the country of their birth at a given moment. While this approach to international migration is valuable in some fields, its limitations must however be stressed, because migration, as the transfer of people, can and must also be studied starting with data concerning the flows of migrants. Stocks of migrants, which are sometimes the only source for comparison between countries, do not allow us to distinguish between or establish a relationship between emigration and immigration for a given country, nor to differentiate between current flows and former flows (expatriate populations, diasporas etc.). By contrast, information on flows, in other words on entries and exits from national territories over a given time (a month, a year), makes it possible to give a clearer picture of the dynamics of the circulation of individuals, where stocks only reflect the net difference between entries and exits, without taking into account the period during which migrants remain there, and without taking into account the movements which take place between two census periods. All depends of course on the questions one asks, but the fact of the matter is that working on stocks does not give a picture of the very essence of migration which is of interest to us here, its dynamic in space, its movement. Quantification of transit migrations with a view to evaluating the economic effect of the charges levied by Nigerien state officials on the migrants is therefore necessarily a quantification of the flows. Now, given the shortcomings of national statistical apparatuses and the limitations of official sources concerning migratory flows in the Sahara, how is one to produce reliable figures on the increasingly clandestine circulation? Given that there is no epistemological incompatibility between the quantitative and qualitative approaches, it is not a question of setting these methodological currents one against the other, but rather of fitting them together (Bourdieu and Wacquant 1992). The question therefore is not whether or not to use quantitative data in an exclusive manner, but rather about the nature and degree of precision in quantitative data concerning the volume of migratory flows which may enhance their qualitative analysis.

In order to get over the problem of reliability in official data, which affects most migratory movements on the African continent, it is possible to produce one's own figures, or at least to try to quantify the flows as observed, and then to suggest extrapolations on the basis of varying criteria. Where migratory flows from sub-Saharan Africa to North Africa via the Agadez region are concerned, the Saharan transit towns provide favoured observation locations, in that they concentrate flows which may take different routes on either side of them. Long-term empirical work, particularly in the transport centres of transit towns, makes a partial evaluation of the circulation of persons possible. Counts (number of passengers per vehicle and number of vehicle departures per day) carried out in sessions lasting several days at a time and at different times of the year, when combined with the patchy official data (from the border police and state police force in particular) and the accounts of various players in the migratory system, make it possible to obtain a very general idea of the size of migratory movements. These may be calculated at several tens of thousands of persons per year; in the opposite direction, i.e. from North Africa towards sub-Saharan Africa, the flows transiting through Niger seem to be slightly smaller (Brachet 2009b).

Based on different hypotheses concerning the number of migrants and the taxes they have to pay, it can be seen that the total amount of currency extracted illegally from migrants by state officials in the Agadez region lies somewhere between 850 million and 3.5 billion CFA francs every year (Table 1).

The accuracy of this estimate is considered sufficient to give an idea of the economic stakes involved in the corruption phenomena we have studied, especially since a more precise extrapolation would necessarily involve a considerable speculative dimension.

Table 1. Estimate of the average annual total of currency illegally taken from migrants by state officials in the Agadez region (2003–2008)

	Conservative estimate	High-end estimate
Agadez (town)	Number of migrants: 40,000 Taxes levied per migrant: 10,000	Number of migrants: 70,000 Taxes levied per migrant: 15,000
Route from Agadez to the Libyan border	Number of migrants: 26,667 Taxes levied per migrant: 6,500	Number of migrants: 46,667 Taxes levied per migrant: 22,000
Route from the Libyan border to Agadez	Number of migrants: 21,334 Taxes levied per migrant: 13,500	Number of migrants: 37,335 Taxes levied per migrant: 31,500
Route from Agadez to Algeria	Number of migrants: 13,333 Taxes levied per migrant: 0	Number of migrants: 23,333 Taxes levied per migrant: 5,000
Route from Algeria to Agadez	Number of migrants: 10,667 Taxes levied per migrant: 0	Number of migrants: 18,667 Taxes levied per migrant: 5,000
Total (CFA francs)	**861,344,500 CFA**	**3,462,726,500 CFA**

Calculations were made on the basis of a number of migrants going from Niger towards North Africa in the range of 40,000 to 70,000 annually, with an average distribution of one-third on the Algerian route and two-thirds on the Libyan route. We considered that on average 80 per cent of migrants travelling to Algeria and Libya return to their country of origin by the same route. It should be noted that the number of migrants being subjected to illegal taxes has no doubt reduced over recent years due to the development of clandestine transport within Niger. *Sources: Surveys 2003–2008.*

The very desire to quantify illegal migratory flows poses a certain number of ethical and political questions. Is it the researcher's job to produce precise figures on the matter when the authorities under whose jurisdiction it falls do not do it, or rather do not have the necessary means? To what is one committing oneself, given that these migratory movements are subject to growing attempts at control by the public authorities in the countries which are involved or feel they are involved? And at the same time, a number of media outlets and public bodies will not wait for results from scientific studies before releasing figures whose origins are uncertain and which are often quite unreliable, for the purpose of sensationalism in the first case, and for political reasons in the second. To ignore the importance of the quantification issue when considering migration between sub-Saharan Africa, the Maghreb and Europe would then play into the hands of these people, whose portrayal of events is based on representations which are partial, in both senses of the word. Especially as, despite the uncertainties mentioned above, the quantitative analysis of migratory flows – both departing and returning – across the Sahara shows that these migrations are first and foremost intra-African. Even if one accepts the highest estimates, illegal migration from sub-Saharan Africa to Europe appears marginal in comparison to the size of these two continents and all the other migratory flows affecting them. Thus the quantitative approach allows one to demolish those arguments which talk of immense crowds of migrants attempting to leave sub-Saharan Africa, and to banish the myth of a migratory danger knocking at Europe's southernmost doors.[7]

CONCLUSION

By highlighting certain dynamics and certain economic stakes affecting transit areas as a result of Saharan and trans-Saharan migration, this work seeks to encourage these areas to be included systematically in the thinking about the migration–development relationship or the effect of migration policies. At the same time, working in the transit areas, and more particularly on transport, enables one to see migration not as a monolithic phenomenon, nor as a succession of fixed stages, but as a fluid process which spreads over time and space. Ultimately, understanding *movement* implies being immobile and observing those who pass by; being mobile and observing those who, through their immobility, appear to pass by; being mobile and observing those who, caught up in the same movement, appear immobile. These three approaches to migration, to movement in migration, are aimed at deciphering the tension between mobility and immobility, between travel, retention and temporary settlement, which is fundamental to all present-day migratory phenomena in North-West Africa. Since these moments in migration are not opposed to one another, but rather make up different facets of a single process, it is not a question of favouring research in the transit areas over that in the departure and destination areas, nor of favouring multiple-site or moving work over work which is fixed in a single location, but rather of stressing the complementary nature of these approaches with a view to gaining a general understanding of migratory phenomena.

Notes

1. This work is based on field research carried out over more than two years in Niger, between 2003 and 2008. During these visits, complete or partial audio recordings of 119 interviews (with migrants, transport operators and state officials) were made. Nevertheless a great proportion of the data from this work were gathered in an informal manner, from observations, reviews and simple discussions.

2. See in particular Bensaâd 2009, Choplin and Lombard 2008, Collyer 2006, Hamood 2006, Nadi 2007, Nyberg-Sorensen 2006, Pian 2007, Streiff-Fénart and Poutignat 2008.

3. Concerning trans-Saharan migration, see for example Bredeloup and Zongo 2005, Goldschmidt 2002, Pian 2007.

4. The crime of extortion consists of receiving or demanding amounts which are not due during the exercise of one's duties, without any service being rendered in exchange.

5. Due to disturbances linked with the resumption of the Touareg rebellion in February 2007, it seems that the state police have left the Toureyet site and there is no longer a checkpoint at this location.

6. Economic Community Of West African States.

7. Also see de Haas 2007, Le Cour Grandmaison 2008.

References

Bensaâd, A. (ed.) (2009) *Le Maghreb à l'épreuve des migrations subsahariennes. Immigration sur émigration*, Paris: Karthala.

Blundo, G. and J.-P. Olivier de Sardan (2001) 'La corruption quotidienne en Afrique de l'Ouest', *Politique africaine* 83: 8–37.

Bourdieu, P. and L. Wacquant (1992) *Réponses. Pour une anthropologie réflexive*, Paris: Seuil.

Brachet, J. (2009a) 'Irrégularité et clandestinité de l'immigration au Maghreb. Cas de l'Algérie et de la Libye', in A. Bensaâd (ed.) *Le Maghreb à l'épreuve des migrations subsahariennes. Immigration sur émigration*, Paris: Karthala.

Brachet, J. (2009b) *Migrations transsahariennes. Vers un désert cosmopolite et morcelé (Niger)*, Paris: Éditions du Croquant.

Bredeloup, S. and M. Zongo (2005) 'Quand les frères burkinabé de la petite Jamahiriyya s'arrêtent à Tripoli', *Autrepart* 36: 123–47.

Choplin, A. and J. Lombard (2008) 'Migrations et recompositions spatiales en Mauritanie. « Nouadhibou du monde ». Ville de transit... et après ?', *Afrique contemporaine* 4 (228): 151–70.

Clifford, J. (1997) 'Spatial practices: fieldwork, travel, and the disciplining of anthropology', in A. Gupta and J. Ferguson (eds.) *Anthropological Locations. Boundaries and Grounds of a Field Science*, Berkeley: University of California Press.

Collyer, M. (2006) 'States of insecurity: Consequences of Saharan transit migration', Working Paper (31), COMPAS, University of Oxford.

Dahou, T. (2002) 'Déculturaliser la corruption', *Les Temps Modernes* 620-621: 289–311.

De Certeau, M. (1990) *L'invention du quotidien. 1. arts de faire*, Paris: Gallimard.

De Haas, H. (2007) 'The myth of invasion. Irregular migration from West Africa to the Maghreb and the European Union', Research report, International Migration Institute, University of Oxford.

Ginzburg, C. (1980) 'Signes, traces, pistes. Racines d'un paradigme de l'indice', *Le Débat* 6: 3–44.

Goldschmidt, E. (2002) 'Migrants congolais en route vers l'Europe', *Les Temps modernes* 620-621: 208–39.

Hamood, S. (2006) 'African Transit Migration through Libya to Europe: the Human Cost', Rapport, The American University in Cairo, FMRS, Le Caire: 85.

Hannerz, U. (2003) 'Several Sites in One', in T. Hylland Eriksen (ed.) *Globalisation: Studies in Anthropology*, London: Pluto.

Le Cour Grandmaison, O. (2008) 'Colonisés-immigrés et "périls migratoires" : origines et permanence du racisme et d'une xénophobie d'État (1924-2007)', *Asylon(s)* (4) : www.reseau-terra. eu/article734.html

Lussault, M. (2005) 'La mobilité comme événement', in S. Allemand, F. Ascher, and J. Lévy (eds.), *Les sens du mouvement : modernité et mobilités dans les sociétés urbaines contemporaines*, Paris: Institut pour la ville en mouvement-Belin.

Marcus, G. E. (1995) 'Ethnography in/of the World System: The Emergence of multi-sited Ethnography', *Annual Review of Anthropology* 24: 95–117.

Marcus, G. E. (1998) *Ethnography through Thick and Thin*, Princeton: Princeton University Press.

Médard, J.-F. (2006) 'Les paradoxes de la corruption institutionnalisée', *Revue internationale de politique comparée* 13 (4): 697–710.

Merleau-Ponty, M. (1999 [1945]) *Phénoménologie de la perception*, Tel, Paris: Gallimard.

Nadi, D. (2007) 'Installations dans une ville de transit migratoire. Le cas de la ville de Tamanrasset en Algérie', in E. Boesen and L. Marfaing (eds.) *Les nouveaux urbains dans l'espace Sahara-Sahel. Un cosmopolitisme par le bas*, Paris: Karthala-ZMO.

Nyberg-Sorensen, N. (ed.) (2006) 'Mediterranean transit migration', DIIS, Copenhagen: 157 (www.diis.dk/sw24384.asp).

Olivier de Sardan, J.-P. (1999) 'L'économie morale de la corruption en Afrique', *Politique africaine* 63: 97–116.

Perrin, D. (2008) 'L'étranger rendu visible au Maghreb. La voie ouverte à la transposition des politiques juridiques migratoires européennes', *Asylon(s)* 4: http://terra.rezo.net/article770.html.

Pian, A. (2007) 'Les Sénégalais en transit au Maroc. La formation d'un espace-temps de l'entre-deux aux marges de l'Europe', thèse de doctorat, UFR de Sciences Sociales, Université Paris 7 Diderot, Paris: 486.

Rodier, C. (2009) 'Externalisation des frontières au sud de l'Europe. L'alliance Union européenne-Libye', in A. Bensaâd (ed.) *Le Maghreb à l'épreuve des migrations subsahariennes. Immigration sur émigration*, Paris: Karthala.

Spittler, G. (1996) 'Explorers in transit: Travels to Timbuktu and Agades in the nineteenth century', *History and Anthropology* 9 (2-3): 231–53.

Streiff-Fénart, J. and P. Poutignat (2008) 'Nouadhibou « ville de transit »? Le rapport d'une ville à ses étrangers dans le contexte des politiques de contrôle des frontières de l'Europe', *Revue Européenne des Migrations Internationales* 24 (2): 193–217.

Chapter 6

⇞•⇜

EXPERIMENTAL DATA COLLECTION METHODS AND MIGRATION GOVERNANCE

Darshan Vigneswaran

INTRODUCTION

Informal migration[1] may be transforming political power and authority in Africa. The presence of large populations of undocumented migrants exacerbates and complicates already fragile relationships between 'states' and 'citizens'. When officials have limited obligations to those that move through and reside in their jurisdiction, it is less likely that they will feel obligated to act within their official mandates. Informal migrants also possess strong incentives to disengage from formal governance structures and in some cases, to deliberately subvert state agents, particularly those that are responsible for enforcing immigration laws. These dynamics compel us to reorient the way we study the relationships between governance, informality and migration. Work on South Africa is particularly cognisant of the fact that governments do not simply struggle to define and limit informal migration, but that migration patterns are increasingly informalising governance structures (Coplan 2001; Ellis 1999; Shaw 2002; Vigneswaran 2010).

The widely acknowledged and much maligned linkages between a) organised crime, b) informal migration and c) the production of fraudulent documents have led international institutions to focus their attention on problems of corruption within immigration departments.[2] Yet, the role of the police in immigration enforcement may be equally problematic. As more states accept that there are limits to border controls as a means of regulating and controlling international migration (Bhagwati 2003; Taylor 2005),[3] many governments are relying on a range of 'internal' controls which limit access to citizenship entitlements and devote added resources to the surveillance of human mobility and residence (Groenendijk 2003; Guiraudon and Lahav 2000; Lahav 2000). As part of this shift, some governments are calling on domestic police forces for help.[4] For example the US has a) empowered police officers with the prerogative to conduct inspections of buildings and make immigration arrests; b) supported police departments with increased access to immigration databases; and c) co-ordinated federal immigration agency activities with local police agencies, particularly for raids and other enforcement operations (Coleman 2007). It is not yet clear how police departments will ultimately utilise these additional responsibilities vis-à-vis immigration enforcement, but it is likely that efforts to increase their involvement will remain a feature of immigration policies for some time.

In recognition of this trend, scholars have also paid additional attention to police enforcement of immigration laws in residential, commercial and agricultural areas and on city streets. While some researchers, particularly those concerned to combat human trafficking, have called for increased police capacity to control human mobility (Derluyn and Broekaert 2005; Mameli 2002) most work has been critical of the involvement of domestic police in immigration enforcement. Police officers rarely possess the necessary language and cultural skills to deal with migrants in a sensitive manner (Culver 2004). They are preoccupied by other policing agendas, and tend to confuse their roles and prerogatives as enforcers of criminal laws with their corresponding powers vis-à-vis immigration offences that are more administrative in nature (Quassoli 2004). At a policy level, scholars have a) questioned whether there is a valid legal mandate for local police officers to implement federal/national immigration laws (Keblawi 2004); b) pondered whether immigration control constitutes the best use of finite law enforcement resources (Barbagli and Sartori 2004; Holmes et al. 2008; Vigneswaran and Duponchel 2009); c) noted adverse affects on both migrants' willingness to report crime and migrant communities' relationship with the police (Kittrie 2006); and d) argued that police enforcement contributes to the negative stereotyping of minority communities (Adler 2006; Romero 2006). Research has also identified a range of police failures to act in accordance with the spirit and the letter of immigration laws. Police officers have been more likely unreasonably to use force to arrest undocumented migrants; commonly verbally abused suspects (Phillips et al. 2006, 2002); unnecessarily harassed particularly vulnerable migrants; and extorted migrants for bribes (Gulcur and Ilkkaracan 2002). This last finding is of particular significance, not simply because it casts doubt on the utility and implications of decisions to move immigration enforcement resources away from the border, but because it also suggests that such policies may be compromising the integrity of states' core law enforcement agencies.

Understanding the evolving relationship between immigration enforcement policies and the development of political institutions in Africa requires improved data. Unfortunately, our ability to speak confidently about informality, law-breaking behaviour and corruption in migration governance has been limited by our lack of suitable techniques to study these phenomena. Potential respondents face disincentives to provide accurate accounts of their behaviour, thereby confounding many conventional interrogatory methods (interviews, surveys, focus groups etc.). This chapter responds to this problem by introducing and reviewing an experimental data collection technique which we have dubbed 'incident reporting'. This approach combines a systematic procedure for sampling observed instances of immigration enforcement with a series of protocols for categorising and coding observations of behaviour by officials. The technique goes beyond conventional methods by: a) decreasing, through the removal of threat of personal or institutional sanction and/or repercussion, incentives for subjects to adjust their behaviour or censor their language; b) increasing our capacity to test causal explanations of informal behaviour by officials; and c) linking the study of the nature of informality in immigration enforcement directly to the study of the extent of these practices. Importantly, this chapter will not specifically engage in a detailed analysis of the findings of this study, which will provide answers to our primary question of how migration governance is transforming the African state. Instead, we adopt the more modest aim of gauging whether, and in what ways the incident reporting technique can help to answer such questions. The chapter concludes that incident reporting could be usefully deployed in a variety of other contexts to collect novel data on informality in immigration enforcement.

METHODOLOGICAL DIFFICULTIES FOR RESEARCH ON MIGRATION POLICING

Journalists and scholars have faced few difficulties in generating anecdotal reports of informal and illegal behaviour by immigration police and undocumented migrants. However, those who seek to generate reliable, representative and comparative data on this subject face a range of obstacles. The 'Blue Code' is a powerful set of moral norms within the police force that encourages feelings of organisational belonging. The code negatively sanctions officers who speak openly and truthfully about police practices, ensuring that even individuals who are not directly involved in illicit activity will be disinclined to provide information about their colleagues' activities (Barker and Carter 1994; Blumberg and Niederhoffer 1985; Kennedy 1977). On the other side of the equation, undocumented migrants are also relatively elusive. They often do not report crimes for fear of reprisal or lack of protection (Kittrie 2006) and under-report in surveys and censuses because of fear of being discovered and deported (Margolis 1995). More generally, 'invisibility' is a crucial tactic which undocumented migrants adopt as a basic survival strategy, to prevent unnecessary targeting by both officials and antagonistic citizens (see Special Issue of *Journal of Refugee Studies* 21 (4)). The fact that the agents and the targets of immigration enforcement activities may be disinclined to provide accurate information compromises the integrity of data on informal behaviour.

Scholars have employed a range of methodological approaches and techniques to combat these problems. Scott Philipps, Nestor Rodrigeuz and Jacqueline Hagan (2006) chose to survey migrants who had already been arrested and deported, instead of resident migrant populations. This approach had two advantages: i) providing the researchers with a relatively easily accessed and relatively representative sample of their target population; and ii) countering fears of reprisals by asking questions of individuals who presumably had 'little to lose' because they had already been discovered and deported at the time they gave responses to surveyors. Switching focus to the official side of this equation, Leigh Culver (2004) used an ethnographic/observational approach, involving 'ride alongs' in police vehicles, to show how a small town police force dealt with invitations to corrupt behaviour. This research relied on the characteristic strengths of participant observation as a research technique; that is, generation of personal trust and subjects' high levels of confidence in the nature and potential impact of the research, to provide entry into otherwise hidden practices of police officials, including their wide use of discretion in the enforcement of immigration laws. On other occasions, researchers have been assisted by official inquiries. For example, Mary Romero's (2006) study of immigration enforcement raids in Arizona benefitted from two separate government inquiries into, among other things, the police mistreatment of minority communities. This material provided her with relatively comprehensive coverage of the raids and the ability to reliably gauge the prevalence of informal and illegal police behaviour in enforcement operations.

Despite this considerable methodological creativity and rigour, research has produced little reliable data on one crucial form of informal behaviour: corruption. 'Corruption' may be broadly defined as the 'improper use of official authority for the pursuit of personal gain'. There are several reasons why it might be particularly difficult to generate reliable data on this topic. The first problem relates to sampling. Groups and individuals that have been successful in securing their release through corrupt means will not be covered by surveys of detainees and deportees. Second, whereas in cases of police brutality and xenophobia, migrants have specific reasons why they might want to provide researchers with information, migrants and migrant groups who have experiences of corruption are invariably implicated in a criminal act, usually one of much greater seriousness than an immigration offence. Hence, there are much stronger reasons for migrants, even those who have already been deported, to under-report or tailor their responses. Third, while ethnographic/

observational research may help to build sufficient levels of trust to encourage police respondents to reveal some forms of 'rule-bending' behaviour, such as their negative attitudes towards minorities and/or their beliefs in the 'virtues' of excessive force, the higher level of sanctions against corrupt behaviour may ensure that these practices remain hidden, even from embedded researchers. Finally, there is little incentive for government officials to attempt to rigorously investigate this topic. Neither pro-law enforcement nor pro-migrant lobbies have much incentive to call on governments to rigorously investigate and document corruption, because this evidence tends to tarnish the reputation of both lobby groups' constituencies.

Given these issues, it is essential, both for researchers of immigration enforcement in particular, and police research more generally, that we develop new techniques to generate more reliable data on the informal practices that take place when police officers enforce immigration laws. With this in mind, this chapter outlines an experimental research technique for studying various forms of law-breaking activities by police. It is possible that this research technique could be applied in multiple ways, to answer a range of different questions about policing. However, the Johannesburg study was specifically designed with a small number of research objectives in mind.

STUDYING SOUTH AFRICAN IMMIGRATION POLICING

This research was conducted as part of a broader collaboration between legal service providers, academic institutions and migrant advocacy groups, to improve the capacity of South Africa's non-governmental sector to address shortfalls in migrant rights protection. As part of its transition from Apartheid, South Africa adopted a new constitution which provides strong guarantees of protection for various categories of migrant rights. However, officials in various government departments have neglected their responsibilities to provide migrants with access to their rightful immigration status, health care and education. One of the most problematic developments has been in the enforcement of immigration laws, where monitoring agencies have noted rampant corruption, abuse and procedural irregularity (CoRMSA 2009; Human Rights Watch 1998, 2006). The actions of the police have received considerable scrutiny. While the Department of Home

Affairs (DHA) is primarily responsible for the enforcement of immigration laws, the Immigration Act (n. 13 of 2002) warrants police officials to question and detain suspected 'illegal foreigners' pending status determination by an authorised DHA 'immigration officer'. In practice, this has resulted in a scenario where police officials do almost all of the 'legwork' involved in immigration enforcement, investigating suspected offences, taking suspected offenders into custody and then handing suspects over to the DHA (Vigneswaran 2008). In a country that deported over 300,000 migrants in 2007, this entails a huge amount of work and a significant outlay of police resources (Vigneswaran and Duponchel 2009).[5] Preliminary investigations of this activity by journalists and advocacy groups have shown that police activity in this area involves significant levels of corruption and worrying examples of physical abuse. Prior to conducting the current study, our programme was also alerted to the possibility that police officials commonly extorted migrants for sexual favours, or simply raped suspected 'illegal foreigners'. Furthermore, during the course of this study, our partner research organisation took up two separate cases of migrant deaths in custody where inappropriate and disproportionate use of force by police officers were believed to be a contributing factor.

The incident reporting technique was employed as part of a broader study which aimed to investigate these claims, examine some of the underlying causes, and generate insights that could be directly utilised in a policy making/advocacy setting. At the same time, we also wanted data that would speak to our broader theoretical interests in the relationship between migration and state transformation in Africa. A number of empirical questions presented themselves as crucial to this overall exercise. First, we needed to understand why the police chose to expend time and resources on immigration enforcement. There is nothing in the immigration legislation which compels a police officer to ask an individual for their documents or to take suspected offenders into custody. Why were the police so heavily involved in this type of enforcement activity? Did it have to do with requests by the DHA for assistance or were the police independently motivated to do this work? Second, it was not clear what sorts of informal police behaviours were occurring, how frequently they occurred and to what extent these were specific to immigration enforcement activities. Our anecdotal reports of police officers breaking the law could not be used to definitively state which, if any of these forms of behaviour (verbal abuse, physical abuse or corruption) was more common and which, if any, were germane to the immigration enforcement process. Third, we needed to understand to what extent more senior officials were involved in any hypothesised form of illegal behaviour by junior officers. Was this a systemic issue involving endorsement by higher level actors or a process driven by the more basic motivations and/or predilections of officers on the beat? By answering these three questions on motivations, extent and organisation we hoped to a) test our initial hypothesis regarding the linkage between immigration enforcement and the informalisation of state practices in Johannesburg, and b) develop a means by which we could then ask the same questions of other cases in South Africa and other parts of the continent.

Contextual origins of incident reporting

Incident reporting constitutes a highly specialised technique that was designed to shed light on specific aspects of these broader questions. The remainder of this chapter will explain how we designed the technique, and then describe some results of our efforts to pilot the procedure in Johannesburg, South Africa. This technique begins with a departure from a core tenet of research on police informality and corruption. Whereas most research on police informality begins with the assumption that the object of analysis will be extremely difficult to locate, we began by presuming that some informal and illegal practices might be highly public in nature and readily and regularly observed in public places. This hypothesis was partially confirmed by a relatively fortuitous encounter. As part of our programme's outreach work, we held partnership meetings with several migrant advocacy organisations who were seeking to increase their research capacity. One of these organisations, which I shall call 'Migrant Help', had set up its own system for monitoring immigration arrests. Using a series of informal contacts and cell-phone communication, this group had mobilised a range of migrant street traders, volunteers and building managers to report cases where police officials had arrested or were arresting undocumented migrants. Migrant Help would send reporters to document what occurred. In those cases where the reporter/

researcher believed some form of rights abuse had occurred or that the police had behaved in an improper manner, they would write a short narrative account of their observations.

Soon after meeting with members of the organisation, I accompanied some of the researchers while they conducted their fieldwork. Their strategy was relatively straightforward. Utilising their experiences of a) having lived in the neighbourhoods in question; b) informally observing police behaviour; and c) participating in local policing forums, the researchers had developed a schematic understanding of the places where police officials commonly stopped migrants and asked them for their documents. The group was notified of instances of enforcement taking place in one of two ways. First, they had established informal agreements with street traders and building managers who worked in the relevant areas to send an SMS to the group's research coordinator whenever they heard about or witnessed a police raid on a building nearby. At this point the coordinator would ensure that a team member would attend the scene, make observations, conduct informal interviews and prepare a report. Second, the researchers, often working in pairs or teams, would comb areas where they knew arrests were likely to take place until they encountered a road block or a patrol car or an officer on the beat. At this point, they would observe the activities of the officials until they stopped and interrogated an individual or group. The researchers often worked without pen or paper, memorising events and words as they went along, and listening to the audible parts of whatever conversations took place. While much more could be achieved in crowded environments, the researchers were able to make relatively detailed observations regardless of the scenario, simply by behaving as 'ordinary' pedestrians and observing what they could of the enforcement action. In the process of conducting this research they gradually learnt the characteristics of ordinary enforcement activities and settled on a series of visible cues, beyond the obvious exchanges of money, which might suggest that an improper or illegal exchange had taken place, such as when an official took a civilian or suspect to another site in the patrol vehicle, or when an individual placed an object on the ground which an officer subsequently picked up. On some occasions the researchers, several of whom were trained journalists, would follow up their observations by attempting to conduct interviews, both with officials and the members of the public involved in the interaction in question. The reports produced by the group contained not only straightforward data such as the racial characteristics of officers and suspects, the nature of the enforcement action and licence plate of the vehicle. The researchers also documented less easily visible characteristics of the interactions between police officers and civilians, such as the amounts exchanged and the types of language used, and could use these insights to build a more reliable portrait of the nature of the exchange itself.

Migrant Help had, by reacting in an intuitive and organised fashion to their group's security and rights-based concerns, established a relatively systematic means of monitoring enforcement-related rights abuses in their vicinity. By side-stepping one of the most prominent *a priori* assumptions of much research on informal police activity, that is, that the object of analysis is invisible or hard to access, they had made it possible to look at this subject from a different angle. Our own programme felt that this approach could be utilised to provide broader insights into the nature and extent of corruption in Johannesburg. However, several large and important questions remained. How representative and reliable were the findings? Could the research strategy be refined to provide for comparative analysis? Finally, was this covert form of research ethically sound? The remainder of this discussion will outline the manner in which we dealt with each of these issues, in collaboration with Migrant Help.

TECHNICAL AND PROCEDURAL DIMENSIONS

Sampling

Our principal aim in working with Migrant Help was to increase the capacity of their project to develop reliable generalisations about police corruption. Following their existing strategy, they could confidently claim to have produced reliable individual reports on police corruption in their vicinity. However, they could not determine whether their data was representative of policing practices in their vicinity or policing more generally. By only writing up cases where abuses of migrants' rights took place, the researchers tended to sample on a dependent variable, excluding other, less problematic enforcement activities of the police and excluding exchanges with

South Africans from their analysis. They tended to conduct more intensive research and write more extensively on cases that they were more ethically or morally opposed to, such as examples of abuse over those of corruption. Finally, while their system for identifying enforcement incidents – involving a network of contacts and personal knowledge of immigration enforcement 'hot-spots' – showed evidence of considerable initiative, it also limited their ability to ensure comprehensive coverage, causing them to focus activities on certain areas to the neglect of others. This problem left their reports open to various forms of critique, particularly the contention that instead of identifying a systemic issue, they had merely identified a small set officers engaging in a fairly uncommon set of illegal activities. In all these respects, their capacity to generalise about police behaviour was severely limited.

We set out to develop a more systematic sampling procedure for the project. This was a difficult task because of the lack of an identifiable sampling frame. Unlike most migration and migration policy research, the object of study and point of access was not a fixed population of police officials, or migrants and their stories, but rather a range of enforcement 'incidents' that were loosely defined and impossible to quantify. The people involved were important characteristics of each incident, but were not the unit of analysis. While we possessed some knowledge, based on previous policing research, about the various categories of police work and the distribution of police labour across these categories, there was no way of identifying a total population of relevant incidents and therefore few ways of either determining an appropriate sample frame or generating a random sample. Instead of aiming for randomness, we tried to make the selection process more systematic. This began with the decision to limit the study to a finite area and period, placing spatial and temporal limits on the number of incidents that could plausibly be included in the sample and the types of claims we would seek to make. We then adopted techniques to increase the likelihood that, regardless of its positioning in space and time, each hypothetical incident (whether it involved problematic or routine policing activity) would have a roughly equal chance of being observed by our researchers. Importantly, while we wanted to sustain a focus on immigration enforcement we also wanted to expand the scope of the study beyond Migrant Help's constituency. This was due to the fact that South African nationals are also commonly stopped and asked to prove their immigration status, and sometimes arrested for not having valid papers (Mabasa 2003; Smillie 2005). Furthermore, we felt that we could only develop an accurate portrait of immigration enforcement if we could compare these operations with interactions between police officers and civilians that did not involve a request to see an individual's papers.

In order to guarantee roughly equal coverage of the area, we decided to adopt a more systematic approach to how we encountered observable incidents. We discontinued the use of fixed reporters in the field and instead built solely upon the strategy of 'combing' the neighbourhood with roving reporters. We began by identifying 22 possible entry/exit points along the boundary of the sample tract. We then placed these numbers in a random order and drew a line between each chosen point and the point immediately following it in the selection. These lines provided us with a template path which we could then use to generate a travel plan, after making adjustments for road and traffic conditions. In order to make this strategy more efficient, we provided the research team with a vehicle. The central idea of the selection strategy, modifying the approach utilised previously by Migrant Help, remained to move through the sample tract until we spotted a police car or official. At this point two researchers would exit the vehicle and observe the next enforcement action in which this car or official was involved. In order to prevent artificial clustering, after they had observed a given incident, the research team would then travel at least three blocks further on the path before beginning to search for the next police vehicle or official. When both teams had completed their observations the driver would retrieve the researchers and resume the journey along the designated path.

After identifying the tract and our procedure for combing through it, we chose a period of two months for the study, allowing for inclusion of a broad range of incidents while ensuring that our research did not go on indefinitely. We then systematically selected the hours in which the researchers worked. The 40 days of the study period were divided up into 80 four-hour work blocks. We randomly selected one-quarter of these blocks in which to conduct research. This sampling strategy had the added advantage of increasing the coverage of the study in terms of time, while economising on our resources.

Using this strategy, a total sample size of 110 incidents was obtained. There is no definitive measure of the representativity of this sample. Nevertheless, two characteristics of the sample population increase our confidence in the reliability of the results. The first is the geographic distribution of the incidents. As expected, there are several cluster points, but a broad geographic distribution of cases may be observed.

The second factor increasing our confidence in the sample is the distribution of incidents across categories of enforcement operation. While there is an expected dominance in the sample of 'street-level' incidents, several inspections of premises have also been observed (see Figure 2). While the researchers observed many incidents where they suspected officers had broken a law of some variety, these numerically exceptional cases could now be contextualised within a broader family of cases of more ordinary policing activity.

Figure 1. Aerial depiction of incident distribution across sample tract

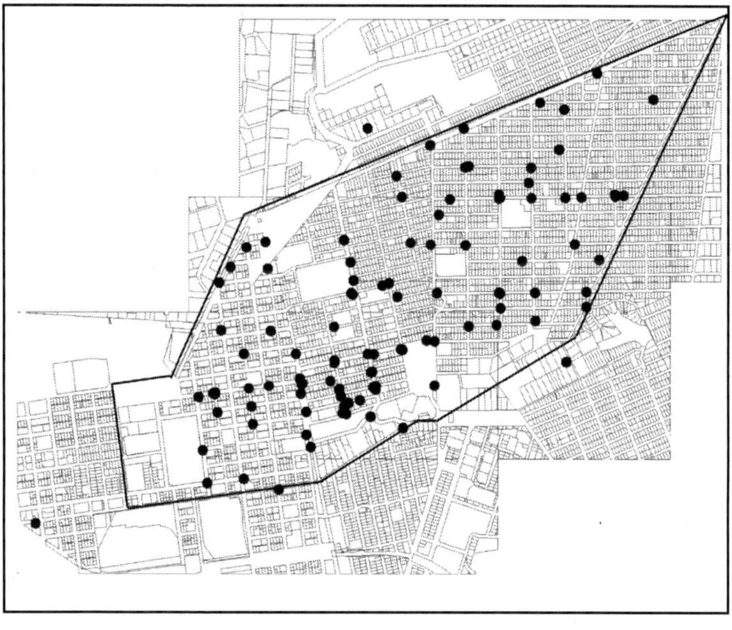

For ethical reasons outlined below, all maps have been deliberately kept anonymous.

Figure 2. Types of operation observed

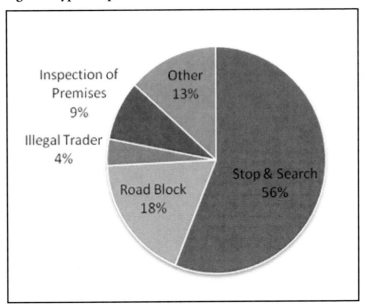

REPORTING

In addition to refining the manner in which we selected incidents, the project also needed to specify how these incidents would be reported. As noted above, prior to engaging in this collaboration, the researchers had tended to respond in a relatively intuitive fashion to incidents, making particular note of those aspects of the incidents that appeared most important, and then recording these details in a short narrative account. There were significant limitations to this style of reporting. In particular, the resulting reports tended to resemble each individual researcher's own narrative predilections, varying from legalistic to journalistic to police investigative styles. Moreover, the material tended to reflect individual researchers' own normative predilections, with particular reporters emphasising cases of police xenophobia and others preferring to fixate on issues of physical or gender-related abuse. These problems were made more complex by the strict practical limits on the amount of data that could be collected. Researchers had a brief 'window' during which they could observe, and in some cases hear, a small set of interactions among police officers and members of the public. Occasionally, these could be supported by short informal interviews with the latter.

In order to refine this approach, we set about reducing the number of categories of information collected. These can be roughly divided into two sets: content data and characteristic data. Content data refers to observations of a particular type of irregular or law-breaking behaviour on the part of the investigating officers. We decided to collect information on three categories of content data:

- *Procedural:* whether an individual had been asked for their documents, verbally abused or read their rights and whether the arresting officers were wearing badges
- *Use of force:* whether force was used, whether the suspect offered resistance and whether the force used was proportional to the resistance
- *Corruption:* whether the officers had solicited payments, whether payments had been made, any amount exchanged, whether any items had been stolen from the suspect and whether the suspect had been taken to a separate venue before being released (a potential indicator of a corrupt exchange)

Each of these indicators was laid out as a series of closed questions which the observational team could answer in a checklist fashion. If their answers involved an observed case of potential irregular or illegal behaviour on the part of the police, the researchers would write a narrative describing the events reported directly underneath their completed report.

Characteristic data refers to observed characteristics of the incident which we planned to use to test causal relationships between the observed incidents and broader factors. Each was selected for their potential utility as an explanatory variable for the empirical questions outlined above as well as the relative ease of generating accurate data without the need for lengthy observation. We recorded:

- *Site:* by placing an 'x' on a map. This information was subsequently translated into geographic coordinates. This material was collected in part as a check on the sampling mechanism, but also to allow for spatial analysis of hypothesised relationships.

- *Time and date:* by analysing the time of incidents in relation to their temporal proximity to pay days, it was expected that this information would allow us to test the degree to which economic motivations might underlie immigration enforcement activity.

- *Type of operation:* based on previous observations and discussions with police officials, we developed six categories of police stop. It was expected that this data could not only help us to check the reliability of sampling but help us to gauge the degree to which official organisation and or endorsement lay behind police malfeasance.

- *Departmental affiliation:* we aimed to use this information to determine levels of organisation involved in immigration policing. For example, the regularity of DHA involvement in immigration enforcement actions could be utilised to gauge the extent to which police immigration enforcement was driven by general immigration policy directives, as opposed to the police departments' independent agendas.

- *Socio-demographic characteristics of officers and suspects:* this information could be utilised to detect instances of discriminatory or profiling behaviour by the police.

While these categories helped to rationalise the reporting process, we still faced a challenge in ensuring that the researchers were uniformly translating their observations into recorded information. In our attempts to refine this approach, we searched for examples of how other research exercises had sought to develop generalisations from relatively sporadic forms of human observation and investigation. Unsurprisingly, criminologists provided some inspiration here. The practice of conducting unobtrusive observations of police stops in public spaces is not an entirely novel research strategy, and has been specifically utilised by researchers to examine issues of police–minority relations before in the literature on ethnic profiling. For the most part, this literature has utilised observational strategies in order to generate reliable benchmarks of driver and offender characteristics which they have subsequently used to aid analyses of aggregate data of police stops. For example, in one study on the Miami-Dade area, researchers were deployed at traffic inspections and instructed to survey which drivers ran red lights, exceeded the speed limit and made illegal turns; and the race and gender of the offenders (Alpert et al. 2007). These observations were then used to generate a baseline of the racial characteristics of the population to examine degrees of racial bias in police officers' decisions to stop motorists. Some studies have taken this approach further to observe police stops themselves. For example, a recent study of racial profiling on the Moscow Metro used this approach, supported by follow-up interviews with suspects, to measure the degree to which police were disproportionately and unfairly stopping non-Slavic travellers (JURIX and Open Society Justice Initiative 2006). Ordinary police data collection processes also provided some inspiration. Many police departments encourage a rigorous process of documentation of both their own activities and reported observations of criminal behaviour made by individuals outside the police force. Although the coverage of these reporting systems varies, this sort of reporting is often designed to be used for the development of statistical generalisations and analysis, as is the case with the US National Incident Based Reporting System. Since police departments have little control over, or capacity to train the citizens who come to them with reports, the key to the reliability of this system is the police officer, who interrogates the reporter and records the data. By interrogating the reporter in line with a series of established protocols, police officials ensure that the data collected conforms to prescribed standards.

Building upon the logic of these two data collection strategies, we adopted two procedures for ensuring consistency of reporting. First, prior to conducting the research, we held a training workshop for our researchers with legal and socio-psychological experts in order to develop a series of appropriate benchmarks, primarily for the most difficult observations: of content data. Second, instead of allowing researchers to work independently, we deployed two researchers to investigate each incident who worked in consultation to prepare each report and write observations. A team leader then read through the entire report with them and confirmed how the information was obtained (through observation, over-hearing or interview) and confirmed or denied their reliability. As a general rule, in cases where it could not be definitively stated whether or not a police officer had acted in a particular way, the team leaders were instructed to record 'don't know' in response.

The reliability of these reporting strategies varied depending on the category of the data being collected. As one would expect, regardless of the efforts to rigorously apply a benchmarking procedure, researchers were more capable of accurately recording characteristic than content data. There were also difficulties in ensuring that researchers erred on the side of caution in their recording of data. This was particularly problematic with regards to questions that were framed as basic features of a particular form of interaction, but could not always be adequately answered for every incident. For example, researchers sometimes included figures of how much money was exchanged in their reporting of corrupt practices on the basis of having sighted the money, but without having conducted an interview with the subject to confirm their suspicions. Many of these issues could be effectively addressed through rigorous cross-checking by the team leader. However, these problems meant that there are several categories of data which we cannot confidently report on. More problematic is the fact that it is not clear whether there were specific forms of policing that may have biased the observational process in one way or another. For example, are there aspects of road blocks that make informal or illegal activities more or less opaque? Do Metro Police officials adopt strategies which make their attempts to use force more or less visible? These types of questions constitute grounds upon which to criticise the findings of this study and show where greater refinement of the technique is required.

ANALYSIS

Despite these limitations, the study produced a range of data that we can confidently report on, and use to refine our claims about the relationship between immigration enforcement and changes occurring within state institutions. The findings help us to refine some hypotheses as to why police officers choose to enforce immigration laws. Confirming our suspicion that police officers spend a significant amount of their time and resources on immigration enforcement tasks, we noted that they asked to see suspects' documents in the vast majority of their daytime patrols and operations (87 per cent

Figure 3. Police stations/agencies involved in observed incidents

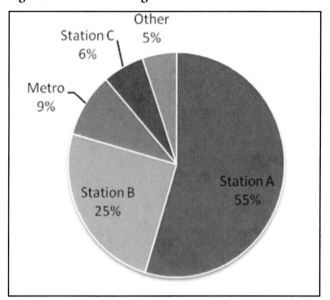

n=75). This type of behaviour was not being specifically provoked by the institutions charged with responsibility for immigration enforcement because none of the incidents we observed involved DHA officials.[6] Instead, we found more support for the claim that police propensity to enforce immigration laws was motivated by the prospect of soliciting a bribe. Crucially, our findings lent support to a less extreme version of the various claims about predatory policing that we had uncovered in our preliminary consultations. Prior to beginning this study, we had received reports that officers from outside precincts were 'moonlighting' within our sample tract for the sole purpose of extorting migrants for bribes.[7] Figure 3 shows that the vast majority of incidents only involved officers from Stations A, B and C, which each had jurisdiction over a part of the sample tract.

The data which showed *where* police officials were involved in enforcement actions was even more compelling (Figure 4). This map showed a close correspondence between enforcement activities and police jurisdiction, with police officials from Station A and B rarely participating in enforcement activities, even in the precincts of adjacent stations.

Figure 4. Aerial depiction of the distribution of station members' incidents vis-à-vis station location

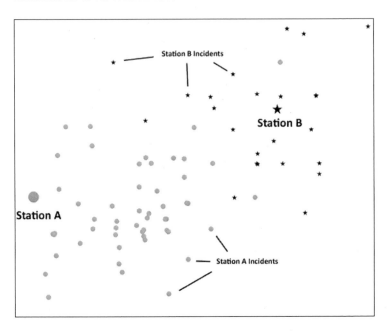

This does not mean that immigration policing was not predatory at all, because officers certainly strategically exploited opportunities to solicit bribes. At a general level, officers were more inclined to solicit bribes on pay days (58 per cent n=19) when returns would be better, than on other days (25 per cent n=36) when returns would be poor. A more pertinent finding for this study was that officers were more likely to solicit bribes in cases where they were investigating immigration offences. Officers were more inclined to solicit a bribe in those cases where they had asked to see an individual's documents (34 per cent n=41), than in cases where they had not (25 per cent n=8). When taken together, these findings suggest the need for revisions in our understanding of the causal relationship between immigration enforcement and police corruption. Rather than the idea that the process of excluding foreign nationals creates occasional opportunities for corrupt exchanges, our findings suggest that the knowledge that immigration laws may provide opportunities

Figure 5. Aerial depiction of the proximity of corrupt incidents to station location

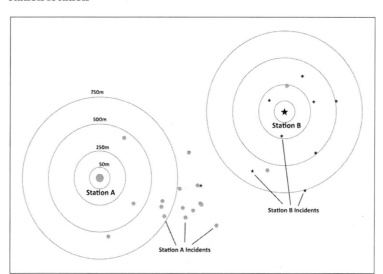

for corrupt exchanges may be part of the reason why police officers regularly ask people to prove their immigration status.

It would appear that immigration enforcement shares a problematic relationship with state transformation, potentially supporting processes which reduce the integrity of officials within key law enforcement agencies. The findings allow us to go further, to gauge the *extent* of such problems. At a general level, our findings suggest that corrupt activity is a pervasive feature of street-level policing. Approximately two in every five incidents we observed (40 per cent n=97) involved at least one of our indicators of corruption: a) the officer solicited a bribe; b) the officer took the suspect to a separate venue other than the police station; c) the officer received money or a personal belonging (often a mobile phone) from the suspect. Importantly, these types of behaviour were more common than other forms of informal and law-breaking behaviour, such as physical and verbal abuse. Officers were more likely to engage in corrupt activity than to use force disproportionately while subduing a suspect,[8] or to abuse suspects verbally (3 per cent n=39). However, it may not only be the presence of foreigners that created these dynamics. Indeed, we found that incidents which only involved South African suspects were more likely to involve corrupt behaviour (67 per cent n=6) than those that only involved foreign nationals (53 per cent n=17). This may have less to do with any propensity of South African or foreign nationals to participate in corruption than the fact that corrupt exchanges cannot take place unless there is some base level of cultural understanding between officer and suspect.[9] Again, these findings suggest the need for revisions in our understanding of the relationship between South African post-Apartheid police transformation and immigration policy. Given the historical role of the police in sustaining the racist and authoritarian Apartheid regime, issues like police brutality and chauvinism have dominated the reform agenda. In contrast, our study suggests that these problematic issues may not constitute the most regularised form of informal/illegal behaviour within the South African police. Furthermore, while international migration may open up more opportunities for corruption, there may be a variety of dimensions of policing which are directed at the broader population, where opportunities for corrupt exchanges emerge. In this sense, immigration offences should be grouped with traffic, gambling and liquor offences which also create opportunities for police corruption.

Thus far, we have shown how immigration enforcement responsibilities may shape the behaviour of street-level officers, and shown that corrupt behaviour in particular is extensive. The next step for our analysis was to determine whether these behaviours were deeply rooted in policing institutions, and more specifically, whether they appeared to be condoned by more senior officials. While it was difficult to generate conclusive evidence on this front, we generated findings on several indicators which suggested potentially interesting lines of analysis. We found evidence to suggest that senior police officials might be able to significantly deter or hinder street-level corruption. Generally speaking, officials involved in street-level policing can be divided into three types: A) Constables and Student Constables who do most of the legwork of patrols, road blocks etc.; B) Captains and Inspectors who supervise the activities of the Constables; C) Superintendents who rarely leave the station, except to inspect the activities of groups A and B. For the most part, the incidents we observed involved only officers from group A, so we used alternative indicators to gauge relationships between the supervisory activities of B and C officials and corruption. For group C officials we deployed a spatial test. We assumed that police officers would not engage in corrupt activity near their own station if they feared the sanction of the Superintendents who worked there. Unsurprisingly, we did not observe any officials engaging in corrupt activity within a 50m radius of their own station. However, we found that Station B officials were more willing to engage in corrupt activity within 500m of their station than Station A officials were. Crucially, this was despite the fact that indicators of corrupt activity were observed in a higher proportion of incidents involving Station A officials (38 per cent n=55) than incidents involving Station B officials (25 per cent n=24).

One interpretation of this finding could be that some senior officials have the *capacity* to limit corrupt activity among junior officials, who deliberately avoid committing illegal acts in areas where their most senior officers might detect this activity. This finding should be weighed against other results which suggest that middle-ranking (Group B) officials may in fact collude with the corrupt activities of juniors.

In order to gauge the impact of Group B officials on policing integrity we measured the incidence of corruption in operations involving varying levels of Group B supervision. We assumed that in 'fixed point' operations like road blocks, a Group B official would usually be in attendance or would at least monitor officials closely. In contrast, in mobile patrol incidents like inspections of illegal traders and stop and search operations, Group B supervisors would have less control. Somewhat surprisingly, higher levels of supervision did not result in lower levels of corruption. Indeed, fixed point operations revealed a higher level of corrupt activity (53 per cent n=19) than mobile patrols (30 per cent n=63). This finding suggests that middle-ranking officials might tacitly condone or actively support corrupt behaviour. From these findings, it seems plausible to suggest that the 'street-level' corruption which commonly occurs in immigration enforcement operations may not be disorganised and random, but may be directly connected to the chain of command in the South African police.

If this preliminary analysis of the findings is accurate, then incident reporting may offer a range of useful means for analysing the relationship between immigration enforcement and state transformation. Our study was limited by a small sample size (n=110), a biased case selection (a high-density migrant area) and a number of untested assumptions (for example, the significance of spatial associations as indicators of causal relationships). Furthermore, we have mostly examined correlations in this review which necessarily require a range of supporting research strategies that can gauge whether our hypothesised explanation for these correlations obtains. Nevertheless, given the highly sensitive nature of the subject matter, we believe that the findings have allowed us to eliminate some of the more outlandish hypotheses, refine central tenets, measure the extent of certain phenomena, and develop new lines of analysis for study. Returning to our central question, we can more definitively state that immigration enforcement is both a product of, and facilitator in, the corruption of the South African police. Furthermore, it seems worth going beyond the level of the individual officer, to examine how organisational forms and institutional norms within the police encourage this type of behaviour. Importantly, and unlike most other highly personalised observational research strategies, the incident reporting technique allows for more reliable comparison across cases and time, to gauge whether these findings are peculiar to the Johannesburg inner-city, or generalisable to immigration enforcement and policing practices in South Africa and beyond.

ETHICS AND SAFETY

Despite the various attractions of this research approach, there are some weighty ethical and safety issues that mitigate the degree to which it can be recommended as a procedure for wider use. While the research approach itself afforded necessary regard to laws on privacy and surveillance, other ethical and safety questions were less easily resolved. Did the study's observational strategy contravene professional ethics on informed consent? Did the study expose researchers themselves to unreasonable and unconscionable risk – particularly in the form of potential reprisals? For researchers who are accustomed to regarding the informed consent as a *sine qua non* of research ethics forms, the decision to conduct unannounced observational research might appear to be the most challenging issue. As Julius Roth (1962) has noted, almost all scholarship involves certain degrees of nondisclosure or secrecy. Professional bodies and the broader literature appear to have only cautiously accepted the use of covert research in strictly circumscribed areas (British Sociological Association 2002: 4). After surveying the literature, we used the following guidelines for determining how and when to employ this type of strategy: a) that the use of such strategies be justified in relation to some explicit humanitarian or public good (Douglas 1976); b) that the information gained through the use of these observational methods could not have been otherwise obtained through the use of ordinary means (Liamputtong 2007; Miller 2005); c) that the research only adopts covert strategies insofar as this is essential to the research process; and d) that we should aim wherever possible not to deliberately misrepresent the research in which we were engaged (Erikson 1967).

The second issue related to the potential danger to which our researchers might be exposed: '[t]he study of policing would appear to be a field where threats to personal physical safety are inevitable' (Westmarland 2000). Our study clearly involved an additional type of risk, that of potential reprisals from police officers or other persons who have strong motivations to prevent the collection and dissemination of information relating to their involvement in a criminal activity. Our approach began with the assumption that there would be incidents where the research activity was regarded as suspicious by officers, and researchers interrogated about their activities. We put in place a series of safeguards and protocols to minimise the potential for any such events to result in harm. This involved ensuring that the researchers were all equipped with mobile phones and able to contact a legal representative and a senior researcher at the university. As noted above, we then established a protocol for responding to questions from the police that involved being relatively candid about the researchers' identities and responsibilities. In total, the researchers were stopped by police officers on two occasions during the study. Based on these brief experiences, it would not appear that the risks faced by virtue of conducting research in a covert manner were of an entirely different order to those presented by more conventional social research strategies in Johannesburg such as survey work and participant observation.

CONCLUSION

As states increasingly deploy their domestic police forces to regulate human mobility, the need for innovative means of examining illegal behaviour by police officers will also rise. While most research on illegality within the service has steered clear of observational strategies on the grounds that this activity is too 'hidden' to be observed, this chapter has reviewed an experimental research technique which begins with the opposite assumption: that much illegal activity takes place in public and can be readily analysed in this way. My central claim has been that the incident reporting technique can provide new insights into this complex and changing field of activity. Having deployed this strategy, we emerge with a more sober and more compelling confirmation of a predatory model of police corruption, one which suggests that the petty extortion of migrants on the street is probably more widespread than other forms of abuse and may have linkages back to more senior level officers at the station. However, rather than placing immigration enforcement outside of other forms of petty corruption, this study suggests that these dynamics constitute part of broader changes occurring within South African policing. Importantly, this study creates the potential for statistical and spatial inferences which can potentially be employed on a comparative basis to multiple research sites or on a longitudinal basis to track changes in police behaviour over time. Given the partial nature of the insights generated by this technique, incident reporting clearly needs to be used in conjunction with a variety of other research methods in order to provide a complete and contextually embedded analysis of police corruption. Furthermore, given the potential security risks and ethical dilemmas involved in this covert research strategy, in the opinion of this author, justifying the employment of this technique also places considerable burdens on the researcher to address issues of broader relevance and humanitarian impact. Nevertheless, this review has suggested that incident reporting is a potentially useful and valid technique, which may provide a variety of new insights into police corruption and policing more generally.

Notes

1. This paper uses the terms 'informal' or 'undocumented' to refer to this particular stream of migration in preference to more pejorative and loaded variants like 'irregular' or 'illegal'.

2. This has been particularly pronounced in efforts to implement the United Nations Convention Against Transnational Organised Crime.

3. This point was made at least three decades ago in relation to the US–Mexico border (Wilson and Cory 1979).

4. In some senses this represents a return to past practices. Prior to the formation of regularised and functionally separated immigration departments, ordinary police officials did most of the work involved in checking migrants' documents and arresting those who did not possess a valid immigration permit (Brannigan and Lin 1999; Lucassen 2002). As immigration policies became increasingly separated from 'ordinary' law enforcement functions in the post-war era, many came to regard the immigration policing as an entirely separate state function from the policing of criminal laws. This was reflected in a concomitant retreat of police forces from immigration enforcement roles and in some more extreme cases, the passage of laws which specifically limited the powers of police officers to make immigration arrests.

5. Statistics obtained from Department of Home Affairs Annual Reports.

6. It is likely that this finding would change significantly if we were able to include raids, which usually occur at night-time, in our sample. Due to safety concerns, we did not conduct research at night.

7. The majority of the 'other' cases, of officers who weren't from the three South African Police Service police stations with jurisdiction within the sample tract, were Metro Police officials who are responsible for the enforcement laws across the city.

8. Only 1 out of 110 cases involved a disproportionate use of force. However, these findings need to be read with caution given that we only observed four cases where force was used to subdue a suspect.

9. An interesting finding from this angle was the fact that corrupt behaviour was not observed in any of the six incidents where both South African and foreign national suspects were involved. It seems plausible to suggest that in such cases, the involvement of multiple nationalities complicated the interaction, making it more difficult for officers and suspects to deploy conventional intra-ethnic or inter-ethnic protocols.

References

Adler, R. H. (2006) '"But they claimed to be police, not la migra!" - The interaction of residency status, class, and ethnicity in a (Post-PATRIOT Act) New Jersey neighborhood', *American Behavioral Scientist* 50: 48–69.

Alpert, G. P., R. G. Dunham and M. R. Smith (2007) 'Investigating racial profiling by the Miami-Dade police department: a muti-method approach', *Criminology and Public Policy* 6: 25–56.

Barbagli, M. and L. Sartori (2004) 'Law enforcement activities in Italy', *Journal of Modern Italian Studies* 9: 161–85.

Barker, T. and D. L. Carter (1994) *Police Deviance*, Cincinnati, Ohio: Anderson Pub. Co.

Bhagwati, J. (2003) 'Borders beyond control', *Foreign Affairs* 82: 98–104.

Blumberg, A. S. and E. Niederhoffer (1985) *The Ambivalent Force: Perspectives on the Police*, New York: Holt, Rinehart, and Winston.

Brannigan, A. and Z. Q. Lin (1999) '"Where east meets west": Police, immigration and public order crime in the settlement of Canada from 1896 to 1940', *Canadian Journal of Sociology-Cahiers Canadiens De Sociologie* 24: 87–108.

British Sociological Association (2002) 'Statement of Ethical Practice'.

Coleman, M. (2007) 'A geopolitics of engagement: Neoliberalism, the war on terrorism, and the reconfiguration of US immigration enforcement', *Geopolitics* 12: 607–34.

Coplan, D. (2001) 'A river runs through it: the meaning of the Lesotho-Free State Border', *African Affairs* 100: 81–116.

CoRMSA (2009) 'Protecting Refugees, Asylum Seekers and Immigrants in South Africa', Johannesburg: CoRMSA.

Culver, L. (2004) 'The impact of new immigration patterns on the provision of police services in midwestern communities', *Journal of Criminal Justice* 32: 329–44.

Derluyn, I. and E. Broekaert (2005) 'On the way to a better future: Belgium as transit country for trafficking and smuggling of unaccompanied minors', *International Migration* 43: 31–56.

Douglas, J. D. (1976) *Investigative Social Research: Individual and Team Field Research*, Beverly Hills, CA: Sage Publications.

Erikson, K. T. (1967) 'A comment on disguised observation in sociology', *Social Problems* 14: 366–73.

Ellis, S. (1999), 'The new frontiers of crime in South Africa', in J.-F. Bayart, S. Ellis and B. Hibou (eds.) *The Criminalization of the State in Africa*, Oxford: James Currey.

Groenendijk, K. (2003) 'New borders behind old ones: Post-Schengen controls behind the internal borders and inside the Netherlands and Germany', in K. Groenendijk, E. Guild and P. Minderhoud (eds.) *In Search of Europe's Borders: Immigration and Asylum Law and Policy in Europe*, The Hague: Kluwer Law International.

Guiraudon, V. and G. Lahav (2000) 'Comparative perspectives on border control: away from the border and outside the state', in P. Andreas and T. Snyder (eds.) *The Wall around the West : State Borders and Immigration Controls in North America and Europe*, Lanham: Rowman & Littlefield.

Gulcur, L. and P. Ilkkaracan (2002) 'The "Natasha" experience: migrant sex workers from the former Soviet Union and Eastern Europe in Turkey', *Womens Studies International Forum* 25: 411–21.

Holmes, M. D., B. W. Smith, A. B.Freng and E. A. Munoz (2008) 'Minority threat, crime control, and police resource allocation in the Southwestern United States', *Crime & Delinquency* 54: 128–52.

Human Rights Watch (1998) 'Prohibited Persons: Abuse of Undocumented Migrants, Asylum-Seekers, and Refugees in South Africa'.

--- (2006) 'Unprotected Migrants: Zimbabweans in South Africa's Limpopo Province'.

JURIX and Open Society Justice Initiative (2006) 'Ethnic Profiling in the Moscow Metro', New York: Open Society Institute.

Keblawi, J. (2004) 'Immigration arrests by local police: inherent authority or inherently preempted?', *Catholic University Law Review* 53: 817–53.

Kennedy, D. B. (1977) *The Dysfunctional Alliance: Emotion and Reason in Justice Administration*, Cincinnati: Anderson Pub. Co.

Kittrie, O. F. (2006) 'Federalism, deportation, and crime victims afraid to call the police', *Iowa Law Review* 91: 1449–508.

Lahav, G. (2000) 'The rise of non-state actors in migration regulation in the United States and Europe: changing the gatekeepers or "Bringing Back the State"?', in N. Foner, R. G. Rumbaut and S. J. Gold (eds.) *Immigration Research for a New Century: Multidisciplinary Perspectives*, New York: Russell Sage Foundation.

Liamputtong, P. (2007) *Researching the Vulnerable: a Guide to Sensitive Research Methods*, London and Thousand Oaks, Calif.: SAGE.

Lucassen, L. (2002) 'Administrative into social control: the aliens, police and foreign female servants in the Netherlands, 1918–40', *Social History* 27: 327–42.

Mabasa, T. (2003) 'SA man may be deported – from SA', *The Citizen*, 16 January, p. 1.

Mameli, P. A. (2002) 'Stopping the illegal trafficking of human beings – how transnational police work can stem the flow of forced prostitution', *Crime Law and Social Change* 38: 67–80.

Margolis, M. L. (1995) 'Brazilians and the 1990 United States Census: Immigrants, ethnicity, and the undercount', *Human Organization* 54: 52–9.

Miller, J. M. (2005) 'Covert participant observation: reconsidering the least used method', in J. M. Miller and R. A. Tewksbury (eds.) *Research Methods: A Qualitative Reader*, 1st ed. Upper Saddle River, N.J.: Prentice Hall.

Phillips, S., J. M. Hagan and N. Rodriguez (2006) 'Brutal borders? Examining the treatment of deportees during arrest and detention', *Social Forces* 85: 93–109.

Phillips, S., N. Rodriguez and J. Hagan (2002) 'Brutality at the border? Use of force in the arrest of immigrants in the United States', *International Journal of the Sociology of Law* 30: 285–306.

Quassoli, F. (2004) 'Making the neighbourhood safer: social alarm, police practices and immigrant exclusion in Italy', *Journal of Ethnic and Migration Studies* 30: 1163–81.

Romero, M. (2006) 'Racial profiling and immigration law enforcement: rounding up of usual suspects in the Latino Community', *Critical Sociology* 32: 447–73.

Roth, J. A. (1962) 'Comments on "Secret Observation"', *Social Problems* 9: 283–4.

Shaw, M. (2002) 'West African criminal networks in South and Southern Africa', *African Affairs* 101: 291–316.

Smillie, S. (2005) 'South African held after failing police's illegal alien "test"', *Cape Times*, 25 October, p. 7.

Taylor, S. (2005) 'From border control to migration management: the case for a paradigm change in the Western response to transborder population movement', *Social Policy and Administration* 39: 563–86.

Vigneswaran, D. (2010) 'Criminality or monopoly? Informal immigration enforcement in South Africa', *Journal of Southern African Studies* 36 (with the assistance of Tesfalem Araia, Colin Hoag and Xolani Tshabalala).

--- (2008) 'Enduring territoriality: South African immigration control', *Political Geography* 27: 783–801.

Vigneswaran, D. and M. Duponchel (2009) 'One burden too many? A cost-benefit analysis of immigration policing in Gauteng, Johannesburg', Forced Migration Studies Programme.

Westmarland, L. (2000) 'Taking the flak: operational policing, fear and violence', in G. Lee-Treweek and S. Linkogle (eds.) *Danger in the Field: Risk and Ethics in Social Research*, London and New York: Routledge.

Wilson, R. and B. Cory (1979) 'Hide and seek at the border - US agents are losing', *Police Magazine* 2, pp. 6–10, 13–17.

Chapter 7

CONGOLESE MIGRATIONS TOWARDS AFRICA, EUROPE, AMERICA, AND ASIA

Agbada Mobhe Mangalu

INTRODUCTION

Having long remained on the sidelines of intercontinental migratory movements, the Congolese have gradually started to emerge from this isolation. This has been happening since the late 1980s and particularly the early 1990s. The growing taste for intercontinental migration among the Congolese population has coincided with the deterioration of socioeconomic conditions within the country (Lututala and Zamwangana 1998; Sumata et al. 2004). The traditional destinations used to be the Congo Brazzaville and Angola in Africa, and Belgium in Europe; new destinations have been added, such as South Africa, Nigeria, France, the United Kingdom and Canada. This intensification of Congolese emigration has been accompanied by a diversification in the profiles of the migrants themselves. The initially elitist migration – basically motivated by professional and study considerations (diplomats and members of their families, along with higher level students) – is now accompanied by other types of migration, most notably migration for economic reasons, currently affecting all levels of society (Mangalu 1998; Lututala and Zamwangana 1998; Gatugu et al. 2001; Kagné and Martiniello 2001).

Despite these considerations of a general nature, knowledge of Congolese migration still remains patchy and little documented; no nationwide study has yet been undertaken on this subject (Zaïre, 1994). But since the end of 2007, this gap has started to be filled. In fact, we have a rich database, the first of its kind, extracted from a probability survey of 945 households and 992 individual biographies. This survey was financed by the French government through the French Centre for Population and Development (CEPED), as part of the FSP7[1] programme: 'International migration, territorial recomposition and development in southern countries'. This study has made it possible to answer a panoply of classic questions about international migration, particularly those to do with the purpose of migration, the destinations, the involvement of the original households in migratory processes, the migrants' profiles and financial transfers. It can also provide answers to more specific issues such as the determining factors for migration, the interaction between migrants' different life experiences (educational, professional, marital etc.), and so on.

The protocol developed for this survey was inspired by that used as part of the Mexican Migration Project,[2] collecting a combination of quantitative, qualitative, transverse, longitudinal, national and transnational, individual and community data. This is what is referred to by Massey and Zenteno (2000) as an *Ethnosurvey*.

In fact, in order in particular to provide some basic answers about widely-held stereotypical views comprising the spread of African migrants to Europe on the one hand, and the brain drain currently being suffered by the African continent on the other, and restricting this purely to the case of the Democratic Republic of Congo (DRC), the main question we intend to consider here is as follows: is there any difference between Congolese emigrants in terms of their socio-demographic and migratory profiles according to their continent of destination and of residence? The purpose is to carry out a comparative study of the different continents, looking at the level, type and purpose of the migration of Congolese people and their profiles and financial transfers.

METHODOLOGY

This section deals with the presentation not only of the central hypothesis on which the whole study rests, the whole process underlying the collection and analysis of data, but also the framework for interpreting the results obtained.

Hypotheses

Given the increasing importance of migration in the country's social, economic and political landscape, and also considering the geographical and cultural proximity to certain countries; the porosity of the borders with certain countries, particularly those in Africa; the toughening of access conditions, particularly in Europe; and the financial costs of travel, the central hypothesis on which this consideration rests suggests that Congolese emigrants will differ in terms of their socio-demographic and migratory profiles (age, gender, level of education, marital status, profession, purpose of migration etc.), depending on the country and therefore the continent of destination and residence. Europe, America and Asia, for example, would be the destination continents for the most educated emigrants, travelling essentially for reasons of study, who would be older and therefore married etc.

To try to answer our initial question and thus to check our working hypothesis, a number of statistical analysis techniques were used: chi-square analysis, analysis of variance, multiple correspondence analysis and logistic regression. The justification for each of these techniques will be provided below. First of all, we shall look at the methods used for data collection and analysis, before ending with a look at the methodology used to interpret the results obtained.

Data collection methods

The techniques for collecting the data used for this research are founded on two main methodological approaches: documentary research and a field survey.

The collection protocol set up for this study was designed with the following characteristics, among others: having both qualitative and quantitative data available; having data available both at household and individual level; having both biographical and transnational data available. However, we should point out that for the purposes of this chapter only the quantitative data from the Kinshasa survey were used, since they were the only data available, with the Belgian part of the study still ongoing.

The quantitative Kinshasa survey was of a retrospective type, with a single sweep of a random sample of 945 households representing the city of Kinshasa and 992 individuals drawn at random from the households surveyed.

Selection of households

The surveyed households were drawn using the same sampling frame of the city of Kinshasa as was used for the very first Demographic and Health Survey (EDS) carried out by the country in 2007. There were four degrees of sampling, initially stratified according to the prevalence of migration in each district of the city. Three strata were thus created: districts with a high prevalence of migration, districts with a moderate prevalence of migration, and districts with a low prevalence of migration. The general design of the sample was as follows:

1. 1st degree: Random selection of 30 urban districts out of the 291 urban districts making up the city, i.e. a sampling rate of around 1/10 (1/9.7)

2. 2nd degree: In each district sampled, four streets were drawn at random

3. 3rd degree: In each street sampled, 8 inhabited plots were drawn in a random fashion

4. 4th degree: In the 8 plots sampled, 8 households were randomly selected and were the object of the survey.

We should point out that, in order to maximise the chances of contacting a large number of households with migrants, those districts with a high prevalence of migration were over-sampled.

Selection of individuals for the biographical survey

In each sample household, all returning migrants found there aged between 20 and 60 years were entered into the survey, and another non-migrant member of the family aged between 20 and 60 years was randomly selected, using the selection grid model used for the Demographic and Health Survey (EDS).

Data collection instruments

Three main data collection instruments were used for this survey: a household questionnaire, an AGEVEN[3] sheet and an individual biographical sheet.

The household questionnaire dealt, among other things, with the identification and characteristics of the current members of the household, and of all former members of the household currently living abroad, the migratory route of these people as told by the head of the household or his partner, and the interaction between the household and its migrants, particularly through contacts and financial remittances etc.

The AGEVEN sheet made it possible to follow changes over time in various aspects of life (e.g. educational, professional, marital) as experienced by those interviewed, from a starting event (e.g. birth, marriage, start of schooling) up to the date of the survey, noting and dating the different sequences of events observed. Thus it allows us to retrace the educational, marital and migratory stories of those individuals who were questioned.

The individual biographical questionnaire was given both to returning migrants and to non-migrants, with a few possible adaptations. Importantly, all were asked to retrace their marital, reproductive, educational and professional histories, changes in their place of residence, family and social networks abroad. For returning migrants, questions were added about their history of international migration and their history of sending remittances to the country during migration. For non-migrants, the special questions looked at their history of attempted international migrations, remittances received, and so on.

Analytical methods

Given the purpose of the study and the nature of the variables present, the following analytical methods were used: chi-square analysis, analysis of variance, multiple correspondence analysis and logistic regression.

Chi-square analysis

Chi-square analysis is a statistical test making it possible to check whether a link exists between two qualitative variables. It therefore makes it possible to study a number of independent groups described by means of a qualitative variable. It can be a preliminary stage in more elaborate analyses such as logistic regression and correspondence analysis. It is precisely for this reason that we resorted to this technique. In fact, the existence or non-existence of links between the different qualitative variables should provide guidance on whether or not to proceed with other types of analysis. The variables entered into this analysis are, on the one hand, the socio-demographic and migratory characteristics of Congolese emigrants (gender, age group, profession, level of education, marital status, reason for migration, foreign residency period grouping, etc.), seen as independent variables, and the emigrants' choice of residence and destination continent, seen as a dependent variable; even though the chi-square test does not automatically impose such a distinction between variables.

Variance analysis

Variance analysis is a statistical technique which makes it possible to test whether the mean values of a number of subgroups are equal. It requires the dependent variable to be of the continuous quantitative type and the independent variable, known as the factor, to be of the qualitative type. For our purposes, this test was used to check whether there were statistically significant differences in terms of age, length of migration and sums transferred to the household of origin over the last 12-month period by Congolese migrants, according to their continent of residence.

Logistic regression

Logistic regression is a technique which makes it possible to study the relation between a dependent variable and one or more independent variables, be they quantitative or not. Unlike linear regression, which is based on a quantitative-type dependent variable, logistic regression demands that the dependent variable be of the dichotomic qualitative type. It is therefore seen as an extension of the chi-square analysis, in that it can be based on a number of independent variables at once. Use of this technique as part of the present study arises from the fact that it allows us to study the effect of independent variables (socio-demographic and migratory characteristics) on the probability of choosing and residing in one continent rather than another.

Multiple correspondence analysis

In addition to the objective of condensing information which is considered too copious, correspondence analysis allows one to sort individuals into different types according to their proximity to the modalities of variables. This leads in fact to the creation of typical profiles for individuals who have roughly the same characteristics across the analysis variables. In this study, the use of this technique is also explained by the fact that the main purpose is to create profiles for Congolese emigrants according to their destination continents.

Methodology for the interpretation and explanation of results

Alongside the methods for collecting and analysing the data, it is still important also to consider the methods used for interpreting and explaining the results obtained. In fact, while data analysis methods lead to the discovery of characteristics, typologies, particularities, and dependency or interdependency between phenomena, the methods used for the interpretation and explanation are there to assess the results obtained against the hypotheses, the theories upon which the hypotheses are founded, and the problems and results of previous known research (Lututala 1996). The idea is to see how knowledge has been built up and how it fits into the ongoing development of the science, or what we might call the *wheels of scientific research*.

More specifically, we have favoured the following explanatory approaches: a functionalist approach, a systemic approach, and a diachronic approach.

Functionalist approach

The basis of this approach lies in the fact that social events are explained in accordance with the functions that they provide in the social system to which they belong. No social event is due to chance; it is dictated by the need to maintain social equilibrium. Migration as currently experienced within the Congolese context certainly results from this approach. In fact, the small amount of research carried out on Congolese migration agrees in recognising that a number of social functions are attached to this migration, including production (through financial and material transfers by migrants) (Mangalu 1998) and reproduction, particularly of migration within households (Lutututala 1982). Furthermore, these migrations are no longer simply isolated actions undertaken by individuals, but are increasingly part of a broader family context. This is also confirmed by the existence of a very close link between the emergence of migration and the acuity of the socioeconomic crisis within the country (Schoumaker et al. 2008).

Systemic approach

If we accept that a system is the end product of interdependencies and reactions between elements of a social organisation operating according to ideologies and norms which govern the roles of the various individuals within it, then we can also see that Congolese migration within the current context is indeed a complete system in its own right. Indeed, in the Congolese migratory system, each player has a particular role to play, in order to guarantee the stability and durability of the system. So the household of origin has taken on a role as provider of the means for migration at the start, while the migrant has taken on a role as provider of remittances, also reproducing migration within their household of origin (Mangalu 1998). This is therefore a system where the different players (migrants and households of origin) are interconnected like links in a chain, and where each group tries to ensure the harmony of the system, playing the specific role expected of them at specific times.

Diachronic approach

The aim of this approach is to seek out the explanation for a phenomenon, starting from its very genesis. Thus the triggering of 'popular' intercontinental migration among the Congolese is associated with the late 1980s and early 1990s. This period covers the decay of the Congolese economy and the outbreak of war.

THE RESULTS

Level of Congolese migration by continent

Among those Congolese emigrants still residing abroad, as identified from within their household of origin, 56 per cent live in Africa, compared with 38 per cent in Europe and 6 per cent in America and Asia. These figures clearly show that the majority of Congolese turn to other African countries rather than other continents. But, as we shall see below, this preference for Africa (apart from Congo Brazzaville and Angola) is very recent.

Gender

Another important factor when analysing data on migrations is the gender of those people migrating. In fact, in the case of migration away from Kinshasa, it can be seen that, contrary to other countries where there is a marked predominance of men among the migrants, here the situation seems a little more balanced. For example, in Africa it is found that just over six emigrants in every ten are male. This situation is even more balanced in Europe, where the two sexes are present in more equal proportions, at around 50 per cent each. But overall the larger proportions of women tend to head towards Europe and America and Asia rather than Africa. The chi-square analysis also indicates a very close link between the gender of migrants and their continents of destination and residence, with a 99 per cent confidence level.

Purpose of migration

The study results also show a difference between the main reasons for migrating, according to the continent of destination or residence (Figure 1). While just over six emigrants out of every ten currently residing in Africa are there for economic reasons, this proportion drops to just under four emigrants out of every ten among those residing in Europe, and just under three emigrants out of every ten currently residing in America or Asia. By contrast, it can be seen that just over four emigrants out of every ten currently residing in Asia and America are there for study reasons, compared with two emigrants out of every ten residing in Europe, and just under one emigrant out of every ten currently residing in Africa. Marriage and family reunification are the motivation for two emigrants out of

Figure 1. Purpose of migration by Congolese emigrants according to continent

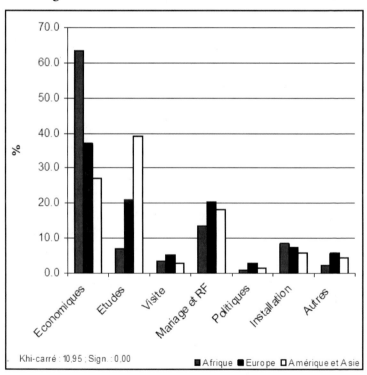

every ten residing in Europe and in America and Asia, and just under one emigrant out of every ten residing in Africa. The chi-square test has confirmed the link between the purposes of migration and the continents of residence, with a confidence level of 99 per cent. So it can be said that Congolese nationals residing in other African countries have gone there essentially for economic reasons, while those who reside in Europe have gone there essentially for reasons of study, marriage and family reunification; those who have gone to America and Asia have essentially gone there for study reasons.

Level of education

In most studies on migration, education is adopted as one of the factors for differentiating between the migratory behaviour of different members of a community. In the case of the DRC, the results also back this up. Indeed, from Figure 2 it can be seen that Congolese nationals residing in Africa predominate among those educated to secondary level or below (primary or no formal education), while those educated to higher levels are clearly dominated by those who reside in America and Asia and in Europe. This could mean that the further away the destination, the more the migrant needs to be equipped with the necessary advantages, particularly intellectual ones, to bring their migratory plan to fruition. The chi-square test indicates a very close link between the continent of residence and educational level, with a significance level of more than 99 per cent. Generally speaking, it could be said that Congolese nationals with secondary or no formal education mainly head towards Africa, while those with a higher level of education mainly head towards America and Asia and Europe (Figure 2). This finding seems to call into question one of the stereotypes used as an attempt to explain migration out of Africa for Europe in terms of misery and poverty. Here it can clearly be seen that it is not the least well-off who take the decision to leave, but rather the most educated who mainly head towards Europe and America. Perhaps they have a clearer perception than others of the difficult conditions affecting the country, which will not allow them to realise their legitimate aspirations to well-being.

Figure 2. Distribution of Congolese emigrants by level of education according to continent

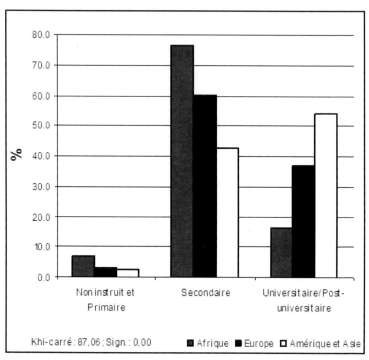

Khi-carré : 87,06 ; Sign. : 0,00 ■ Afrique ■ Europe □ Amérique et Asie

Marital status

The distribution of Congolese emigrants by marital status according to continent of residence indicates that a little over four emigrants out of every ten residing in Africa are single, whereas the proportion is only around two emigrants out of every ten residing in Europe and in America and Asia. By contrast, it is seen that more than seven emigrants out of every ten residing in America and Asia are married (Figure 3). The proportions are seven out of ten for emigrants residing in Europe and just over five out of ten for those residing in Africa. As can be seen, there is therefore quite a close link between marital status and continent of residence. Furthermore, the chi-square test

Figure 3. Distribution of emigrants by marital status according to continent

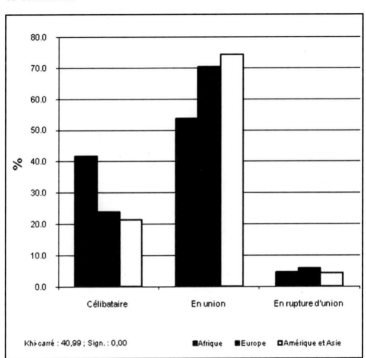

Khi-carré : 40,99 ; Sign. : 0,00 ■Afrique ■Europe ▢Amérique et Asie

shows significance greater than 99 per cent. In the light of these results, we can say that Africa is the continent of single Congolese nationals, while Europe, America and Asia are the continents of those who are married. This could be explained in particular by the relatively high ages of those going to Europe and America compared with those going to Africa. Likewise, following the adoption of more and more restrictive migratory policies by most European countries, only family reunification presented itself to most candidates for migration to Europe as the single purpose for going there.

Professional occupation

In relation to professional occupation, Figure 4 shows that three Congolese emigrants out of every four residing in Africa had a professional occupation at the time of the survey, compared with just

Figure 4. Distribution of Congolese emigrants by employment according to continent

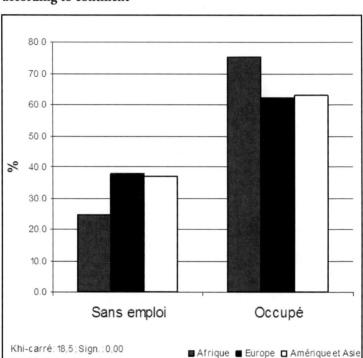

Khi-carré: 18,5 ; Sign. : 0,00   ■ Afrique ■ Europe □ Amérique et Asie

over six emigrants out of ten residing in Europe, America and Asia. Even though emigrants residing in Africa have the greatest proportion in work at the time of the survey, the proportion of emigrants working on other continents is not negligible. Later analyses will determine the nature of this employment.

Period of residence abroad

The migrant's period of residence abroad is particularly important, since knowledge of its duration allows us in particular to anticipate the links that the migrant is expected to maintain with his or her household of origin, and even the remittances that he or she can transfer for its benefit. Table 1 shows that migrants who have gone to other African countries predominate among all duration categories of less than five years, while those living in Europe, America and Asia predominate among those with at least seven years' residence abroad. The chi-square test also shows a fairly close link between the duration and the continent of residence, with a 99 per cent confidence level. Migrations towards Africa seem therefore to be more recent than those towards Europe, America and Asia.

Table 1: Average length of stay of Congolese migrants according to continent of residence

Continent of residence	N° of obs.	Average length (years)	Difference in means (years)	
			Continents	Differences
Africa	610	6.6	Europe	-4.2***
			America and Asia	-3.7***
Europe	418	10.8	Africa	4.2***
			America and Asia	0.5°
America and Asia	70	10.3	Africa	3.6***
			Europe	-0.5°
F = 41.00***				

***: *Significant to 99%;* °: *Not significant*

The test for mean equality applied to these data confirms these results, and indicates that the average period of stay for Congolese migrants residing in Africa is 6.6 years, compared with 10.8 years for those residing in Europe, and 10.3 years for those residing in America and Asia. This enables us to say that migration to Africa would be, on average, four years more recent than migration to Europe, America and Asia. These differences are statistically significant at the 99 per cent threshold. By contrast, there is no statistically significant difference between Europe and America and Asia in terms of the period of residency of migrants.

Age at survey

Table 2. Average ages of Congolese migrants according to continent of residence

Continent of residence	N° of obs.	Average age (years)	Difference in means	
			Continents	Differences
Africa	614	35.0	Europe	-4.4***
			America and Asia	-3.8***
Europe	419	39.4	Africa	4.4***
			America and Asia	0.6°
America and Asia	70	38.8	Africa	3.8***
			Europe	-0.6°
F = 33.6***				

***: Significant to 99%; °: Not significant

From Table 2, it can be seen that four emigrants out of every ten were aged 30 to 39 years at the time of the survey. Furthermore, this is the age group most in evidence irrespective of continent. It can also be seen that emigrants residing in Africa are slightly younger than those residing in Europe or in America and Asia. In fact, just over seven emigrants out of ten residing in Africa are under 40 years of age. This proportion is just a little more than five emigrants out of ten in Europe and in America and Asia. The chi-square test also indicates a fairly close link between age and continent of residence.

The variance analysis also confirms these results and indicates that Congolese nationals residing in other African countries are aged 35 years on average, and are four years younger than those residing in Europe and in America and Asia. This age difference is statistically significant to greater than 95 per cent. The results also indicate that the average ages of emigrants residing in Europe and those residing in America and Asia are not statistically different; they hover around 39 years.

EFFECTS OF EMIGRANTS' SOCIO-DEMOGRAPHIC AND
MIGRATORY CHARACTERISTICS ON DESTINATION

To measure these effects, we opted for logistic regression. In order to meet the requirements of this technique we created a dichotomic variable 'Reside in Africa' with two values: 1, if the migrant is resident in Africa; and 0, if the migrant is resident outside Africa, i.e. in Europe, America or Asia. These last three continents were grouped into a single value for the simple reason that the analysis of most of the socio-demographic characteristics used in this study did not reveal any statistically significant differences between them.

The results of this analysis show that migrants with no formal education and those educated to primary level have approximately six times more chance of going to and residing in Africa than anywhere else when those with higher and university level education are taken as the reference (Table 3). Those at secondary level are twice more likely to go to Africa than anywhere else compared with the reference modality. These two results are significant to 99 per cent.

Single people are about 1.5 times more likely to go to Africa than elsewhere when married people are taken as the reference; the result is significant to 95 per cent. Although migrants who have separated are 1.3 times more likely than married people to go to Africa, this result is not statistically significant. Migrants in work at the time of the survey are twice more likely to reside in Africa than anywhere else compared with those who are unemployed. This result is significant to 99 per cent.

As for the reasons behind migration, it can be seen that migrants who have travelled for study reasons are 4.5 times less likely to choose Africa than other continents when those who have travelled for economic reasons are taken as the reference; this result is significant to 99 per cent. Those who travel for holiday reasons and for other visits are 2.4 times less likely to choose Africa compared with those who travel for economic reasons, used here as the reference; this is significant to 95 per cent. Those who gave marriage and family reunification as the reason are 2.2 times less likely to choose Africa than the reference modality, with a confidence level of 99 per cent. Those who travel for political reasons are five times more likely to choose continents other than Africa, with a 99 per cent confidence level. However, those who decide not to return to the country following migration, i.e. to go and settle for good in their new place of residence, choose one continent or another indiscriminately.

In relation to age, it can be seen that an extra year of age among migrants reduces the probability of choosing Africa by 6.4 per cent; this result is significant to 99 per cent. Finally, even though women are 1.2 times less likely to choose Africa than the other continents when compared to men, this result is however not statistically significant.

Regression analysis has made it possible to identify factors which are likely to explain Congolese emigrants' choices regarding continents of destination and residence. For Africa, these are basically education to secondary level and below, single status, economic reasons, the fact of having work and the relative youth of migrants. By contrast, for the other continents these are education to higher or university level, study and training reasons, visits, marriage and political reasons, being older in relative terms, and the lack of work. These factors already give an idea of the profiles of migrants heading for and residing in each of these continents. Multiple correspondence analysis will attempt to confirm this trend.

Profiles of Congolese emigrants

Having separated the links between emigrants' socio-demographic and migratory characteristics and their continents of destination and residence on the one hand and the factors likely to explain their choice of these continents on the other hand, it is now our task in this section to draw up typical profiles for Congolese emigrants according to their continents of destination and residence, using multiple correspondence analysis.

The results of this analysis rely on the first two factorial axes, which together explain 21 per cent of the total variance of all initial variables. From this analysis it can therefore be deduced that the first factor clearly contrasts migrants residing in Europe, in America and in Asia with those residing in Africa. Those who reside in Europe, America or Asia are educated to higher or university level, aged at least 40 years, and their journey is essentially explained in terms of study; meanwhile, those who reside in Africa are educated to second-

Table 3. Net effect of emigrants' socio-demographic and migratory characteristics on choices regarding continents of destination or residence (probability of having migrated to Africa)

Variables	Exp (B)	Wald	DL
Level of education			
No education and primary	5.62***	16.90	1
Secondary	2.43***	26.68	1
Higher and university (MR)	-	-	-
Marital status			
Single	1.47**	4.44	2
Married (MR)	-	-	-
Separated	1.28°	0.48	1
Professional occupation			
Unemployed (MR)	-	-	-
Employed (MR)	1.85***	13.26	
Purpose of migration			
Economic reasons (MR)	-	-	-
Study and training	0.22***	41.13	1
Visit	5.04**	5.92	1
Marriage and family reunification	0.46***	11.88	1
Political	0.22***	6.56	1
Settling for good	0.81°	0.61	1
Other reasons	0.32***	9.84	1
Age	0.94***	39.10	1
Gender			
Male	-	-	-
Female	0.82°	1.21	1
Constant	5.28***	15.00	1

*****: Significant to 99%; **: Significant to 95%; °: Not significant*

ary level or below, aged under 40 years and their main motivation for travelling is made up of economic reasons. This first factor also contrasts men with women. Men are mostly single and working at the time of the survey, and have travelled mainly for economic reasons, whereas women are not working, either married or separated, and have travelled principally for marriage and family reasons.

The second factor characterises unemployed women, aged between 20 and 29 years, educated to secondary level or below, who have travelled for marriage and family reasons, and to visit. These women are contrasted against men who are employed, aged between 40 and 49 years, educated to higher and university level, and who have travelled for economic and study reasons.

In the light of these results, we can draw up the following profiles of Congolese migrants according to their continents of destination and residence.

Table 4: Profiles of Congolese emigrants according to continents of residence

Europe and America and Asia	Africa
Essentially women	Essentially men
Older (40 years and above)	Younger (aged under 40)
Higher and university level	Secondary level and below
Married	Single
Separated (essentially the women)	Employed at the time of the survey
Unemployed at the time of the survey (essentially women)	Travel essentially for economic reasons
Purpose of migration linked to study (tertiary stage)	
Purpose of migration linked of marriage and family reunification (essentially women)	
People aged 60 years and over, coming for visits (essentially women)	

MIGRANTS' REMITTANCES

The last result is the remittance behaviour of Congolese emigrants according to their continents of residence. It should be borne in mind that remittances from migrants are one of the main reasons why households become involved in their members' migratory movements. The results show that there is certainly a link between the continent of residence and the probability of emigrants transferring resources. The chi-square test shows a very close link between these two variables with a 99 per cent confidence level. In fact, nearly seven emigrants out of ten residing in America and Asia carried out a remittance of finances to benefit their original household in the 12 months leading up to the survey. The proportion is just over six out of ten for emigrants residing in Europe compared with just under five out of ten for those residing in Africa.

In addition to the differences seen in the proportions of those remitting, according to their continent of residence, differences can also be seen in the volume of financial remittances made by migrants to their households over the same period. In fact, migrants residing in America and Asia showed themselves to be more generous towards their households than the others.

During this period they transferred US$552.70 on average compared with US$512.30 and US$334.30 for those residing in Europe and Africa respectively.

As can be seen, those residing in Europe remitted on average US$178 more than those living in Africa. This result is significant to 95 per cent. And those residing in America and Asia remitted US$218 more than those residing in Africa; this result is significant at the 90 per cent confidence level. By contrast, although those residing in America and Asia remitted on average US$40 more than those residing in Europe, this difference is not statistically significant.

Table 5. Average amounts remitted (in US dollars) by Congolese migrants according to continent of residence

Continent of residence	N° of obs.	Average transfer ($US)	Difference in means (in $US)	
			Continents	Differences
Africa	282	334.3	Europe	-178.0**
			America and Asia	-218.4*
Europe	269	512.3	Africa	178.0**
			America and Asia	-40.4°
America and Asia	48	552.7	Africa	218.4**
			Europe	-40.4°
F = 3.5**				

*** Significant to 95%; *Significant to 90%; °: Not significant*

DISCUSSION OF RESULTS

It should be borne in mind that the main objective of this research was to highlight the socio-demographic and migratory characteristics of Congolese emigrants according to their continents of destination and residence. From the analyses we have performed, we are able to highlight the following key results: in terms of the level of Congolese migration, and contrary to received ideas, Africa comes out as the top destination. These results are not fundamentally different from those we found in 1997, which indicated that 52 per cent of Congolese emigrants were residing in Africa compared with 42 per cent in Europe and 6 per cent on the other continents (Mangalu 1998: 50).

Moreover, these results necessarily call into question the assumption of neo-classical theory which states that migrations arise from differences in salary levels from one country to another and that migrants tend to maximise their profits by heading towards the countries with the highest salaries (Todaro 1969; Piore 1979; Massey et al. 1993). In fact, the general situation in the other African countries to which the majority of Congolese go is not much different from that in the DRC. Therefore, we need to find theories and explanatory factors other than those put forward by neo-classical theories. In fact, for the average Congolese national, the ideal is therefore to leave the country regardless of destination and even how long the journey might take. For most migrants, travelling in steps is a strategy which is well integrated into their migratory travels (Lututala 2005). In this sense, Africa would appear to be a transit continent before the journey continues to more distant shores. The facts that the period of residence in Africa is shorter and that African migrations seem to be more recent also fit this strategy.

If one looks at the reasons why Congolese nationals migrate, combined with their levels of education, ages, and matrimonial status, it can be seen that those who head towards Europe are distinctly older, educated to university level, go there essentially for study reasons, and are mostly married. This fits well into the framework of migratory selectivity. The 'education' variable has thus changed the orientation of Congolese migration from Africa to Europe. Moreover, even back in 1976, Byerlee et al. were already observing that even though economic factors were predominant in the decision to migrate, their importance was reinforced by the 'education' variable. In fact, education not only creates new aspirations, which are not generally satisfied at the local level for the majority of Congolese nationals, but also provides recipients with certain abilities which enable them to judge situations in terms of their aspirations and possibly to decide to go where they think their aspirations may be more easily realised (Mangalu 1998).

Given the difficulty of obtaining other types of visa to go to Europe in particular, and the relative ease of obtaining a visa for study reasons, more and more Congolese nationals wait to finish their second-year university studies before launching themselves into a migratory venture in Europe and America. Considering the length of time taken by university studies in the DRC, it is only natural that these migrants should be comparatively older, and also married, particularly where women are concerned.

Moreover, the importance of education in Congolese nationals' migratory strategies, particularly where Europe and America are concerned, is not a new phenomenon. Back in 1994, the National Report on Population presented in Cairo was already denouncing this state of affairs in the following terms:

> ... of all known cases of emigration, we should highlight
> the most common form, concerning the brain drain.
> Here, every year, teachers, doctors, engineers, artists,
> sportsmen and other intellectuals leave the country to
> go and provide their services abroad. (Zaïre 1994: 31).

Similarly, during our study in 1997, to which we have already referred, we found that 63.7 per cent of Congolese emigrants held a secondary level and/or university qualification on leaving the country (Mangalu 1998: 43).

The consideration of all these variables fits well into the context of the social function ascribed to migration (particularly to Europe and America) in the Congolese context. Indeed it has been demonstrated that Congolese migrations are more and more becoming part of a strategy adopted by households with a view to enlarging their living space in order to ensure production and even reproduction (Lututala 1982; Mangalu 1998; Sumata et al. 2004). Within the confines of this strategy, it is only those with a high likelihood of achieving successful integration abroad who are sent or encouraged to leave, particularly for distant shores. And these judgements are generally founded on age, gender, level of education, marital status and profession. This strategy seems close to the interpretation of migration inspired by the 'Human capacity theory' developed by Schultz (1960).

As for financial remittances made by emigrants to benefit their households of origin, this could well fit into the systemic approach. In fact, in this migratory system, each player has a particular role to play, as we have said. The households have the role of providing the means for migration (Root and de Jong 1986; Gregory et al. 1986; Nelson 1981 quoted by Lututala 1995), while migrants have a role to play in production (through sending funds) and reproduction (by supporting migration by other household members) (Pessar 1986; Lututala 1987; Gregory 1988; Mangalu 1998). From the findings on remittances it can clearly be seen that the further away the continent of residence, the higher the proportion of emigrants who remit, and the bigger the total sums remitted. The profiles of emigrants residing in Europe and in America and Asia could also hold some explanation for this difference in remittance behaviour.

As for the emergence of migration on the Congolese social and political landscape, several studies place it around the end of the 1980s and the start of the 1990s (Lututala and Zamwangana 1998; Sumata et al. 2004). We have also found that the rise in emigration by Congolese nationals started around 1985, with a first peak around 1992 and a second around 2000 (Schoumaker et al. 2008). Likewise, the average length of stay of Congolese migrants, the longest calculated with these data, i.e. around 11 years for Europe, places the year of departure at around 1996. For those familiar with the DRC's recent history, the period running from the end of the 1980s to the end of the 1990s is a period of great socio-political disorder, marked in particular by the end of the Mobutu regime, the start of two wars and the assassination of President Laurent-Désiré Kabila.

CONCLUSION

The purpose of this study was to perform a comparative analysis of the socio-demographic and migratory characteristics of Congolese emigrants according to their continents of destination and residence. The initial hypothesis was that these characteristics would be differentiated according to continent. To check this hypothesis, we used data from the migration survey conducted in Kinshasa in 2007 – a retrospective-type representative survey. A certain number of data analysis methods were used to enable verification of this hypothesis. At the end of this exercise, our central hypothesis was proven to be valid. Indeed, whether we looked at the level of migration or other elements of the socio-demographic and migratory profiles of Congolese emigrants, we found that there were considerable statistically significant differences according to the continent of residence. Africa stands apart from Europe, America and Asia. In fact, the profiles of Congolese migrants going to these last three continents appear similar and are clearly distinct from those who go to Africa. Africa is seen as the continent of recent migration, emigrants educated to a low level (no formal education and primary), young people, single people, those who travel for economic reasons; meanwhile, elsewhere, they are generally married people, people with a high level of education (secondary and further), travelling essentially for study reasons. Where financial remittances are concerned, emigrants residing in Europe, America and Asia have shown themselves to be more generous – both in the number of times they send funds and in the total value of funds transferred – than those residing in Africa. In the light of these results, it can therefore be stated that the continent of destination or residence is a differentiating element in the profiles of Congolese emigrants.

Although the results shown here seem valuable in more than one respect, they are still subject to certain provisos. First, the nature of the phenomenon studied here means we must keep our conclusions in perspective. Second, the type of approach used for collecting the data also means we must keep our conclusions in perspective. In fact, the 'descendant questionnaire' (Gendreau 1993: 189) to which we referred has a number of drawbacks, particularly the fact that the people questionned are not those who have experienced the phenomenon. This could be a possible source of errors. Finally, the territorial spread of our results also calls for caution. In fact, the survey which was conducted is highly representative of the city of Kinshasa. Could the results be extrapolated across the whole country? Ten years ago, the immediate response would have been in the affirmative, in that virtually all departures (legal and by aeroplane) for foreign countries from the DRC were from Kinshasa, thanks in particular to all foreign embassies and chanceries being established there, along with the only international airport at that time. All legal emigrants therefore had to stay there for many months and sometimes years before leaving to go abroad. But this is no longer the case today, with the establishment of some consulates in other secondary cities (Bukavu, Goma, Lubumbashi), but also the opening of other international airports in the provinces (Kisangani, Mbuji-Mayi, Lubumbashi).

Despite all this, the results given here can be seen as representative, firstly for the city of Kinshasa where the study was undertaken, but also to some extent for the country as a whole. Indeed, the questions put to the heads of families and their spouses to identify members of their family living abroad were not restricted solely to those who lived in Kinshasa before going abroad. All those who currently live abroad, regardless of their places of departure, have been listed, and information has been obtained about them; the whole country is represented here, clearly with large numbers of departures from Kinshasa.

The results of this study shed new and unexpected light on international migration from the DRC, and certainly help to fill a gap.

Notes

1. Priority Solidarity Fund: a fund set up by the French government and managed by the Institut de Recherche pour le Développement (IRD), dedicated to financing research in the countries of the South which come into France's priority solidarity area.

2. This is a multidisciplinary and transnational study analysing Mexican migration to the US every year. It involves both American researchers from the Office of Population Research of Princeton University and Mexican researchers from the Department of Investigation of Social Movements of the University of Guadalajara. Migrants are monitored both in the US and during holidays in Mexico.

3. AGEVEN: Acronym for Age and Event. This is a data collection sheet which makes it possible to situate the main events experienced by a survey subject in relation to the date they occurred or the individual's age at the time the event being studied occurred.

References

Byerlee, D., J.L. Tommy and H. Fatoo (1976) 'Rural Urban Migration in Sierra-Leone: Determinants and Policy Implication', *African Rural Economy Paper*, n° 13, Michigan State University.

Gatugu, J., A. Manço and S. Amoranitis (2001) *Valorisation et transfert des compétences : l'intégration des migrants au service de co-développement. Le cas des Africains en Wallonie*, Paris: L'Harmattan.

Gendreau, F. (1993) *La population de l'Afrique, Manuel de démographie*, Paris: Karthala.

Gregory, J. W. (1988) 'Migration et urbanisation', in D. Tabutin (ed.) *Population et Sociétés en Afrique au Sud du Sahara*, Paris: L'Harmattan.

Gregory, J. W., M. H. Saint-pierre and A. B. Simmons (1986) 'Structure démographique des ménages et comportement migratoire en Haute-Volta', in D. Gauvreau et al. (ed.) *Démographie et sous-développement dans le Tiers-monde*, Centre for Developping-Area Studies, n° 21, Université MacGill, Montréal.

Kagné, B. and M. Martiniello (2001) 'L'immigration subsaharienne en Belgique', in Courrier hebdomadaire, n° 1721, CRISP.

Lututala, M. B. (1982) 'Migrations internes et dynamiques démographiques en Afrique : Une analyse méthodologique', Mémoire de maîtrise, Faculté d'études Supérieures, Université de Montréal.

Lututala, M. B. (1987) 'Dynamique des migrations au Zaïre. Réseau de Kinshasa', thèse de doctorat, Faculté des études supérieures, Université de Montréal.

Lututala, M. B. (1995) 'Les migrations africaines dans le contexte socio-économique actuel. Une revue critique des modèles explicatifs', in H. Gérard and V. Piché (eds.) *La sociologie des populations*, Montréal: PUM/APELF-UREF.

Lututala, M. B. (1996) 'Initiation à la recherche scientifique. Notes du cours de Méthodes de recherche en Sciences Sociales', Cours à l'intention des étudiants en Sciences Economiques, Faculté de Sciences Economiques et de Gestion, Université de Kinshasa.

Lututala, M. (2005) 'L'élargissement des espaces de vie des familles congolaises sur des migrants à Paris', in K. Vignikin and P. Vimard (eds.) *Familles au Nord, Familles au Sud*, Louvain-la-Neuve: Academia-Bruylant.

Lututala, M. B. and T. Zamwangana (1998) 'R.D.C : Terre d'asile ou pays d'exil ?', in Departement de Demographie (Université de Kinshasa), *La question démographique en République démocratique du Congo*, Kinshasa: DDK-FNUAP.

Mangalu, M. A. (1998) 'Etude de la chaîne migratoire familiale des Congolais, mémoire de licence en démographie', DDK-FASEC, Unikin.

Massey, D. S. and R. Zenteno (2000) 'A validation of the ethnosurvey: the case of Mexico-U.S. migration', *International Migration Review* 34(3): 766–93.

Massey, D.S, J. Arango, G. Hugo, A. Kouaouci, A. Pellegrino and J. E. Taylor (1993) 'Theories of international migration: a review and appraisal', *Population and Development Review* 19(3): 431–66.

Pessar, P. A. (1986) 'The role of gender in Dominican settlement in the United States', in J. Nash and H. Safa (eds.) *Women and Change in Latin America*, South Hadley: Bergin et Garvey Publishers, Inc.

Piore, M. J. (1979) *Birds of Passage: Migrant Labor and Industrial Societies*, New York: Cambrige University Press.

Root, B. D and G. F. de Jong (1986) 'Family Migration: Conceptualizing the Migrating Unit in a Developing Country', paper presented at the Annual Meeting of the American Sociological Association, New York.

Schoumaker, B., S. Vause and J. Mangalu (2008) 'Political turmoil, economic crises and international migration from Africa to Europe: evidence from event-history data in Kinshasa', poster presented at the 20th Conférence Européenne sur la Population, Barcelona (Spain), July.

Sumata, C., T. Trefon and S. Cogels (2004) 'Images et usages de l'argent de la diaspora congolaise : Les transferts comme vecteur d'entretien du quotidien à Kinshasa', in T. Trefon, Ordre et désordre à Kinshasa. Réponses populaires à la faillite de l'État. Coll. Cahiers Africains, n° 61–2, pp. 134–54.

Schultz, T. W. (1960) 'Capital formation by education', *The Journal of Political Economy* 68: 571.

Todaro, M. P. (1969) 'A model of labor migration and urban unemployment in less developed countries', *The American Economic Review* 59(1): 138–48.

Zaïre (Republic of) (1994) 'Rapport national sur la population', presented at the Conférence Internationale sur la Population et le développement, Cairo, Egypt.

Chapter 8

⟫⟩◆⟨⟪

COMPARING DOGON AND SONGHAI MIGRATIONS TOWARDS GHANA

Isaïe Dougnon

INTRODUCTION

In the anthropology of African migrations, one issue which has yet to be studied in detail concerns the comparison between the migratory models developed by rural communities from a single country who have emigrated to other African countries. Up to now, each researcher has specialised, in accordance with the classic methods of anthropology, in a specific ethnic group confined to a particular site. This research is an attempt to reverse this trend through a comparative analysis of emigration from the Dogon and Songhai communities to Ghana.

In terms of migratory models, the Dogon and Songhai have been going through a period of transition for the past two decades. This has entailed a change from the old form of migration, which was a constant coming and going between their villages and the towns and cities of Ghana, and led to the creation of their respective communities in certain Ghanaian towns and cities, to a more complex form of mobility in terms of destination, work, duration and networks (Boesen and Marfaing 2007).

Alongside these two forms of migration there has also been further displacement leading numerous Dogon and Songhai families to settle permanently in the fertile lands in southern Mali or elsewhere. Overall, these two groups have maintained certain aspects of their ancient forms of movement and display similarities in their present forms, enabling a fruitful comparison to be drawn.

Cohesion within each group was robust enough to maintain support links between the migrants and their family members who stayed behind in the village. However, the after-effects of two major droughts in 1972 and 1984 and the upheaval experienced by the national economies of several countries in the sub-region following the Structural Adjustment Programme and civil wars plunged the migrant societies into a threefold economic, political and cultural crisis so intense that the old forms of migration and social organisation changed. For three decades, in Dogon and Songhai homelands alike, migration has served as a reminder of the two droughts which have affected stock-rearing and agriculture, and the great displacement of the hungry populations from the Dogon Plateau, the Gourma interior, the Niger Valley and the Lake area towards the south of Mali and elsewhere.

In an attempt to resolve these problems and to stabilise the nomadic and sedentary populations of the North, a number of development projects were launched in the 1970s and 1980s. However, these projects are far from having a limiting effect on migration: those living in the countryside voice their support for the introduction of new agricultural techniques, and yet refuse to give up their seasonal migration, which reduces the effectiveness of the introduction of such techniques (Dougnon 2005).

The general purpose of this work is to perform a comparative analysis of the migratory behaviours of the two communities. This comparison will be set into a historical perspective. First, it aims to show the causes of migration, the diversity of destinations, the intensity of migration and the migratory models of each of the two communities in Ghana. Second, it aims to analyse the process whereby Ghanaian towns and cities adapt to immigration through activities and social organisation. Our surveys show that despite a similarity in the causes of migration, each community has developed its own specific adaptation process, specialising in those activities for which it feels most gifted. Hence a comparative analysis of the processes whereby the Dogon and Songhai adapt through their activities enables us to understand the whole configuration of the ethnic division of labour within the immigrant community in colonial and post-colonial Ghana as a whole.

In order to arrive at a full understanding of the elements in this analysis, it is necessary to connect both migrant communities at once to their mother societies in Mali and to the social life of the Ghanaian community in its colonial and post-colonial totality. For such an exercise, it is necessary to describe some of the sociological and physical characteristics of the migrants' departure and arrival sites.

A COMPARATIVE STUDY WITH A HISTORICAL PERSPECTIVE

The value of the comparative study

The use of the comparative method in surveys of internal migrations in Africa remains trustworthy as a way of understanding the adaptation process for immigrant communities. In Mali, a number of empirical studies dealing with migration have been conducted since independence (Daum and Dougnon 2009). These studies consist for the most part of theses by students at the Ecole Normale Supérieure (ENSUP) and the Faculté des Lettres, Langues, Arts et Sciences Humaines (FLASH), and partly of works written by Malian researchers who are based locally or are part of the diaspora. In addition to work conducted by nationals, it is important to mention works by French researchers from the Institut de Recherche pour le Développement (IRD). In addition to this there are consultation reports sponsored by the International Labour Office (ILO) or the International Organization for Migration (IOM) and studies commissioned by European and African NGOs.

For the most part, these studies are conducted in a Malian village or a district of Paris. One of their characteristic methodological weaknesses is the lack of a conceptual framework which can enable researchers to exchange work among themselves, to evaluate it and to improve it collectively, and most particularly to create a historiography of Malian migration. This lack of historiographical work explains the redundancies in the research which use the same fields and questions as their framework. The lack of a framework which would allow the comparison of empirical studies explains why it has been so difficult to produce a clear picture of migratory trends among the Malian population and as a result to devise a real national policy on the issue.

From the thematic and methodological point of view, empirical studies on Malian migrations are organised around three main themes. The first productive field concerns internal migrations within Mali, from the rural setting to the urban setting and from one rural setting to another. The regional approaches which lie at the heart of the work often lead to an observation of the strategies of one particular regional or ethnic group in its migration and its appropriation of certain niches within the labour market, be they urban or agricultural. Another field concerns intra-African migrations. Here, researchers have concentrated either on pendular migrations (agricultural work, commerce) or the history of migration to one country or another, or the transformation of seasonal or work-based migrations into permanent settlement migrations. So there has been a certain number of studies concerning Malians in Ghana, Ivory Coast, the Congo and other countries in East Africa among others (Manchuelle 1997; Dougnon 2007; Tounkara-Gary 2008). Finally, the last area in question touches on international long-distance migrations, particularly migrations to France and, more recently, Spain and Italy.

This study attempts to show that the new forms of migration, be they of young single Songhai or Dogon people, or family migrations to more fertile lands, are inseparable from the old forms of migration. They are interlinked, within a single migratory dynamic (Capron and Kohler 1976). Their shared roots are buried deep in the colonial past. Today's migratory models and the models of the colonial era are just different expressions of the same dynamic. The comparative approach aims to bring out the specific traits of the different migratory forms, their development and their foundations. It is a question of establishing a general interpretive framework within which all the specific forms can find their true meaning.

The current intensification of research into Africa–Europe migration is being driven strongly by the political and social demands of the European Union. This gives the impression that African migratory flows are essentially directed towards Europe. However, the geography of African migration paints quite a different picture (de Haas 2007).

In Mali, for example, surveys carried out by state institutions estimate the number of Malians in the diaspora at between two and four million, whereas only 100,000 Malians live in Europe. The vast majority live in Africa, south of the Sahara, of whom 1.5 million are in Ivory Coast.

Now for comparative research to be carried out, this requires research to be centred on migration within Africa, considering, as Zélinsky (1980) suggests, a series of concepts which could explain the whole panoply of migratory phenomena in Africa. So there is a need to describe and explain former and present migrations, as well as those which will occur in the future.

In this study, we propose a comparison of Dogon and Songhai migrations to Ghana. Migration from these two communities has gone through three historical periods corresponding to the advent of the colonial labour market, the effects of drought, and the acceleration of urbanisation in Africa. The 1920s (and their European effects) and the 1970s–1980s (with their chronic drought) are the two key periods in relation to which all migratory currents can be contextualised and analysed. The first of these key periods was a time of migration for prestige, while the second was one of migration for survival.

Sources and methods

Two main sources have provided base data for this comparative study of Songhai and Dogon migration. The present-day situation was ascertained using data from ethnographical surveys in the Dogon country, in the Timbuktu region, and in Ghanaian cities, particularly Kumasi and Accra. Meanwhile, for the historic perspective, we turned to colonial reports (French and English) from labour inspectors, border police and Cercle (district) commanders or commissioners. These reports were sourced from the Koulouba archives in Bamako, and the Ghanaian archives in Accra, Kumasi and Tamale.

The colonial sources give statistics which make it possible to gauge the extent of migration in the colonial era, which was 99 per cent male. They also add to the picture from recollections given by immigrants concerning certain aspects of colonial work (work hours, changes in pay, promotion and social security). The surveys were conducted in two stages: between 2000 and 2003, as part of a doctoral thesis, then between 2003 and 2004, as part of post-doctoral research. Seven months of surveys were necessary: three months in the country of departure and four months in Ghana.

The use of the anthropological and historical literature enabled us to look at migration over the long term and to consider one of the fundamental questions of the migratory dynamic, namely: how do the new forms of migration (agricultural migration and mobility) take root in the ancient forms?

However, it is beyond our reach to consider all Songhai groups in order to compare them with the Dogon groups. The two communities are scattered across the whole of Ghana. The Songhai are just as present in the towns as in the villages of Ghana, while the Dogon are concentrated mostly in Accra. So we shall limit our study to the Dogon in Accra (a city of considerable development under the colonial regime) and the Songhai in Kumasi (a trading town).

In the Songhai region of origin, our survey took place in the Cercle of Rharous in the Timbuktu region. We worked in the following villages and hamlets: Gourma-Rharous, Gaberi, Sherifen, Kel-wan, Kano, Chiba-Chiba, Kardjiba, Tourchawene, Gourzougueye, Banikane, Timbuktu and Gossi. In each of these localities, we interviewed between five and seven returned migrants, using the so-called snowball method.

The Cercle of Rharous extends over roughly 50,000 square kilometres. Its population was estimated at 85,433 in 2006, with residents distributed across 44 villages and 173 nomadic fractions,[1] whereas it was as high as 100,000 in 1976. Here the effect of migration on the Cercle's demography is clear. This population consists of the Songhai, Tamashek, Arabs, Peul and Bozo (Doumbia 1986). The Cercle comprises a fluvial area which is 5 to 30km wide, making up the agricultural valley which extends a distance of 150km and is eminently suited to agriculture. The Songhai of Rharous live essentially on agriculture, stock-rearing and fishing. Small businesses play an important role in economic life through village fairs and crafts (tanning and pottery). The dominant crop is floating rice (moberi, kossa etc.) produced in the plains, depressions and low-lying lands which can be flooded, a few kilometres from the villages. Other crops (wheat, market garden crops and especially tobacco) are secondary to this.

In the Dogon country, we selected ten villages on the basis of their age and the magnitude of migration. In each village, we worked with returned migrants, talking to three older ones (who migrated during the 1960s) and two younger ones (who migrated in the 1990s), once again using the snowball technique. We surveyed the women to collect songs about Ghana or the town of Kumasi. The great majority of the Ghana Dogon come from the Cliff and Plateau areas. We carefully photographed ancient objects brought back from Ghana: shoes, male symbols, hats, knives and lances. In addition, we talked to the country dwellers about the role of the imported objects in social ceremonies.

The working language was chiefly Dogon, which is our mother tongue. The multitude of Dogon speakers was not a handicap, in that we belong both to the Plain and to the Plateau, where the tinku so, toro so and djamu sai languages dominate respectively. The speakers of these languages form the overwhelming majority of migrants in our research sites. For example, in Ghana, djamu sai is spoken by all the migrants.

In the Songhai areas (in Ghana, as in the Timbuktu region), we were able to make use of interpreters, particularly by turning to former students and an old Songhai migrant who had been living in Kumasi since 1952. A lack of knowledge of the Songhai language was made up for by the cousinage system which exists between the Dogon and Songhai.

From 'migration for prestige' to 'migration for survival'

We talk of 'migration for prestige' when someone leaves their village to go and work elsewhere with the sole aim of buying luxury items (clothes, perfume and other modern items) or to seek out new horizons or cultures (colonial cities and learning foreign languages), and we use the term 'migration for survival' in the same way as André

Marty (1987): displacement with a view to feeding oneself and one's family who have stayed behind in the village.[2]

Migration to Ghana, among the Songhai in the Cercle of Gourma-Rharous (Timbuktu region) and the Dogon, took off in the 1920s when Ghana became the largest centre both for colonial development and for agricultural production in colonial West Africa.

In the colonial period, young Dogon and Songhai country dwellers would migrate in search of clothes and money to pay taxes, or simply to avoid forced labour in French Sudan. According to Mr Abdoulaye Dunbane from the village of Mandiakoye, a former immigrant who returned to the village after more than 20 years in Ghana, migration has been practised since 1973 by people from the valley looking to feed themselves and their families who have stayed behind in the village. In essence, this is what he says:

> In the time of our fathers, the Gold Coast [the colonial name for present-day Ghana] was a 'promised land'. Anyone coming from there had everything: perfume, fine clothes. The girls were mad for the perfume. Some even left their fiancés to go after the Ghana idje [those returning from Ghana]. The women sang their praises. Unlike the generation of migrants who left to find luxury items, the 1973 generation left to find grain. This year (2003) I brought home two tonnes of millet.

In the 1920s, food was plentiful and all basic needs were met, said one old man in the village of Kardjiba. People migrated to buy clothes because there was nothing lacking at home. He says that livestock rearing and rice growing complemented one another, which guaranteed that the people would have a stable and sustainable economy. In 1973 this balance was destroyed and a single sector of activity was not enough to meet the population's food needs. For more than two decades, the rains have been unreliable and insufficient (200mm of rain nowadays compared with 700mm in the 1920s). Well-off country dwellers use motorised pumps to irrigate their rice paddies. The only alternative is irrigation, which is expensive for the overwhelming majority of small farmers. So young men migrate elsewhere to find what is lacking. A good many country people have rebuilt their livestock thanks to migration. In the past, between the villages of Gossi and Douentza, thousands of flocks could be seen on either side of the road. In 1984, catastrophe struck. The nomads sold their cattle at a knock-down price (1000 Malian francs, 500 CFA francs) to migrate to Ghana, Libya, Saudi Arabia and Southern Mali. The majority of the people to whom we spoke stressed the contrast between the country they left and the country where they arrived. The first was a country of famine, lack of clothes, inadequate resources for work, shortages of money and markets. The second country was quite the opposite: in other words there were opportunities to access the basic necessities. Are all these contrasts really true? Whoever visits the river belt during the floods (August to January) would say the country people here are spoilt by nature: water and green plains everywhere. However, in the dry season (February to June), this same Mother Nature creates a scene of calamity. The river is both a jewel and a source of misery. The country people lack the means to control it while it destroys their fields.

Mr Ageymadidi Aboubacrine Maïga maintains that men and women cannot remain in the Niger River Valley without migrating:

> You can't live here without leaving. The pools rely on the rain. The IVPs rely on taxes. And to pay the taxes you have to go elsewhere. If a man stays away and doesn't find anything, then he has to return home to do what he was doing before he left. My sister left Gourzougeye in 1984 for Ghana, but she came back for good in 2003 with all her family.

In fact, there is no such thing as a permanent return, for all those returned migrants whom we met in the three valley communities said that if the contrast between their region of origin and the region to which they emigrated continues to increase, they would go back again to the place from which they had returned. If however the contrast decreases, they are prepared to stay in their villages.

THE FIRST GENERATIONS OF SONGHAI AND DOGON MIGRANTS IN GHANA (1920–1950)

> Here, we don't know Bamako, the capital of Mali, but Accra, which is Ghana's; the people here don't know Bamana,[3] but they speak Hausa, English and Ashanti.
>
> *A former migrant from the village of Tourchawene, in the*
> *Cercle of Rharous*

Settlement by the Dogon and Songhai in Ghana could not have been predicted at the start of the British occupation of the Ashanti lands in 1870. One would have predicted the arrival of the Ashanti's neighbouring ethnic groups: Mossi, Hausa, Kotokoli from Togo, ethnic groups from the Northern Territories and so on,[4] but not people from the Dogon Plateau or Niger Valley. These were situated, quite literally, on the periphery of the new colonial development zone. However, even during the first decade of the twentieth century, the Dogon and Songhai had acquired considerable experience of crossing transcolonial borders as well as a vast pool of knowledge on English working methods, on trade in the Kumasi market and the customs of the different ethnic groups in Ghana. In the 1920s and 1950s, 'going to Kumasi or the Gold Coast' was quite a well-developed practice among first-generation migrants, namely those who belonged to the Kumasi boys among the Dogon or the Kumasi boys among the Songhai.

Going to Kumasi and bringing back luxury items were the basis of the mature man's identity: open-spirited, and achieving physical and mental perfection. And the man who decided to settle there would thereby guarantee his prosperity. This new idea of the journey to Kumasi was so popular that French colonial administrators took steps to halt the stampede of their subjects to Ghana (Dougnon 2007).

The motivations of first-generation migrants

In Central and Southern Africa, the Katanga and Rhodesian copper mines and the Rand mines drew thousands of men from Mozambique, Angola and Rwanda. In West Africa, it was the cocoa and coffee plantations, the ports and the mines which created a major demand for workers.

The first movements by the Songhai and Dogon were the result of the attractive modernity of colonial Ghana. Because of its geographical proximity to the British growth areas as compared with the French ones, the Dogon and Songhai started thronging to Ghana from the early twentieth century. It is possible to identify three major periods in the history of Dogon and Songhai migration:

- The early decades of the colonial period saw migration for prestige developing in an exclusive way.
- The 1930s to 1950s saw further migration among the Dogon and Songhai populations, in addition to migration for prestige, triggered by the effects of the colonial economy which, through tax and food production levies, the recruitment of workers and military conscription, and multiple forms of contracts and exploitation introduced by the French administration and passed on by the heads of cantons, caused many country dwellers to flee and settle in Ghana.
- During the 1970s and 1980s, the Dogon and Songhai populations bore the full brunt of two major ecological disasters, hence the numerous departures for permanent settlement by the Songhai in Ghana and cities elsewhere in Africa.

Thus, in their search for work, many migrants from the French territories (Burkina Faso, formerly Upper Volta, and Mali, formerly French Sudan) came to work in Ghana.[5] Relying on migrants' accounts and colonial reports, it is possible to identify four reasons or motivations which explain the coming and going of young people between Ghana and their rural regions of origin:

- Prestige and the new identity of the successful male. On returning to the village of his birth, the migrant often takes great pleasure in an ostentatious display of the treasures he has brought back (Bouju 1984). Nor will he hold back from telling stories of the great people he has met and a thousand and one other marvels. These tales from the distant traveller have had a decisive effect on other young people considering leaving their village. The young village dwellers also notice how the returning male wins the heart of a beautiful girl who was a designated fiancée of an old man in the village. His fellows also notice that he has developed an independent and entrepreneurial attitude.
- The desire of young country dwellers to improve their economic standing. Young people who have not migrated realise that they have no private property. They work for their family and the local chiefs. They are bound hand and foot by the social values of the wider family and the village. Seeing the improved position of returned migrants, these

young people feel frustrated and in their turn leave the village in secret to embark on this adventure.

- The Sahelian migrant's wish to sell his capacity for work rather than his cattle, in order to have sufficient money to pay his taxes.
- Urbanisation and the loss of control over young people by their elders. There are rarely any statistical data on this subject, but it is known that the villages empty during dry seasons. The older people say that such a record can be explained by the fact that they have little control over the young people, who set off whenever they want.

It has already been mentioned that the majority of these migrants return to the village to farm the family's fields. However, it is reckoned that more than 5 per cent of these migrants stay at their migration destination, and this number is increasing each year. As for the Dogon, the percentage is twice as high.

An analysis of the cultural and economic influence of the migrant who has returned to the village echoes the relations between the different generations of migrants in the host countries. In both cases, it is always the immigrant's economic success which determines his status in respect of his family, his loved ones, and the community as a whole. The migrant who returns with plenty of resources through being successful adapts better to the conditions in the village, which are often precarious, and finds it easier to escape the shackles of tradition. In his host location, he has more opportunities to adapt to the host culture, while retaining his own culture and maintaining regular links with his family in the village (sending gifts and making frequent visits). These are still the reasons put forward by young people to justify their leaving their village for African cities and for Europe.

The city of Kumasi or 'paradise on earth': the myth of Ghana in the Dogon country

Ghana exerted a strong attraction across the regions in the Niger River Bend, particularly in Ségou, San, Mopti and Bandiagara. The main occupation in the colony was agriculture. In the Ashanti lands and Togo, the natives cultivated cocoa for export. Revenue from the sale of this product was used for importing manufactured goods such as clothes, foodstuffs, bicycles, phonographs, motorbikes and other luxury items whose use has become commonplace over the past few decades thanks to contact between Africans and Europeans.[6] Margaret Peil gives an idea of the economic and political position occupied by Kumasi, which was known as the 'Garden City' in the 1960s. In particular, she writes:

> With the coming of the railway line from Sekondi in 1903 and the development of cocoa as an export crop, Kumasi became a great marketing centre. Migrant workers on the gold mines and cocoa farms stop in Kumasi to purchase goods before returning to their homes all over West Africa. A popular saying has it that: 'he who has not been to Kumasi will not go to paradise.' (Peil 1972: 7).

During the 1930s, in the Dogon country, Kumasi was seen as the 'mother' city of the Ghanaian territory. Exchanges such as: 'Where are you coming from?' 'I'm coming from Kumasi. Where are you coming from?' 'I'm coming from Sokindé. Where are you coming from?' 'I'm coming from Accra. Where are you coming from?' 'I'm coming from Obuasi. Where are you coming from?' 'I'm coming from Cape Coast', were heard every day in the villages. Young people would meet up in the evenings in the square, after their hard work in the fields. Conversation would often revolve around the desire harboured by some of them to leave for Kumasi. If one said, 'after the growing season, I'm leaving for Kumasi', another would respond, 'I'm going too', and so on, and the craze for leaving would take hold of the whole group. The decision to leave had to be kept secret; the elders must not know, because they could have caused the plan to be aborted. Three generations of migrants made this trip in turn: the first (1910 to 1940), known as the 'foot-travellers', made their way through the Dogon villages to the cities of Ghana on foot. The second (1950 to 1980) travelled by car, and the third and final generation are the children born in Ghana (Dougnon 2003). The account which gets to the very heart of the main question in this article is the one given by this former migrant, who has been settled in Accra since 1939:

> At the time, the young people lacked nothing in the Dogon Country, just the clothes. To celebrate the buro and dama ceremonies in fitting style, they had to go and

> get clothes in the Gold Coast. [Abdoulaye Kodio, immi-
> grant from the Dogon Plateau to Accra-Madina]

With his words, this migrant shows the full cultural significance of migration, since it establishes a link between the highly symbolic and ritualistic local festivals of the Dogon Country and the European clothes brought back thanks to migration. As a harvest festival, buro is the Dogon's biggest traditional festival. It can often last for more than a week. Dama, or the end of mourning, is a funerary festival, celebrated three years after the death of one or more elderly people. Its purpose is to accompany their souls to the ancestral heaven. There were perfectly good local forms of dress for these events, but they became devalued when compared with the clothes imported from the Gold Coast, which were grandly displayed in the local markets.

MIGRATION AND ETHNIC DIVISION OF LABOUR

Two ethnic groups, two career paths

The Songhai and Dogon immigrants originated from the same geographical region of Mali (the north-west). In the migrant districts, known as *zongo*,[7] they developed two completely different ways of adapting. A Songhai community – although originally country dwellers in the Niger River Valley – becomes liberal, entrepreneurial and capitalistic to a degree which would be hard to find in their villages of origin. However, next door lives a Dogon community which basically relies on the security of colonial work.

The history and culture of the two ethnic groups' country of departure has had a fundamental effect on the choice of work and adaptation strategies. The Songhai, founders of an empire which developed thanks to trans-Saharan trade, and the inheritors of an Islamic civilisation, soon responded by engaging in commerce and quickly prospering at it. In the cities of Mali (Mopti, Bamako, Niono, Koutiala and Sikasso), seasonal migrants from the regions in the North have over the past three decades become associated with the *koroboro*[8] *butiqini*, literally 'the little Songhai shop'. The multiplication of these little shops, their quality, the diversity and the prices of the products on offer there have become the chief characteristics of the Songhai migrant. Moreover, a great number of them would not hesitate to say that commerce is all a Songhai knows. This description was until then reserved for the Soninke, good farmers at home and good traders elsewhere (Whitehouse 2003).

By contrast, the Dogon have transferred their ancestral notion of work to Ghana. According to this concept, the value of work is a function of the total effort needed to perform it. In other words, it is the quantity of sweat expended that determines the value of the work. Agriculture, their main activity, basically consists of working the fields. It conjures up the idea of pain, effort and tenacity. Its product, the cereal crop, is a basis of human life. The rigour of agriculture is linked to the physical environment. The Dogon cultivate plots on the plateau, holding back the earth with low walls and retaining structures constructed from stones simply placed one on top of another. In the light of this notion of work, it is easy to understand how Dogon migrants state that the hard work of the white man (mines and public works), were by definition a Dogon activity which suited their abilities.

In pre-colonial Africa, customs and traditions decided the type of work that a man of a given status was authorised to do or not to do (Rouche 1955). In societies where caste systems exist and where cultural forces tend to crystallise the form of social organisations and institutions, certain occupations are hereditary: healers, priests, commerce and tanning etc. (North 1926). With colonisation, the local division of labour changed overnight. Upheavals linked to the displacement of people, production methods and the extension of borders for trade and labour had a violent impact on ancestral work prerogatives.

Songhai immigrants in Kumasi's central market (1930–1948)

Of all professions, commerce is the one which demands the greatest mobility and contact with other groups. Competition between these groups can often turn to conflict. Political management of these conflicts is generally to the detriment of the least integrated or the most stigmatised.

In Ghana, the Songhai were known by the curious name of *kayakaya*, literally 'carry on the head'. The notion of *kayakaya* was used to refer not only to a particular type of work – as head porters – but also to the community which engaged in this activity. In the 1930s, they were officially called the *kayakaya* or Gao community.[9] In fact, *kayakaya* expresses their new identity as migrant workers in Ghana, whereas the name Gao referred to their geographical origin. The word *kayakaya* had a pejorative connotation because the work to which it referred was reserved for migrants. The stigmatisation of the *kayakaya* community and their work is linked to the fact that these communities were perceived as being foreigners despite the length of their stay in the Ashanti country. In addition, no Ghanaian native would agree to work as a head porter, which was seen as degrading.

Having been denigrated in the past, the *kayakaya* community has over time become a community of respectable businessmen. They have gone on from being head porters for others to become traders in their own right (Dougnon 2005).[10] This new status has enabled them to occupy a large part of Kumasi's central market and thus to dominate the trade in basic commodities. This control of commerce by communities who, in the natives' eyes, have become masters after having been mere servants, has not been well accepted. In April 1948, a ruling by the municipal authorities in Kumasi gave the *kayakaya* one month to vacate the market. After this deadline, their goods were to be seized and they would be expelled by force. According to a rumour which gained wide currency, the Songhai were responsible for price inflation affecting basic essentials. And this inflation had been caused deliberately, because the Songhai knew that they had established a monopoly on the trade in foodstuffs at the market in Kumasi. Despite appeals to the colonial and traditional authorities of the Ashanti region, and mediation by the *zongo*'s religious and political leaders, the ruling was implemented.

The Dogon and the 'white man's work'

The proactive economic approach of the Songhai is in contrast to the conservatism of the Dogon community, which has tended to stick to jobs in the service of the colonies and to prefer the regular rhythm of the white man's work. In Ghana, the concept of 'white man's work' refers to two fields of activity: public works and mining. Security and caretaking work has appeared on the list since the 1950s and 1960s.

Souleyman Goro, a former worker on the manganese sites in Nsuta, included the following in his account:

> I left my village for Kumasi, but there was no work in that city apart from kayakaya [carrying loads on one's head]. This wasn't the sort of work for Dogon. They can't do that. The Dogon work in mines, in P. W. (Public Works). Kayakaya is for the Songhai, the Bella, the Hausa and the people from round here. The Dogon, no.

In Kumasi, there were two activities: land and wood. The Dogon did not want that, which is why they continued on to Accra, where they were convinced they would find the 'white man's work', said one old Dogon woman, who has been settled in this city since 1942. Migrants chose the 'white man's work' for different reasons:

- The 'white man's work' provided money so that they could take luxury items back to the village. The young migrants were aged between 15 and 30. No one came to Ghana to stay there. According to Abdoulaye Kodio, who left for the Gold Coast in 1940, the young people would become engaged in the village before leaving. If no news was received from the departing young man in three years, his fiancée would leave him for another. A number of young men would come back to prepare for their marriage and to take part in the traditional festivals of buro and dama. During the various celebrations at the local festivals and in the markets, the former migrants would dress in their finest clothes for display and to celebrate in fitting style. They had to go and get these clothes from the Gold Coast.

- They guaranteed the security of regular work. According to Baba Yacoub, the three-year cut-off point was so deeply rooted in the minds of the young migrants that no one would dream of committing to work which would not allow them to honour the deadline. In agricultural work, the contract often ran for one year. The worker was paid at the end of the year. Sometimes he would receive payment in kind. Any migrant who wanted to keep within the three-year limit had to choose the 'white man's work'. The whites paid their workers by the month or even at the end of each week. Even here, young people avoided work which required a long apprenticeship, such as mechanical work, carpentry, build-ing, driving and so on.

- A number of migrants say that 'white man's work' was sought because of its finite nature. This was an everyday activity where the hard worker could keep his job right up until retirement. However, the blacks or the Levantine traders would recompense the employee once the work was finished. A number of pensioners say that the reason they receive a pension is because they did 'white man's work'.

- It enabled professional qualification. There are many who chose 'white man's work' because they were fascinated by the resources, the methods and the nature of the work.

To sum up, here is how Baba Yacoub explains the Dogon's choice of 'white man's work':

> How could someone who has come for money turn down the 'white man's work' and take on the 'black man's work'? The 'black man's work' was certainly there: the cocoa and coffee plantations, the tomato, pepper and maize fields. At that time, the Dogon didn't do 'black man's work'. It was the Zerma, the Peul and the Bella who did that.

Old Baba's words show that the 'black man's work' was considered the preserve of the other migrants. What emerges from his account, like several others, is that difficult work was by definition a Dogon activity; the white man had work which matched their abilities.

The end of the 'white man's work' slowed the migration of young Dogon to Ghana. These then headed like their Songhai compatriots towards Southern Mali and other countries in the sub-region.

NEW MIGRATORY TRENDS IN THE DOGON AND SONGHAI COUNTRY

Over two decades, the two Dogon and Songhai communities have experienced a period of transition in their migratory model. What are these new trends? Since the mid 1980s, the Dogon have been looking for arable land in the south of Mali. Like the Songhai, they are also involved in seasonal migration in the sub-region. These new forms of migration are inseparable from the ancient forms. For two decades, the young people from the two communities have been coming and going between their villages and the towns in the south of Mali or in neighbouring countries (Ghana, Ivory Coast etc.). Here they are called seasonal workers and there are four types of seasonal worker to which we shall return later. They cover territories where the distances involved can vary considerably. The organisation of their migration has also seen some changes, due to economic and political difficulties in the countries of departure and arrival.

Migratory models among the Dogon and the Songhai

There is abundant literature dealing with migration in Africa south of the Sahara (Caldwell 1969; Thaddeus 1996; Ferguson 1990; Macmillan 1996). However, the majority of ethnographic data are drawn from Southern and Central Africa where, since the colonial era, mining companies which import labour have dominated the scene. One of the specialists on this part of Africa, James Ferguson, maintains that the migratory model most conceptualised by anthropologists is the 'two-phase' one:

> The least elaborate possible version of this progression, of course, is a simple two-phase model: in one period workers were 'migrant labourers', making short work-trips to the towns and often leaving their families behind; in the next they become 'permanently urbanised' (Ferguson 1990: 387).

Ferguson has set out his critique of this model, which he describes as simplistic. On the basis of his field surveys undertaken in Kitwe in Zambia, he maintains that the migratory trend from 1920 to the present day has undergone both complex changes and significant continuity which is not suggested by the classic model based on the theory of modernisation or the process of African urbanisation. Nevertheless, he does acknowledge that this model has some value in analysing the social life of migrant communities in the 1940s to 1960s. Following his criticisms, Ferguson has not constructed an alternative migratory model. He has simply demonstrated the complex character of the relationships between the migrant and his family members who have stayed in the village, and the importance of women in the lives of immigrant men.

What is the migratory model currently applicable to the Dogon and Songhai country? When the researcher works in the immigrant districts of Accra and Kumasi, he discovers a model comparable to that described above by Ferguson. But when he conducts his research in the villages of departure, he identifies several types of migrants using different displacement models. Who is the migrant in these two areas? Where is he going, and why? How can one ask such a question in an area where there is not a single man who has not migrated during his working life? The enquirer must wonder how to proceed. Should he take a sample at the risk of missing out on the best individual experiences? Or instead should he start asking around all the men in the village? Taking into account the amount of time set aside for the survey, we decided to interview chiefly the seasonal workers who have come back for the farming and those who have come back for good, for whatever reasons that may be. In Kumasi and Accra, we interviewed more than 100 migrants who belonged to the first generation.

Four types of seasonal workers

Today, four types of seasonal migrants can be distinguished by virtue of the differing migratory experiences of the populations of Gourma-Rharous and the Dogon country:

- The regular seasonal migrants are those who leave each year after the harvest and return for the growing season. The length of their absence ranges between three and six months.
- The multi-seasonal migrants are those whose exodus lasts more than one year. The migrant transfers his family (wife and children) to his host country if his income is sufficient, but takes it back to the village as soon as his situation deteriorates.
- Irregular seasonal migrants meanwhile only migrate when the spectre of famine becomes inevitable. In the case of good harvests they do not move away.
- Finally, visiting migrants have finished work migration for reasons of age or illness, but they continue to visit their fellow countrymen who have settled abroad. The length of the visits ranges from one to six months, and may be as long as a year.

In the cities of Mali (Mopti, Koutiala, Bamako, Sikasso), migrants who find employment doing casual work fall into the first group. They say: 'we're escaping hunger'. Their return to the village depends on the food situation within the Niger River Valley and the Dogon Plateau. Migrants heading off to Ghana or Ivory Coast for more than a year belong to the second group. However, seasonal migrants who go from one town to another in Mali and elsewhere are from a group which we could call 'floating', in the same way as Marty (1987). These say: 'we're migrating to look for that bit extra'. In the north, these are generally the former slaves, deprived of land and cattle. These days, this group also includes country dwellers who have lost their lands following land disputes. These people are obliged to migrate. The migratory model for this group is more complex. The group's members are often looking for a suitable area for permanent or provisional settlement within the country. Failing this, they will group together in a neighbouring country to conduct their village activities. This is the case of Malian nomads in Niger, Burkina Faso and Mauritania, and Bozo and Songhai fishermen in the village of San Fatou in Ivory Coast.

Seasonal migration works on the basis of an active network and inter-family solidarity, two factors which must be considered when trying to understand the current dynamics of migration. The long establishment (since 1920) of the migration which affects several generations in these two localities and the economic dynamism of certain migrants in their host country also help with understanding the choice of destination for new candidates.

A long and short migratory distance

The choice of destination is not a function of physical distance, but of the existence of migratory networks. Seasonal migrants most often opt for places where solidarity between new and old migrants operates like an institution. 'The Songhai goes where his relatives are', claimed one old man in the village of Kardjiba. According to Whitehouse, 'while the geographical distance between the origin and a given point is fixed, the social distance may diminish over time with the growth and strengthening of migratory networks. However, it may increase in response to political and economic conditions.' (Whitehouse 2003: 6). The main destinations which crop up are as follows:

- Ghana is the top destination among the Dogon and Songhai as well as all populations from the north-east of Mali (Peul, Bobo, Bella). However, populations from the south-west of Mali leave for Senegal and Gambia (Bamana, Soninke, Kassonké, Peul).

- Mopti was initially just a mandatory staging town for Songhai migrants coming from Kumasi. It was here that they would buy provisions for their brothers from the village. But from the 1970s onwards, this town has become the main destination for many seasonal Dogon and Songhai migrants. It is here that they would build up their initial capital before continuing their journey further south through Mali or towards the Ivory Coast, Liberia or Sierra Leone.

- Niger is the favoured country for the people of Gao. Among the peoples living in the Cercle of Gourma-Rharous, it is the Iklan (former slaves) who most regularly travel to this country.

- Bamako started to emerge as a destination at the same time as Mopti, with the emergence of migration symbolised by 'the little Songhai shop', security and caretaking work, and domestic work among young Dogon girls and boys.

- The Ivory Coast was the second most important destination outside of Mali, after Ghana, because of agricultural and fishing resources in the area around Bio, a small town located in the centre of the Ivory Coast. This flow has reduced due to conflicts.

- Senegal is the favoured destination for those living in the Cercle of Niafounké, as well as the Kano, Gaberi and Samar in the Cercle of Rharous.

- Finally, Mauritania, Libya and Saudi Arabia are also favourite destinations among the Tamasheq and Moorish populations. Saudi Arabia is also the destination for Dogon girls from the Cercle of Bankass. Libya is experiencing increasingly larger Songhai migration.

Structure and organisation of migration

'Prior to the 1980s, migration was more or less well organised', said one old country dweller in Rharous. For example, in a family with five boys, three would take care of the crops while two would leave. At harvest, the first migrants would return for the work, while three who had grown the crops would head off for Ghana. The five would not leave together in case of an agricultural disaster.

In the Rharous and the Dogon country, migration affects everyone, be they free, freedmen, landowners or landless. There is no fixed age for migration; as soon as the boy feels capable of travelling and working, he is free to go. The destinations vary according to work opportunities or the economic situation. The first destination was Ghana, followed in the 1980s by Nigeria, Ivory Coast, Niger and some cities in Mali such as Mopti, Koutiala and Sikasso.

The duration of this migration is difficult to determine. According to some migrants, the return journey does not occur until their objectives have been reached, and the period of absence can range from eight months to a year or a year and a half, depending on how lucky the migrant has been and the needs which he has to satisfy. Migrants state that one year away will enable an immigrant to bring back clothes for the whole family and to buy two bulls. While in the colonial era the purchase of clothes was the main objective, since the 1970s and 1980s food and taxes have become the migrant's main preoccupation.

CONCLUSION

By adopting a method which gives great importance to the historical perspective, we have been able to show the different factors, be they cultural or ecological, which have caused the Dogon and Songhai to change from migration 'for prestige' to migration 'for survival'. This process also explains why migration which was initially centred on Ghana has extended to other countries in the Ecowas[11] as well as other African countries. Moreover, the boom in transport since the 1970s, making it accessible to large numbers of people, has increased the spread of seasonal migration, which now covers the Ecowas zone, enabling migrants to engage in small-scale trade and casual jobs.

The comparative approach, meanwhile, has shown how each ethnic group has adapted during migration to specialise in the field for which it feels best prepared. The Dogon, who have favoured colonial work over self employment, have found themselves in an unenviable economic situation in the post-colonial period, while the Songhai, who have excelled in commerce, have made their mark over several years as key economic players in the fuel and building sectors, and the trade in foodstuffs. Despite being expelled from Kumasi's central market in 1948, the Songhai have lost none of their entrepreneurial spirit.

Economic success has allowed the Songhai to develop a more complex system than the Dogon of co-operation with native populations. In addition to marrying Ghanaian women, they have been able to develop good business relations with the local authorities (in this case, the Ashanti). This cohabitation arrangement was partly destroyed following the trade conflict in 1948. With the end of the 'white man's work', the old Dogon (particularly those from the first generation) have developed a homesickness for their natal land and have an ambition to return there. The historical analysis has also helped with understanding current trends in migration and has revealed that migration is no longer monopolised by the young men, as was the case in the years prior to 1970.

Notes

1. Project to Mobilise Food Security Initiatives in Mali (PROM-ISAM), 2006.

2. Jonathan Crush et al. (1991: 131) observed the same model in the 1970s among Bantustan populations in South Africa. Following the collapse of agriculture and the reduction in arable land, these people depended for their survival on the income from their relatives who had left to work in the mines and administrative departments of the great South African cities.

3. Bamana is the national language of Mali, since more than 70 per cent understand and speak it. Hausa, English and Ashanti are the three most popular languages in Ghana.

4. This territory, located in the North of Ghana, had a different status during the colonial period from the regions in the South

of Ghana. From the cultural, social and geographical point of view, this area was quite distinct, since it was not part of the Gold Coast. The ethnic groups of the Northern Territories were affiliated to the neighbouring ethnic groups of Burkina Faso and Togo. As such, their workers arriving to work in the South were seen as immigrants.

5. See 'The Annual Invasion of the Gold Coast by French and Northern Territories Subjects in Search of Labour', ADM 11/1076, Accra Archives.

6. Dossier, Labour, 1927, 'Note to the Governor on the emigration of the Sudanese workforce to Gambia and the Gold Coast', *Fonds Récents*, Archives de Bamako.

7. *Zongo* is a Hausa word meaning 'foreigners' district'. During the colonial era, it was the mining companies who, on the colonial government's instruction, established the *zongo* so that they could settle the migrant workers there.

8. The term *koroboro* signifies a man who lives in the village, and by extension the town. The antonym is *gandjiboro*, which means a man who lives in the bush. These dichotomous terms illustrate the images of the two main societies in the North: that of the shepherd or nomad, who follows his animals through the bush, and that of the Songhai farmer who lives in the villages along the valley and later in the political centres of the Middles Ages: Gao and Timbuktu.

9. Gao was the historic capital city of the Songhai Empire up to 1591, the date of the Moroccan invasion.

10. We have described at length the cultural and economic implications of this word *kayakaya* in our article: 'From head portering to trade: The Songhai migrants or *kayakaya* in the market at Kumasi, Ghana 1930–1948', presented to the symposium *Between city and desert: Mobility, activities and urbanity in the Sahara-Sahel region*, Berlin, 8–10 December 2005.

11. Ecowas: Economic Community of West African States, within which it is possible to travel without a visa.

References

Boesen, E. and L. Marfaing (2007) *Les nouveaux urbains dans l'espace sahara-sahel un cosmopolitisme par le bas*, Paris: Karthala-ZMO.

Bouju, J. (1984) *Graine de l'homme, enfant du mil*, Paris: Société d'Ethnologie.

Capron, J. and J. M. Kohler (1976) 'Migration de travail vers l'étranger et développement national', paper presented at the seminar 'Méthodes de Planification du développement Rural', Ouagadougou, 3-6 March.

Caldwell, J. C. (1969) *African Rural-Urban Migration: The Movement to Ghana's Towns*, Australian National University Press.

Crush, J., J. Alan and D. Yuldelman (1991) *South Africa's Labor Empire : A History of Black Migrancy to the Gold Mines*, Oxford: Westview Press.

de Haas, H. (2007) 'Le mythe de l'invasion: Migration irrégulière d'Afrique de l'Ouest au Maghreb et en Union européenne,' International Migration Institute, University of Oxford.

Daum, C. and I. Dougnon (2009) 'L'Afrique en mouvement', *Hommes et Migrations*, N0 1279, mai-juin 2009.

Dougnon, I. (2003) 'Les Ghana boys et le prestige de l'habit européen au Pays Dogon (1920-1960)', in R. Bedaux and Van Der Waals (eds.) *Regards sur les Dogon du Mali*, Rijksmuseum voor Volkenkunde, Leiden: Snoeck Gand.

Dougnon, I. (2005) 'De l'assistance au développement : la participation paysanne en question, le cas de la région de Tombouctou', AEGIS Conference, London, 29 June–2 July.

Dougnon, I. (2007) *Travail de Blanc, Travail de Noir : la Migration des Dogon vers l'Office du Niger et le Ghana, 1910-1980*, Paris: Karthala.

Doumbia, Z. (1986) 'Programme de Relance et de Consolidation du Mouvement Coopératif en 6è et 7è Région du Mali', Note à la coordination de Programmes Euro Action-ACORD, Tombouctou.

Ferguson, J. (1990) 'Mobile workers, modernist narratives: a critique of the historiography of transition on the Copperbelt [Part One]', *Journal of Southern African Studies* 16(3): 385–412.

Manchuelle, F. (1997) *Willing Migrants Soninke Labor Diaspora, 1845-1960*, London.

Marty, A. (1987) 'Etude-Programmation Socio-Economique Gourma, Traitements des Questionnaires Généraux Janvier-Mars 1987', Documents de l'Aide d'Eglise Norvégienne, Gossi.

North, C. C. (1926) *Social Differenciation*, Volume II, London: Routledge.

Peil, M. (1972) *The Ghanaian Factory Worker: Industrial Man in Africa.*, Cambridge: Cambridge University Press.

Rouche, J. (1955) 'Migration au Ghana (Gold Coast) (Enquête 1953-1955)', *Journal de la société des africanistes* XXVI(1-2): 1–3, 33–196.

Tounkara-Gary, D. (2008) *Migrants soudanais/maliens et conscience ivoirienne. Les étrangers en Côte d'Ivoire (1903-1980)*, Paris: L'Harmattan.

Thaddeus, S. (1996) 'Labor migration in colonial Tanzania and the hegemony of South African historiography', *African Affairs* 95: 581–98.

Whitehouse, B. (2003) 'Rester Soninké: La migration, la multilocalité et l'identité dans une communauté sahélienne', Thèse de M.A, Brown University, Providence Island, USA.

Zélinsky, W. (1980) 'The impasse in migration theory: a sketch map for potential escapees', in P. A. Morrison (ed.) *Population Movements: Their Forms and Functions in Urbanization and Development*, Liege: Ordina Edition.

Chapter 9

⟾⬥⬦⟾

COLLECTING DATA ON MIGRANTS THROUGH NGOS

Tara Polzer Ngwato

INTRODUCTION

Surveys are often equated with representativity. There are various forms of representativity depending on the goals of the research. Where a survey intends to produce findings which are generalisable to a wider population on the basis of statistically significant extrapolation from a sample, the necessary tool to achieve representativity is generally considered to be a random sample. In migration research, however, there are many contexts in which there is no established sampling frame for the population of interest, posing an 'unassailable barrier to the textbook ideal type' of a survey based on random sampling (Bloch 2007: 213). Most surveys of mobile populations therefore have to creatively compromise and work with certain generalisability limitations and biases.

The survey I describe is a study of cross-border migrants, asylum seekers and refugees in urban areas of South Africa, and their levels of access to and experiences with basic socio-economic services in health care, education, housing, employment and social welfare. This survey was administered through 'service provider organisations' (SPOs), meaning non-governmental organisations and religious organisations which provide different kinds of services to cross-border migrants. Conducting research on refugees and migrants through NGOs has been criticised for not being methodologically rigorous (Jacobsen and Landau 2003). It is seen as an 'easy' form of access and it clearly introduces a series of biases. However, I argue that in addition to producing genuine and useful knowledge about a hard-to-reach population, working with and through SPOs can also have particular process-benefits if the relationship between researchers and SPOs is explicitly collaborative, builds capacity, and contributes to the translation of research findings into improved conditions for the populations being studied.

This chapter discusses an example of research explicitly designed to inform and change non-governmental and governmental action towards migrants. I argue that working collaboratively with SPOs can be particularly valuable in this form of research. However, this should not be understood as suggesting different standards of methodological adequacy for action- or policy-oriented research versus research primarily aimed at the academy or concerned with broader theory-building or hypothesis-testing. To be credible, and indeed ethical, action- and policy-oriented research must be based on methodologically solid research at all times (Jacobsen and Landau 2003). All research with urban self-settled migrants has to deal with the same technical challenges of a missing sampling frame, accessibility, trust, and logistic feasibility. Finally, while action-oriented research has a more obvious need to build an implementing audience as part of the research process, theory-building and -testing research should nonetheless consider how it relates to a practitioner audience and how the generated data is likely to be used and by whom. This is especially the case if the research is concerned with vulnerable groups or with forms of vulnerability (Turton 2003).

In the rest of the chapter I briefly summarise some of the recent methodological literature on surveying migrants, in particular in (South) Africa, with a focus on common biases and limitations encountered in attempting large-scale surveying of migrant populations who live dispersed among host populations. I then present a description of my case study: first a very brief note on migrant populations in South Africa and what makes them a difficult population to survey, and then an outline of the service-provider survey method we employed. This is followed by an analysis of the biases introduced by this method, an evaluation of how these biases relate to biases in other survey techniques, and their possible impacts on the usefulness of the data. The limitations discussed include urban, nationality, documentation, gender and vulnerability biases, as well as respondent duplication, strategic responses and 'intermediary' quality control and interests. Finally, I outline the key benefits of the service-provider survey approach, which are logistical and financial feasibility, research capacity building within the migrant rights service provider sector, and a more direct connection between data collection and data use.

SURVEYING MIGRANTS: RECENT SCHOLARSHIP

After a long phase of relative silence on methodological issues in forced migration research (Jacobsen and Landau 2003), methodological reflection has recently expanded significantly (see *Journal of Refugee Studies* Special Issue 20(2) in 2007, for example). Since refugee and migration studies are multi-disciplinary fields, the role of large-scale quantitative studies is contested, although they are much more established in demography-centred migration studies than in legal and political-science-centred refugee studies. While some see surveys as generally inappropriate for capturing what is really important about refugee and migrant experiences (Rodgers 2004), others see surveys, in all their imperfection, as fulfilling important academic and, not least, strategic goals. In the latter camp, Jacobsen and Landau argue that large-scale, quantitative data on migrants is important for making well-founded policy recommendations, which cannot appropriately be supported only by isolated and small-scale case studies (Jacobsen and Landau 2003).

It is well known that surveying cross-border migrants in a representative fashion poses a series of difficulties. Over 20 years ago, Fawcet and Arnold (1987) enumerated four common problems. These are the lack of a sampling frame; high costs of national studies; high non-response rates; and the likelihood of dishonest and strategic responses (Fawcett and Arnold 1987: 1531–2). Fawcet and Arnold also note the common tendency of researchers to use unrepresentative sampling methods to address the lack of a sampling frame, including organisation-based or snowball sampling, or sampling from areas of high concentration of out- or in-migration (Fawcett and Arnold 1987).

Alice Bloch (2007), in a recent review of methodological challenges in surveying refugees, adds to and elaborates on several issues raised by Fawcett and Arnold. These include the usefulness of a trusted intermediary between researcher and respondent to address issues of fear and suspicion (Bloch 2007: 234, 236), and the dangers of gatekeeping and limited networks if respondents are identified by snowballing from a limited number of refugee organisations (Bloch 2007: 235). Bloch also notes the importance of language in ensuring accessibility to respondents and comparability of translated questionnaires across communities (Bloch 2007: 240), which links with her discussion of appropriate modes of data collection (e.g. face-to-face, written self-completion, etc.). She concludes by emphasising the need for extensive exploratory work with the target community and flexibility during the field-work process in order to enable good research quality.

To address the lack of list-based sampling frames for migrants, such as voters' rolls or census lists, surveyors often use spatially defined sampling frameworks such as house-to-house sampling. However, authors critically evaluating recent surveys of migrants and refugees in South Africa note the inadequacy of most spatially-defined random sampling frameworks for studying mobile populations in inner-city areas (Vigneswaran 2007). Logistical issues of safety and low response rates are also highlighted as key challenges in the inner-city context (Vigneswaran 2007). Singh et al. (2008) present a highly involved spatially-defined sampling methodology which claims to enable representative sampling within specified neighbourhoods and nationality groups, but they also encounter extensive and expensive logistical difficulties in implementing this framework. While the creative efforts made by these researchers to approximate representative sampling methods are valuable, they highlight the usefulness of considering non-spatially-defined sampling frames.

The key concern of all these methodological discussions is the quality of the *data collection process*. They do not discuss what is to be done with the data once it has been collected, nor whether any link exists between modes of collection and later data use. Some researchers see extensive consultation with 'communities' and migrant organisations before and during the research as mainly about improving the quality of the data by enabling access, identifying where 'hidden' migrants are located, and ensuring cross-cultural comparability of concepts and terms (Bloch 2007; Parrado et al. 2005). While the connection between research process and data use is purportedly central to 'action research' approaches (Melrose 2001), there is also not much written about the details of how this is to be achieved. This is a gap in the methodological literature that my discussion of service-provider-based surveying aims to address to some extent.

Addressing the Sampling Frame, Logistical Feasibility and Data Use

Given these recognised challenges in surveying migrants, there are three arguments for SPO-mediated surveying, each addressing a different kind of methodological problem. The first problem is the most commonly written about, relating to the nature of the population being studied: the lack of a sampling frame. One of the possible ways of addressing this is a methodology which aims to approximate generalisability through a combination of large sample size, data diversity and comparative data analysis techniques.

Working through SPOs allows for larger overall sample sizes because surveys are cheaper to run over larger areas and longer periods of time compared to fieldworker-conducted surveys. For the same reasons, they allow for a diverse sample, since it is less financially and logistically necessary to restrictively sample only specific neighbourhoods or nationalities. Of course, large samples are not inherently less biased than small samples if the selection process is biased, but larger samples do allow for more robust disaggregation and stratification of the collected data. Post-hoc stratification of the data enables us to monitor whether previously identified groups such as women, certain nationalities, or undocumented migrants are sufficiently included in the final sample. If there is sufficient knowledge of the population distribution from other surveys, the data can be weighted to compensate for under-sampling of certain groups.

This is why SPO-mediated surveys are useful particularly in contexts where they are complementary to other studies. While the collaborative process elements of SPO-mediated surveying are valuable on their own, the usefulness of such research for helping to understand the characteristics of the study population is especially great if it is coupled with other surveys using other sampling access points. For example, the survey under discussion here was also administered to a random sample of people waiting in line to apply for asylum at four Refugee Reception Offices around South Africa. Since this is also a biased sample, including only those attempting to access asylum, it would have been ideal also to conduct a door-to-door version of the survey in city neighbourhoods with large migrant populations. This was not financially feasible, but previous door-to-door surveys covering other research questions gave us some indication of the migrant population composition in particular urban neighbourhoods by gender, nationality and documentation status. While no single survey results in a sample which is representative of the overall national population of migrants and refugees, comparing the different sample compositions allows us to be conscious of probable biases which can then be included in the interpretation and reporting of the findings.

The desire for larger sample sizes brings us to the second problem, which is very familiar to most researchers: the question of financial and logistical feasibility. Some research organisations are able to raise and dedicate the resources required for a national survey of migrants with thousands of respondents and tens of fieldworkers, and such surveys are very valuable. In practice, however, such surveys are few and far between and many organisations with worthy research questions and agendas cannot afford them. Given limited resources, small research teams and inhospitable survey sites, how can one achieve the broadest and largest possible sample of migrant respondents? I argue that working with and through existing organisations is a very cost-effective strategy and may be the only financially feasible option in some cases.

Third, and in my opinion most important, is the data use problem, which is in effect an ethical problem. What will the collected data be used for and who will use it? Although good research methodology textbooks always state that data collection techniques should be designed with a clear data use in mind, there is rarely any discussion in these textbooks, or in the methodological literature, of data dissemination techniques and how these might relate to data collection. This is particularly striking in migration and forced migration research, in spite of the oft-claimed advocacy goals of the research (Polzer 2007). Without privileging policy-oriented research over other research (Bakewell 2008), data use is fundamentally an ethical question. If researchers choose to explicitly ask migrants, refugees or other vulnerable people about their current problems and needs, this creates an obligation for active engagement with the needs that are then expressed (Jacobsen and Landau 2003; Turton 2002). By working with service provider organisations to collect the data, I argue, researchers can help to integrate the research findings into the work of existing organisations, therefore increasing the likelihood that the data will be used to the benefit of the surveyed populations.

This discussion therefore acknowledges that conducting refugee and migrant research through NGO or community-organisation intermediaries can be a question of convenience (as mentioned critically by Bloch 2007; Jacobsen and Landau 2003) but that, if carefully done, it can also be a more reflected and conscious process in terms of the values of ethical research.

THE MIGRANT RIGHTS MONITORING PROJECT PUBLIC SERVICE ACCESS SURVEY

The appropriate method for surveying migrants depends to a large extent on the context of migration in a country. South Africa is a regional economic hub as well as one of the most stable and prosperous countries on the continent, and so has been at the centre of a centuries-old regional labour migration system as well as attracting new flows of forced migrants from across the continent since the early 1990s (Wa Kabwe-Segatti and Landau 2008). South Africa has a policy of urban integration for asylum seekers and refugees, meaning they live dispersed throughout the general population rather than being constrained to camps. Economic migrants are also widely dispersed throughout the country. Important and large groups of migrants are undocumented, including many economic migrants from the region, most Zimbabweans fleeing economic and political crisis since 2000, and significant numbers of refugees who are not able to access the inefficient asylum application system (CoRMSA 2008). Methodological implications of this migration context, as in many similar contexts, are the lack of clear spatial or bureaucratic sampling frames, logistical and language difficulties in accessing dispersed and diverse populations, and widespread distrust of researchers.

Because of the urban dispersed settlement policy, most basic welfare needs are expected to be met by public services (schools, clinics, etc.) and by the migrants themselves through the market (rental accommodation, employment, etc.). There are a wide range of non-governmental organisations that provide services to migrants, refugees and asylum seekers, but mainly in an auxiliary capacity, without providing complete care. Types of service provider organisations include legal advice offices, basic welfare organisations, shelters, special-issue advocacy organisations (e.g. access to education or health), faith-based organisations, and refugee self-help organisations. There are widely differing levels of organisational formality and reach, with some working nationally and many limited to one locality. Mandates are also affected by whether the organisation is a formal implementing partner to the United Nations High Commission for Refugees (UNHCR), in which case they are supposed only to serve recognised asylum seekers and refugees. Other kinds of organisation, for example faith-based groups, generally do not discriminate by legal status. There are some existing networks among these organisations, including city-based networks and a national network under the Consortium for Refugees and Migrants in South Africa (CoRMSA), but apart from holding regular information-sharing meetings, these networks do not have many shared activities.

It is in this migration and organisational context that the Migrant Rights Monitoring Project (MRMP) was developed by the Forced Migration Studies Programme in the University of the Witwatersrand.[1] The MRMP is a multi-year research programme whose aim, as the name suggests, is to monitor the extent to which the legal rights of migrants and refugees in South Africa are being upheld in practice, and to provide national data showing change over time in rights protection. The data collected is explicitly designed to inform advocacy activities by other organisations in civil society for the protection of migrant and refugee rights, and to inform govern-mental action. The MRMP covers a wide variety of rights, including access to documentation, rights during arrest and deportation, and socio-economic rights. We use a wide variety of methodologies to monitor these rights, including several different surveys, in-depth case studies and qualitative methods. This paper will focus only on the MRMP Public Service Access Survey (PSAS). Apart from cover-ing basic demographic information about migrant respondents (sex, age, length of time in country, documentation, education level) the PSAS focuses on access to socio-economic rights in education, health care, housing, employment and social welfare.

To provide a sense of the survey's scope, here are some brief examples of the kinds of information produced by the PSAS:

- Only 12 per cent of surveyed respondents have school age children with them in South Africa, but 19 per cent of those school age children are not attending school.

- 59 per cent of the respondents have never required health care since their arrival in South Africa, and 67 per cent of those who have did not experience any problems accessing health care. Language problems and lack of documentation were the main kinds of problems experienced.

- 66 per cent of respondents live in privately rented flats, with 60 per cent of these in sub-tenancy arrangements. The dom-inant accommodation challenge is overcrowding, which is significantly more common for undocumented than for documented migrants.

- Regarding employment, the well-educated respondents (with tertiary degrees) are no more likely to be working than the less educated (with primary education). There are sig-nificant differences in unemployment rates by nationality, with Congolese reporting higher unemployment rates than other nationalities. Police harassment was the most com-monly noted concern among those who were working.

Between July 2007 and December 2008, the PSAS collected 1864 questionnaires through ten partner service provider organisations in the four main urban areas of South Africa (Johannesburg, Pretoria, Cape Town and Durban).[2] The SPO selection was intended to be as broad as possible for each city, but with an initial focus on established and institutionalised NGOs over smaller community-based and refugee-self-help organisations. This is because partner organisations were required to use their own, existing staff resources to contribute to the project. Furthermore, working through refugee organisations would have biased the sample too strongly towards documented and political migrants, while we were also interested in undocumented and economic migrants. In practice, however, this bias remained in place by working through established NGOs as well, as discussed further below.

Data collection and respondent sampling has had several characteristics which have been important to the success of the project so far: a) continuous collection of data over 18 months, b) maximum coverage but flexible sampling of SPO clients; and c) ease of engagement with the survey instrument by SPOs and respondents.

The data collection was continuous, reaching each new client as they arrived into the service provider programmes, rather than being concentrated in a short time period. On the one hand, this gives the data a continuous element over time, through which changes in migrant experiences can be traced month by month over time when aggregated. This gives the survey (especially after its 18 month running time) a significant advantage over other surveys which have either been one-off cross sections (CASE 2003) or repeated cross sections with significant breaks in between (such as the FMSP 'African Cities' Johannesburg Study in 2003 and 2006). As importantly, the continuous process has meant that SPOs could fit the data collection into their ongoing work rather than taking time and resources out of their programmes to focus on data collection for an intensive period of time.

This leads into the maximum coverage but flexible sampling method adopted. Each SPO was requested to include as many of their new clients as possible in the survey, preferably all new clients, but it was up to each organisation to decide on how this would be accomplished. In some cases, clients would complete the questionnaire while waiting to see legal counsellors or social workers, while in others the questionnaire would be built into regular rights-awareness training workshops. In other organisations, it was included in the exit-interview after a six-month welcoming programme for new migrants, or into English classes for French-speakers. In practice, there were some problems with continuity of commitment by SPO staff, partly due to insufficiently regular check-ups by myself, so that actual coverage of migrant clients was not close to complete. This introduces an additional element of uncertainty into the sampling. However, given the emphasis on sample size and diversity in the overall sampling concept, this does not invalidate the entire approach, since it was understood from the beginning that regularity and comparability of the sub-samples making up the surveyed whole would not be possible in any case.

The comparability of responses was brought in through the use of a relatively simple and accessible questionnaire of closed, pre-coded questions, used by all SPOs. This questionnaire was translated into English, French, Swahili, Somali and Portuguese.[3] Complementing the flexibility premise above, the questionnaire was designed to allow for self-completion on the SPO premise, or for assistance/interviewing by an SPO staff member. To facilitate SPO assistance to respondents without requiring staff to speak all the relevant languages, the non-English versions of the questionnaire also include the English original for each question. This still created problems for respondents who were not literate in their home languages or whose home languages were not included in the translations if no SPO staff could speak their language; an issue, as elsewhere, which was particularly noticeable for Somali women, as reported by SPOs.

Because of the relatively long time-frame of the 'data collection phase' of the research, and the commencement of 'data analysis' and 'data use' while data was still being collected, some level of iterative adaptation of the research process was possible. For example, the original group of participating SPOs expanded, and there was a shift from initially not providing any funding to partner organisations to providing some organisations with small monthly stipends to support data collection interns or volunteers. This change, while increasing the volume and predictability of monthly data collection, may also have impacted on data quality issues by creating new incentives for falsifying data.

The long time-frame and continuous, iterative engagement with SPO partners enabled the most important element of this survey methodology: namely the partnership and capacity building element. The survey instrument was designed after consultation visits with all partners and a draft was then discussed with them again and adapted on the basis of these discussions. Each SPO was visited individually and trained in the purpose and use of the questionnaire. Each SPO was also called regularly to provide feedback on the data collection process. Completed questionnaires were posted by SPOs to the Forced Migration Studies Programme as soon as a stack was collected, and so data entry was continuous. The entered data was analysed twice during the data collection process (in January 2008 with 317 completed surveys and in June 2008 with 890 completed) and findings shared with all SPOs in a data summary report. These reports included the raw percentages of answers to each question as well as narrative analysis of the key findings and basic advocacy pointers arising from the findings. The initial January 2008 data summary was discussed with all SPOs to ensure that the format was understood and useful. All SPOs were encouraged to request specific analysis of the data to suit their specific advocacy or programming needs, e.g. pulling out comparative data on education access across cities, or comparing Zimbabwean access to education with other nationalities. This offer has so far been used only by two organisations, but in those cases has successfully contributed to local advocacy and awareness-raising campaigns, based on feedback from the partner organisations.

LIMITATIONS OF SURVEYING THROUGH SERVICE PROVIDER ORGANISATIONS

Surveying migrants through SPOs in South Africa brings certain biases with it, many of which are likely to apply in other country contexts as well where there are integrated and diverse migrant populations who are served by NGOs. These include urban, nationality, documentation, gender and vulnerability biases. Other data problems are respondent duplication, strategic responses and the quality of SPO staff as 'researchers', as well as their potential interest in constructing certain outcomes in the data. I will comment briefly on each of these issues and note the extent to which they pose greater or similar liabilities in data quality compared with some other recent South African migrant surveys.

Urban bias

Working through SPOs in South Africa introduces two kinds of urban bias: urban versus small town and rural bias, and inner city versus township and informal settlement bias. Virtually all migrant-oriented SPOs are based in the main metropolises in South Africa (Johannesburg, Pretoria, Cape Town and Durban). These are the same cities where the government's Refugee Reception Offices are located, apart from Port Elizabeth, where there is an RRO but relatively few established migrant SPOs. While there are clearly large concentrations of migrants in these cities, there are also important and large non-citizen communities in the rural border areas (especially bordering Mozambique and Zimbabwe), and largely unstudied but significant non-citizen populations in smaller towns and secondary cities around the country (CoRMSA 2008).

The urban/non-urban distribution of migrants is of course not random: there are important differences between the average characteristics of urban migrants (more refugees and asylum seekers, more educated, often from urban backgrounds, some women and families), small-town migrants (mainly single, young, entrepreneurial men from specific national communities such as Somalis, Ethiopians, or Pakistanis who may or may not have asylum documentation), and rural border area migrants (mixture of long-term residents and circular labour migrants, less education, often from rural backgrounds, very few with asylum and refugee documentation). Furthermore, the different contexts lead to different experiences for non-citizens in terms of access to basic services and relations with host communities.

Regarding the second kind of urban bias, most migrant SPOs are based in or close to inner cities. This means that they are well-located to serve migrants resident there, but not necessarily easily accessible to residents of townships and informal settlements more removed from the city core. The Excelsior Centre in Cape Town is an exception to this in our set of partner SPOs, as is the Mthwakazi Arts and Culture organisation which does regular outreach to Zimbabweans in townships and informal settlements around Johannesburg. Some of the legal organisations have clients who travel from outer-city areas and even other towns to seek assistance. In spite of these exceptions, people living outside the inner city are relatively under-serviced by

SPOs, and are therefore also not reached by our survey. As above, this is important because the nationality, gender, employment and demographic characteristics as well as experiences of inner-city and informal settlement-based migrants are likely to be significantly different. For instance, the 10 per cent of survey respondents who report living in informal settlements are significantly more likely to be Zimbabwean, undocumented, less educated, and unemployed than those living in inner-city accommodation.

Most previous surveys of migrants in South Africa share these forms of urban bias by either explicitly limiting the geographical areas of focus to specific neighbourhoods in inner-city Johannesburg (Singh et al. 2008; Vigneswaran 2007), or Johannesburg and other cities (McDonald et al. 1999), or surveying through urban-based Refugee Reception Offices and urban-based refugee communities (CASE 2003). Exceptions are the national migration survey carried out by the South African Human Sciences Research Council in 2001–02 which included rural and peri-urban areas (Kok et al. 2006).

Nationality bias

People of different nationalities have different likelihoods of using formal service providers. For example, Somalis, Ethiopians and Eritreans do not use the mainstream migrant rights SPOs very often, and certainly less than their respective percentages in the overall non-citizen population in South Africa. Mozambicans are the most extreme case. After Zimbabweans, they are the largest foreign nationality in the country but only make up 0.3 per cent of the survey respondents. Asian migrants from Pakistan, Bangladesh and China also do not make use of migrant NGOs. In contrast, Congolese and Zimbabweans are well-represented among SPO clients, but not according to their respective prevalence in the overall population. Congolese make up 37.5 per cent of the survey respondents, followed by 29.3 per cent Zimbabweans, even though there are probably four times as many Zimbabweans in the country overall than Congolese. Nationality bias in this survey is exacerbated by the inclusion of some nationality-based SPOs. For example, in the initial group of SPO partners, our only Johannesburg-based partner was an organisation catering mainly to Zimbabweans. This meant that the Johannesburg data was not comparable with other cities, since it only reflected the experience of one nationality, and one with a significantly different profile than other nationalities. It was possible, of course, to compare the experience of Zimbabweans across cities. We later added additional SPOs in Johannesburg and achieved a more balanced sample.

Again, other migrant surveys (as well as qualitative studies) in South Africa commonly address problems of cost and research focus by limiting the nationalities they sample. The 2006 African Cities Project in Johannesburg only surveyed Somalis, Congolese, Mozambicans and South Africans (Vigneswaran 2007), while Singh et al. focused exclusively on Somalis, Congolese, Zimbabweans and South Africans (Singh et al. 2008). The Southern African Migration Project selected Basotho, Mozambicans, Zimbabweans, Malawians, Nigerians and 'Francophone Africans' as target groups, with other nationalities included in small numbers under sampling rubrics such as 'traders' (McDonald et al. 1999). The overall effect of such inbuilt nationality bias is that certain nationalities are almost never included in surveys (such as Ethiopians and Eritreans, or East African migrants). Apart from specific targeting of certain nationalities by surveyors, ethnographic research in Johannesburg confirms that certain nationalities – particularly Mozambicans – are particularly keen to remain 'hidden' from official or public eyes (Madsen 2004; Vidal 2007), showing their heightened resistance to surveying in general, and not only to SPO-based sampling.

Documentation bias

Documentation bias is very common in migration studies around the world. Our SPO survey had two kinds of documentation bias: self-selection and mandate-based selection. Undocumented migrants are often afraid to ask for help, do not trust institutions or do not think they have any rights which SPOs could assist them to claim. In addition to this self-selection, some organisations, especially those who are implementing partners of the UN High Commission for Refugees, have mandates to assist only documented asylum seekers and refugees. The result in our survey is that only 21.1 per cent of respondents reported being undocumented. This might be an undercount, since respondents may have claimed documentation they did not really have. In the overall migrant population in South Africa, the undocumented are in the majority, compared with documented asylum seekers and refugees.

The common problem of estimating wider documentation levels from migration surveys is illustrated, as one of many examples, by the SAMP survey which sampled its 501 respondents through a version of 'snowball' sampling starting from migrant community insiders. On the basis of this non-random sampling system, the authors then state that 93 per cent of respondents had some kind of official documentation. While they claim that this disproves the stereotype of migrants in South Africa not having documentation (McDonald et al. 1999:174), it is just as likely to be a sample self-selection and mediator-selection effect. The 2003 National Refugee Baseline Survey explicitly incorporated documentation-bias by only interviewing documented asylum seekers and refugees (CASE 2003). Door-to-door surveys such as the African Cities Project have high refusal rates, which are likely to be biased by documentation status as well.

Gender bias

Overall, the migrant and refugee population in South Africa has relatively few women, but the lack of a detailed sampling frame does not allow us to judge how the percentage of women accessing SPOs relates to their percentage in the population. SPOs may either over- or under-sample women, depending on the kinds of assistance programmes they offer. While our PSAS data cannot on its own tell us in which direction there may be bias, other data suggests that there may not be a very large bias overall. The service access survey that we conducted at the Refugee Reception Offices, e.g. where respondents were not pre-selected for persons who were already accessing SPO assistance,[4] suggests that there is no significant difference between male and female respondents on whether they reported ever having received welfare assistance from an NGO.

Most other surveys of migrants in South Africa either explicitly stratified their samples to include a certain gender balance or reported various gender-related biases, such as women being more likely to be at home during the day when surveyors were active (Vigneswaran 2007). Singh et al. went to great lengths to ensure random selection of respondents within households while taking into account cultural sensitivities about women only being interviewed by other women, and so were likely to have overcome most gender bias in their sample (Singh et al. 2008).

Vulnerability bias

While urban, documentation and gender bias are well-known and commonly discussed biases in migration surveys in general, vulnerability bias is a key bias when working through SPOs and has two elements: the need for assistance, and the ability to seek assistance. SPOs clearly only serve those people who need some kind of help, thereby excluding those from the sample who have no immediate legal, welfare or counselling needs. Non-citizens with enough resources (financial, social, informational) to look after themselves are therefore invisible. This is a serious concern if the goal is to achieve an overall picture of migrant life and service access in South Africa, since many positive experiences will be missed and negative evaluations may be over-emphasised. On the other hand, people who have needs may still be excluded from this survey if they do not have enough resources to reach SPOs in search of assistance. When comparing results from the Refugee Reception Office survey with the SPO survey, we see that respondents at SPOs are significantly more likely to have at least a completed secondary education than those at the Refugee Reception Offices.[5] This suggests that the least educated either have fewer assistance needs (which seems unlikely) or that they face barriers in accessing SPO assistance.

Non-SPO-based surveys might be assumed to have less vulnerability biases, but often levels of vulnerability are hidden in other biases, such as location and time-of-day biases. More economically successful migrants might be less likely to live in the oft-sampled 'migrant neighbourhoods' in the inner city, while working migrants are less likely to be at home in day-time house-to-house surveying.

Respondent duplication

In addition to these common respondent selection biases, there are several further data quality issues which relate to the actions of respondents and research 'intermediaries' once the respondents have been identified. One of these is respondent duplication. The reliability of surveys depends on each respondent only being recorded once. This was identified as a potential problem early on in consultations with SPOs, who are very aware of the fact that migrants often go to several SPOs in a city for different kinds of assistance. We therefore specifically included a note at the top and front of the questionnaire asking respondents not to fill in the questionnaire again if they had already done so elsewhere. This was also clearly articulated in SPO training regarding how to introduce the questionnaire to respondents. However, it is possible that some respondents will have overlooked this, or ignored it on purpose, wanting to pretend that they had not already sought assistance from another SPO. In a worst case scenario, respondent duplication could make up a large percentage of responses in each city. While it is possible to check the data for identical or very similar responses, it is possible that repeat respondents might change some of the responses they provide from one place to the next. Since the data 'intermediaries' (e.g. SPO staff) are different at each location, in contrast to 'normal' survey field workers who move from location to location, this data quality danger is also unlikely to be uncovered 'on the ground' by recognising repeaters.

Strategic responses

Similar to respondent duplication, strategic responses are probable, due to the likelihood of respondents perceiving a connection between the answers they give on the survey and the kinds of services they are hoping to receive at the SPO. The questionnaire introduction clearly states that it is separate from the SPO at which it is being completed, and that answers will in no way influence the services respondents get from the SPO. It is nonetheless possible that respondents feel that their responses will in some way influence immediate or future services in spite of the anonymity of the questionnaire. This means they might misrepresent potentially damaging information, such as claiming to have documentation when they do not, or exaggerate needs, such as the kind of accommodation they are in or employment needs.

The same kinds of strategic reporting bias are likely in other kinds of migration or social service related surveys as well (Bloch 2007: 242). The actual results of our survey, however, suggest that this bias is not as large as one may assume. Very few respondents reported that they were homeless, for example, with most stating they were in rental accommodation, even though access to accommodation is commonly identified as a key need and desire of migrants. Such strategic reporting might also have been reduced by the fact that there were virtually no questions about immediate food, clothes or money needs, with welfare-handout-related questions only dealing with whether such services had ever been received in the past. It is possible that past assistance may have been under-reported in order to justify claims for future assistance.

A corollary of strategic bias might be the ethical question of whether respondents felt they could refuse to participate in the survey without incurring penalties from the SPO. The right not to take part or to skip certain questions was stated in the written introduction to the survey and SPO staff were trained to emphasise this when assisting respondents or when handing out the questionnaire for self-completion, but it is likely that this message was not always received or believed by respondents. Although SPOs were requested to report back regularly on refusal rates, particularly on specific groups who refused more than others, this information was not provided systematically. Many SPOs relied on their clients to fill in the surveys themselves while in waiting rooms, where there was no-one to actively monitor who chose to complete the survey or not. Alternatively, many different SPO staff members assisted with the survey completion and did not then compare and compile observations on refusal rates. The potentially very important quality and ethical control measure of refusal rates therefore could not be monitored effectively with this method.

Intermediary characteristics: mandate and quality

Researcher-effects are omnipresent in social science research, but 'textbook' quantitative surveys are intended to minimise these effects with the aim of generating 'objective' results allowing for a comparison of 'real' differences between respondents (Neuman 2000: 69). When working through SPOs, there are two kinds of intermediary effects that can impact on the data. One is at the organisational level, as already mentioned above, where different mandates and focus areas can produce nationality, documentation and vulnerability effects. For example, people coming to a legal organisation are likely to have different kinds of problems than those coming to a faith-based basic welfare organisation.

The second intermediary effect lies at the level of the individuals within the SPOs who assist respondents with the questionnaire. This is a question of quality control. Since the implementation of the survey is, so to speak, radically decentralised in an SPO-based model, the overall research co-ordinator has little ability to carry out immediate quality control by conducting spot checks or repeat interviews, or by getting to know field staff well enough to judge whether they are filling in questionnaires on their own, or similar 'cheating'. Everyday quality control is therefore left to the individual SPO's management, where it is likely to get little if any attention, given that the management does not get any personal or organisational remuneration for contributing to the survey. Such quality control is extremely difficult even in professionally managed large-scale 'representative' surveys, as evidenced by the evaluation of the 2001–2002 Human Sciences Research Council Migration Survey which found extensive 'cheating' by field workers (Van Zyl 2006), and so is by no means a liability unique to decentralised SPO-based surveying. It is theoretically imaginable that an SPO or its staff members might try to systematically adjust the questionnaire responses to fulfil a particular political agenda, although this might be identified through careful analysis of the resulting data to identify any suspicious differences or patterns in responses between SPOs. There was no evidence of this when such an analysis was done of the PSAS. A much more common problem is simply wastage, where questionnaires are incomplete or wrongly or unclearly filled in, and then cannot be followed up once they have been sent in to the central collection point.

IMPACTS OF THESE LIMITATIONS ON DATA USE

Since the stated purpose of the Migrant Rights Monitoring Project is to produce data that is useful for advocacy purposes, what impacts do these biases and data limitations have on the usefulness of the survey findings? Clearly, as with other non-probability samples, an SPO-based survey can not be used to extrapolate or estimate various widely desired numbers, as a fully random national sample might. It cannot tell us the overall number of non-citizens in the country; the overall number of any national group or relative percentages of different nationalities in relation to each other; the overall gender-breakdown of non-citizens, or gender-breakdown within any national group; the overall documentation breakdown of non-citizens, or documentation breakdown within any national group; or overall levels of vulnerability and need among non-citizens or the vulnerability profile within any national group.

However, there is much valuable data which the survey can nonetheless provide. These include a nationality, gender, documentation and vulnerability profile of those non-citizens who access SPO assistance. This can then be compared with other sources of data, such as surveys conducted at the Refugee Reception Offices, or conducted door-to-door in migrant residential areas in Johannesburg, to identify differences in profile and therefore who is not accessing SPO assistance. For improving SPO services and outreach, this is useful. Also possible are comparisons between profiles and vulnerability levels of those national groups who access SPOs. Such an analysis clearly shows that Zimbabweans are more vulnerable than other groups in terms of documentation and accommodation access, but not in terms of health care access, for example. It is also possible to make comparisons between cities on migrant profiles, especially with the use of regression analysis to ensure the exclusion of confounding factors, such as different nationality profiles by city.

One key drawback of SPO-based sampling is that it might impact adversely on the communication of the results to policy makers if they perceive the survey methodology to be illegitimate. 'Representative sampling' is a powerful signal phrase for policy makers, whether or not actual representative sampling is achievable.

BENEFITS OF SURVEYING THROUGH SERVICE PROVIDERS

While SPO-based sampling might not have the same assumed policy legitimacy as complex, multi-stage approximations of random sampling – which are also useful and legitimate exercises, of course, and should continue to be pursued where logistically and financially possible – it has several important benefits which can directly increase its policy impact. These relate to the 'do-ability' of the research in the first place, but also to the level of involvement in the overall research design by the same organisations who are intended to make use of the data, thereby shortening the distance and time-lag between the research process and the use of research findings, and broadening the application of research findings.

Financial and logistical feasibility

A key barrier to conducting large-scale quantitative studies of migrants is often that they are too expensive. An SPO-based survey requires paying an experienced researcher to design and pilot the questionnaire, build or expand on a network of SPOs, train and maintain contact with the partners, analyse the data, and train partners in how to use the data. Data entry, once it has been collected monthly or sent in to a central place by the partners, can be outsourced or done by students. The major cost and logistical difficulty of a 'normal' survey falls away, however, which is hiring, paying and managing fieldworkers, and transporting and accommodating them around the country. Even if small stipends are made available to SPO-based interns or staff members, this personnel expenditure has the added impact of sustainably, strengthening the capacity of partner SPOs, and therefore the ability of the data not only to be collected but also to be used effectively.

SPO surveying also deals with other key logistical challenges commonly experienced during house-to-house research in (South) African cities, including researcher safety (Vigneswaran 2007). In addition, SPO-based surveying greatly reduces the non-response rate, which is high in house-to-house and street-based surveying of migrants. A national randomly selected household survey on migration conducted by the Human Sciences Research Council in 2001–2002 (N=4000 households) had a 43 per cent non-response rate from cross-border migrants (Van Zyl 2006: 148). Response rates are higher in SPOs because the respondent is in a place they already trust, to some extent, to be on 'their side', and because the person, by coming to that place, often has time on their hands and does not have other work to do. This does not mean that there are no refusals or that trust is assured; some partner SPOs reported outright refusals or partial refusals to complete the questionnaire especially when they attempted to use it during outreach activities with new clients.[6]

Active networks

As mentioned above, there are existing networks of migrant and refugee rights SPOs in South Africa, including city-based networks and a national network called the Consortium for Refugees and Migrants in South Africa. These networks formed the basis for approaching SPOs to partner on the survey, although not all network partners were survey partners and some survey partners were not part of the formal networks.

The existing networks are generally used for basic information exchange and to some extent for co-ordinating advocacy campaigns, but there are very rarely joint activities over any period of time among network partners, except on a bilateral basis. The survey was a practical and ongoing joint activity, which directly linked the organisations in a shared endeavour beyond their general shared interest in migrant rights. This was especially important for the smaller SPOs whose work is usually limited to their specific local clientele and who therefore said that they appreciated the feeling that their work and experience was feeding directly into a larger, national project. Activating a network through a shared activity such as a survey can have several side effects, such as encouraging other kinds of regular information exchange within the network, catalysing bilateral collaborations, and generally energising local outreach and advocacy efforts. The mention of all the participating SPOs in all written material based on the collected data also profiles the individual organisations to a broad audience as well as illustrating their embeddedness in an active network.

Research capacity building for evidence-based service provision and advocacy

Most migrant rights SPOs in South Africa do not have research experience. There are some large SPOs with extensive experience but often this experience is limited to specific people in the organisations or to policy research rather than client-based research. Furthermore, most SPOs, including the large and established ones, are focused on implementing programming rather than conducting basic profiling research on their own clients or the wider pool of possible clients, and their needs. The MRMP, by working with and through SPOs, therefore fulfils a triple function: a) using SPOs to access migrants for information about the wider needs of non-citizens in South Africa; b) profiling the SPOs' current and potential clientele to enable better internal services management and sector-wide service planning; and c) building capacity within individual SPOs and the sector at large in conducting and using research as both an advocacy and a management tool.

Just as the SPO-survey is an imperfect but nonetheless useful instrument for the aim of gathering overall data on migrants in South Africa, so it is also imperfect and useful as a management tool. Due to wanting to prevent respondent duplication, for example, no SPO was able to consistently survey all their clients, even if they wanted to make the requisite staff effort. The questionnaire was also not designed to evaluate existing SPO services, but rather to establish broader migrant needs and the extent to which rights are met by public institutions. Nonetheless, several of the larger NGOs have recognised the management value sufficiently to build the MRMP questionnaire into their internal client tracking processes, enabling them to more effectively compare and link their own work with that of other organisations. Other partners report using the survey data about their own clients, and the aggregate data for their city, in internal and network-wide strategic planning exercises to identify key areas for intervention.

SPOs can benefit from learning more about research practice so that they are better able to plan and conduct their own research, even if it is small-scale, on issues affecting their clients. It also assists them to learn how to use research conducted by others more effectively in informing their local work. The collaborative MRMP survey process assisted in building this capacity through formal training sessions in using the questionnaires and in how to use the summarised data outputs, but also through the more informal learning experience of regularly using the questionnaire and therefore having an example of a research instrument that SPO staff become familiar with over time. For many SPOs, a key benefit is overcoming the fear and mystique of conducting research by seeing it as something they can be part of themselves. The latter learning experience was repeatedly stated by the smaller partner organisations in feedback discussions and trainings.

Finally, the lead researchers at FMSP also gained from the close collaboration with SPOs. Compared with the more common arrangement of working with specifically hired and trained short-term field workers, SPO staff often have more grounded experience of their clients/respondents and can contribute productively in the research design and data analysis phases to ensure the relevance of the questions asked and the ways in which analysed data is presented.

The Migrant Rights Monitoring Project's experience shows that this form of engagement with SPOs also poses challenges for researchers. One challenge is that it requires teaching and training skills which are not usually associated with research. Longer time-frames for building and maintaining the partnerships are also needed, making this approach less appropriate for research projects with short project cycles or the need for fast data production. Even though the data collection process is effectively 'outsourced' to SPOs, the management time and effort required from a lead researcher is actually the same or greater than when data collection is done by trained field workers. Without a significant investment of time and energy into the consultation and training process, SPO-based surveying loses much of its potential. This leads us to the final and most important point of this chapter, which is how SPO-mediated surveying can narrow the gap between research and data use.

From data collection to data use

In the social sciences, and also in research on migration and refugees, there is often a gap between research process, research findings and the use of those findings in advocating for or implementing changes in policy or practice.

Often, research is conducted by different people than those who can use it to advocate for change. Researchers, advocates and implementers are usually not only in different institutions, but act at completely different levels: local organisations are assumed not to be able to use national data and national organisations are assumed not to need or be able to use local data. Linking local organisations and the data they can collect in a nationally comparative study to some extent overcomes these divisions between institutions and levels of action and analysis.

Moreover, advocates and implementers often cannot use research findings because they do not know about them. This is especially the case for local organisations, who may not hear about research that is conducted in other, but similar, locations or nationally. If they do hear about it they cannot imagine how they can use it locally. There is also often no way for them to contact the researchers to be able to adapt the findings to their local needs. Participating directly in data collection allows such organisations to think about how to use it on a regular basis.

Finally, from the perspective of national professional advocacy organisations such as the Consortium for Refugees and Migrants in South Africa, while they may have access to national or local research findings, they often miss opportunities for using data effectively because they are not present on the ground in different regions/cities. Local SPOs know more about when a local decision is about to be made about health care access or housing policy or street traders, for example, where research data could be used to good effect in influencing that policy. Similarly, local organisations do not have the capacity or knowledge to bring their local knowledge into national policy debates unless they are linked through such a collective survey.

CONCLUSION

This case study of the Migrant Rights Monitoring Project's Public Service Access Survey aims to illustrate two main points concerning methodological approaches to surveying migrants. First, migrant and refugee service provider organisations should not be seen as a 'bad practice' convenience solution to survey sampling, but as potentially valuable research collaborators. As with other sampling strategies, there are important representativity challenges and biases of working through service provider organisations and any researcher choosing this option must engage with these biases consciously and carefully. Ideally, a service provider-based survey should be conceived of as complementary to surveys using other sampling strategies so that differences in the samples can be compared to identify particularly important biases.

Second, and more generally, considerations of how data will be used and by whom should be incorporated directly into planning the data collection process. Working with service provider organisations so that they can use the data they collect requires time and particular forms of training and continuous engagement which must be planned into the methodology and not just appended to other common survey methodologies. It is important to note that there are of course many strategies for including service provider organisations in research processes without necessarily running a survey through their offices and staff. The option of conducting a service-provider mediated survey should therefore be seen as part of a larger catalogue of productive research partnerships where the appropriate form of partnership is determined by the intended research outcome. Similarly, the service-provider mediated survey should only be chosen when appropriate to the specific research question being asked. When both these conditions are fulfilled, then service-provider mediated surveys should be considered an important and legitimate tool in the migration studies and broader social sciences methodological arsenal.

ACKNOWLEDGEMENTS

Thanks go to Loren Landau, Darshan Vigneswaran and Hein de Haas, among others, for their comments on earlier versions of this chapter.

Notes

1. The MRMP is, in turn, part of a larger migrant and refugee rights programme funded by the Atlantic Philanthropies foundation in South Africa. FMSP gratefully acknowledges the support from Atlantic Philanthropies.

2. These SPOs are the African Disabled Refugee Organisation, Bechet School, Cape Town Refugee Centre, CARE (Johannesburg), Excelsior Empowerment Centre, Lawyers for Human Rights, Mennonite Central Committee (recently renamed Refugee Social Services), Mthwakazi Arts and Culture, South Africa Red Cross Society and the Scalabrini Centre.

3. The translations were confirmed by an independent second translator familiar with the project to enable identification and discussion of possible misunderstandings.

4. The Pretoria (Marabastad) survey was conducted by trained field workers over the space of two weeks in November 2007 (N=364), and the Durban survey was conducted in February 2008 (N=300). Both used the same questionnaire as the SPOs.

5. The effect remains highly significant even when taking differences of nationality and sex into account.

6. Comments made during feedback session 26 September 2007.

References

Bakewell, O. (2008) 'Research beyond the categories: the importance of policy irrelevant research into forced migration', *Journal of Refugee Studies* 21(4): 432–53.

Bloch, A. (2007) 'Methodological challenges for national and multi-sited comparative survey research', *Journal of Refugee Studies* 20(2): 230–47.

CASE (2003) 'National Refugee Baseline Survey: Final Report', Johannesburg: Community Agency for Social Enquiry.

CoRMSA (2008) 'Protecting Refugees, Asylum Seekers and Immigrants in South Africa', Johannesburg: Consortium for Refugees and Migrants in South Africa.

Fawcett, J.T. and F. Arnold (1987) 'The role of surveys in the study of international migration: an appraisal', *International Migration Review* 21(4, Special Issue: Measuring International Migration: Theory and Practice): 11523–540.

Jacobsen, K. and L. B. Landau (2003) 'The dual imperative in refugee research: some methodological and ethical considerations in social science research on forced migration', *Disasters* 27(3): 185–206.

Kok, P., J. Van Zyl and J. Pieterson (2006) 'The history and methology of the HSRC Surveys', in P. Kok, D. Gelderblom, J. Oucho and J. Van Zyl (eds.) *Migration in South and Southern Africa; Dynamics and Determinants*, Cape Town: HSRC Publishers.

Madsen, M. L. (2004) 'Living for home: policing immorality among undocumented migrants in Johannesburg', *African Studies* 63(2): 173–92.

McDonald, D. A., L. Mashile and C. Golden (1999) 'The Lives and Times of African Migrants and Immigrants in Post-Apartheid South Africa', SAMP Migration Policy Series, No. 13.

Melrose, M. J. (2001) 'Maximizing the rigor of action research: why would you want to? How could you?', *Field Methods* 13(2): 160–80.

Neuman, W. L. (2000) *Social Research Methods: Qualitative and Quantitative Approaches* (4th Edition ed.), Boston: Allyn and Bacon.

Parrado, E. A., C. McQuiston and C. A. Flippen (2005) 'Participatory survey research: integrating community collaboration and quantitative methods for the study of gender and HIV risks among Hispanic migrants', *Sociological Methods Research* 34(2): 204–39.

Polzer, T. (2007) 'Disseminating research findings in migration studies: methodological considerations', Johannesburg: Forced Migration Studies Programme.

Rodgers, G. (2004) '"Hanging out" with forced migrants; methodological and ethical challenges', *Forced Migration Review* 21.

Singh, G., B. Clark and K. Otwombe (2008) 'Creating a frame: random sampling in a non-homogeneously distributed urban migrant populations', DRAFT.

Turton, D. (2002) 'Forced displacement and the nation-state', in J. Robinson (ed.) *Displacement and Development*, Oxford: Oxford University Press.

Turton, D. (2003) 'Conceptualising Forced Migration', RSC Working Paper, 12.

Van Zyl, J. (2006) 'Evaluating the 2001-02 HSRC Migration Survey', in P. Kok, D. Gelderblom, J. Oucho and J. Van Zyl (eds.) *Migration in South and Southern Africa; Dynamics and Determinants*, Cape Town: HSRC Publishers.

Vidal, D. (2007) 'Living in, out of and between two cities: the migrants from Maputo in Johannesburg', *Inclusive African Cities*. Johannesburg, South Africa, 6–7 March 2007.

Vigneswaran, D. (2007) 'Lost in Space: Residential Sampling and Johannesburg's Forced Migrants', FMSP Migration Methods and Field Notes, 4.

Wa Kabwe-Segatti, A. and L. B. Landau (eds.) (2008) 'Migration in post-apartheid South Africa - Challenges and questions to policy makers', Paris: Agence Française de Développement.

Chapter 10

ANTHROPOLOGICAL APPROACHES TO STUDYING THE MOBILITY OF CHILDREN IN WEST AFRICA

Abdou Ndao

INTRODUCTION

Since the start of January 2008, Plan's West Africa Regional Office has been undertaking research on the mobility of children and young people in West Africa, with support from Plan UK and in collaboration with Terre des Hommes (Regional Technical Support Unit based in Togo), delegations from Terre des Hommes in Benin and Togo and LASDEL-Benin (Laboratory for Analysis and Research into Social Dynamics and Local Development), along with Plan's national offices in Benin and Togo. The objective was to carry out an ethnographic study of the mobility of children and young people along the main routes through Benin, Togo, Ghana and Nigeria.

There are two fundamental reasons behind undertaking a study of the mobility of children. First, we wanted to break through the 'negativistic' image which goes hand in hand with child mobility, and whose importance had been indicated in many studies. We seriously wanted to consider the efforts made by children and young people in the region. A pragmatic approach to the behaviour of children and young people should enable us to support them better. Mobility is not just a negative thing. Fundamentally, it is even positive. This positive understanding of mobility derives in particular from the children's experiences described in previous studies. Fall and Massart (2007) documented the importance and effectiveness of mobility among children and young people, both to obtain financial resources of their own, in order to realise their aspirations for emancipation (Guinea Bissau) and to tackle the difficulties of recreating their own communities (Niger). Indeed, children here seem to be active players in the contemporary world.

Then, it appeared to us – in the light of the available official statistics – that the overwhelming majority of mobile children are first and foremost within the African continent, and particularly West Africa. This view contrasts sharply with the view which gives greater significance (at least in the media) to South–North mobilities over intra-African mobilities (Chronique du CEPED 1998). We saw this readjustment of perspectives to be essential for greater understanding of the mobility of children and young people. There is certainly a multiplicity of studies and approaches to this problem, and there is no shortage of those which concentrate on slavery.

However, approaching the subject via children's mobility is quite novel, and is a response to the desire to move away from the inflexibility inherent in the concept of migration, and to refine our understanding of mobility described as slavery in the light of the experiences of the 'victims'. In short, the notion of mobility allows us to picture the movements of children and young people in their full empirical complexity. Greater empirical refinement will enable us to design better programmes and to respect the efforts made by these thousands of people.

The objective of this research is to understand how the mobility of young people and children is organised in West Africa, particularly in Benin, Togo, Ghana and Nigeria. In more practical terms, this research tries to answer the following questions: Why do children move on? What routes do they follow? What forms of mobility are observed? What are their motivations? What are their strategies?

What difficulties do they encounter? What is their perception of these difficulties? What are their responses and what is the thinking behind their decision to travel? What are the impacts of their mobility practices and what resources do they use in their mobility?

RESEARCH METHODOLOGY

Research sites

The research sites covered the coastal countries around the Gulf of Guinea, particularly Benin, Togo, Ghana and Nigeria. The choice of sites was made on the basis of several criteria such as the density of internal mobility, the plurality of professional areas where children are involved, the institutional value for Plan and Terre des Hommes of documenting certain routes more specifically, and the relationship between the local (mobility within each country) and the transnational (abroad).

In this ethnographic survey, these four countries are seen as a coherent historical entity. In fact, approaching the subject from the mobility angle goes beyond the administrative demarcations which do not determine the movements of children, but which constrain them by creating both difficulties and opportunities. The wish to identify these historic continuities and discontinuities in mobility within the coastal area led to a diversification in the survey sites. In choosing these sites, we considered a number of variables such as the range of mobility (local/transnational), the setting (rural/urban), ethnicity (Fon/Mina etc.), gender (apprentice blacksmiths/porter girls), and according to production modes and sectors (agricultural/non-agricultural/commercial). The diversity of these variables in the choice of sites made it possible to document various forms of mobility and to monitor children with sociologically diverse profiles. Table 1 summarises the main sites surveyed.

Table 1: Research sites

Benin	Togo	Nigeria
The forge in Dantokpa	The daily markets: the great market of Adawlato, Edjranawé, Abattoir	Abeokuta quarries in Ogun State
The Dantokpa market	Porter houses	Lagos
The Salesian Sisters' centre at Dantokpa market	Vo: Vogan, Akoumape-Apeyeme, Sadaga-Apeyeme, Yohonou, Bokototsoanyi,	
Oasis centre	Vo-Kponou, Ative-Kossidame	
	Lacs: Anfoin Aname	
	Afangnan: Attitogon, Avoutokpa, Keyome	
	Yoto: Kouve, Ahepe, Tabligbo	
The Brigade for the Protection of Minors Centre		
The village of Kpanoukpade in the commune of Misserete		
North Benin in the cotton plantations: Gounade, Nodi, Dassari, Materi, Mari, Kounde, Makirou-Gourne, Ounet, Toura, Sirikou, Goumori, Anmanki, Ndaly, Bogodori		

Different criteria were adopted for the choice of the children to be surveyed, who were aged 8 to 25 years in nearly 75 per cent of cases. In particular, these were: 1) children working in fixed production areas (Dantokpa market forge), to give a better understanding of the routes followed by the children as well as the tactics used by them in migration; 2) children working in markets and not fixed to any precise place, but moving according to the opportunities offered to them by the informal economy; 3) children working at production sites considered dangerous (stone quarries in Nigeria), to give a better understanding also of the mechanism for their socialisation in the workplace and the complexity of the transnational routes followed (from Benin to Nigeria); 4) children taken in by NGOs such as Terre des Hommes in Togo and Benin and put into OASIS centres, until they can be re-housed or receive other forms of legal protection (such as through the Brigade for the Protection of Minors).

Data collection through play

This ethnographic research relied on a number of different qualitative tools which can be grouped into two types. The first group is made up of classic ethnographical tools such as interviews, focus groups, informal discussions and participant study. The second contains more play-related methodologies such as the news of the future, lifelines, the shining sun, and the use of theatrical and photographic means of expression. These new methodologies – highly suited to studies into childhood – have become standard practice over the past three years within the research team from Plan's West Africa Regional Office (Dénommée 2007).

Methodological Note 1: News of the future

The objective is to learn the future plans of children and young people through the use of radio interviews. For this exercise, subjects are put into pairs: journalist and interviewee. The children are asked to imagine and prepare the radio news as it might be five years into the future. They are the stars of the show and must prepare the questions and the answers they will use. Each one carries out an interview with the other. The interviewee projects himself or herself five years into the future and, ideally, indicates: where they are, what they are doing, and with whom. Go through the conversations with the young people. Ask for explanations or clarifications of aspects which seem obscure. Discuss the activity with them, their opinions and possible modifications. Take the opportunity to ask them for their permission to use the interviews at a later date (Dénommée 2007: 12).

These play methods have several clear advantages in the context of research into childhood in Africa. While continuing with the tried and tested classic methods (focus groups, interviews etc.), these methodological innovations make it possible to ensure greater involvement of children in the process of producing and organising knowledge. In fact, the primary objective is to hear what children are saying and to give greater consideration to their preoccupations in the process of assembling and validating knowledge.

Methodological Note 2: The shining sun

'The shining sun' is a game which was initiated by ethnographer Carole with a view to enabling us subtly to collect information from the children relating to their respective journeys. Six chairs need to be set out in a circle, and then seven children play the game, with six of them sitting on the chairs and one of them in the middle of the circle.

The rules of the game consist of the leader (the child in the middle of the circle who has no chair) drawing on their own personality and experiences (regions travelled, activities undertaken, etc.) to come up with statements, while each of the other six will think individually to see whether they can identify with each of the statements. Then, when the signal is given, all the children who identify with a given statement will get up to swap seats. Given that there are fewer chairs than there are players, the slowest one will be left without a chair and takes their predecessor's place in the middle of the circle. They will then come up with new statements for the other players to consider, and so on...

However, there are a number of difficulties, methodologically speaking. One of these is the relationship between the research areas and tools, and between the children and the researchers in validating the ethnographic body of data produced. Questions can arise over which types of knowledge to prioritise: the children's knowledge or the researchers' knowledge.

The second limitation is linked to the relationship between artificiality and naturalness, particularly regarding the use of tools of expression which place the children in a play situation. This can lead to questions over the simulation and the sincerity of the information provided. Certainly, scientific credibility is not a characteristic of the use of these forms of expression through play. This limitation is generally inherent in the epistemological and methodological foundations of social and human sciences. But nothing is expressed outside of a specifically organised framework. Within the context of this research, we saw that these settings stimulated the children's creativity, since they felt more at ease. Under these conditions, the researcher finds himself or herself obliged to bring their skills into play, to compare their observations with those of the children.

Methodological Note 3: Lifeline

Equipment required: 1 long rope, 10 flower heads, 10 stones, 2 to 3 sheets of drawing paper, coloured pencils (or felt-tipped pens). The 'Lifeline' exercise helps to break the ice rapidly between people and uses creative media, enabling the child's trajectory to be mapped out in a playful way. In fact, this simple technique works so well that the authors have been able to apply it with conclusive results to adults from different cultures, especially when it was difficult for the person to reconstruct a clear chronological sequence of events in their life.

Moreover, after three months in the field, ethnographers gathered a considerable mass of qualitative data which were stored and analysed using NVIVO 8.0 software, namely 81 group interviews, 112 individual interviews, 20 focus groups and 3 future news programmes.

MOBILITY TYPES AND STRATEGIES

This section will distinguish between the different forms of mobility among children and young people which we were confronted with during the empirical research phase. This is a descriptive typology.

Agricultural mobilities

These occupy an important place and can be identified in this study in the north of Benin, in the cotton plantations. Thus we use the term 'agricultural mobility' to describe mobilities which involve work in the agricultural sector. A great number of these mobilities rely on the existence of a cash crop (cotton in the case of Benin). Children are a significant workforce. Ethnography conducted there suggests that four mobility factors/aspects can be identified in agricultural mobility. A description of these factors can give us a clear idea of the kinds of life experiences gained by these children and young people (Imorou 2008). First, we have what might be termed simple territorial mobility, where the children and (often) their parents migrate in a more or less temporary or permanent way according to the severity of their reasons for leaving. They are looking for more fertile land and/or employment as agricultural workers in cotton production.

A second mobility factor concerns inter-employer mobility which happens when there is a change of employer within a single village, often without the child's consent. The employer's attitude thus has very significant consequences for this type of mobility,

depending on whether or not he honours his contractual engage-
ments and whether or not he is aggressive. Considerable cohorts of
children can be seen changing employer, looking for better day-to-
day living conditions or simply fleeing economic exploitation (they
are not paid) or violence which they have to endure, along with
harassment, name-calling and so on. This inter-employer mobility is
very frequent in agricultural systems.

A third mobility factor concerns mobility of status arising
from 'the process of the change of status for former agricultural
workers (...) similar to ascendant mobility' (Imorou 2008). This
sub-form of mobility reveals the mechanisms and strategies for the
positive redeployment of agricultural workers. These compel respect
and consideration from their native environment, for what they represent and what they have endured during their migratory process.
However, these redeployments may turn out to be negative.

Mobility of role is the fourth factor. The value of this notion is
that it can give a more balanced assessment of the nature of power
struggles between employers and employees. Indeed, as Imorou
(2008) has noted, the quality of these relationships is proportional to
the extent to which employers respect their contractual obligations
towards children. When the employers do not honour their obligations, they find themselves in a situation where the children often
make formal complaints in order to receive what is due to them.

In conclusion, it could be said that experiences of agricultural
mobility are extremely varied and, apart from the immediate purely
economic opportunities, the attractiveness of certain areas which
are rich in land or cash crops, and the types of workplace relations
encountered, will determine movements. This observation shows the
migrant's vulnerability in social settings which are poorly regulated
or run in an arbitrary manner by the employer, the native community or the owner.

During the ethnographic survey, national agricultural mobilities
were identified (such as those we have documented in the North
of Benin), but also international mobilities (particularly into Ghana
and Nigeria). Similar phenomena have been documented in Ghana
(Sabates-Wheeler et al. 2005).

Environmental mobilities

This category of mobility is principally due to environmental degradation which has had a lasting effect on ecosystems. Thus we have seen progressive and lasting problems such as soil infertility, shrinkage, successive drought, flooding and so on. Many of these children mention 'malfunctioning climate' when explaining their mobility. Since their areas of departure are 'pathogenic', one of the possible solutions seems to be to go somewhere else. It is as if the climate, or rather the physical environment, is the embodiment of the environment in general; it is seen as negative, with no leisure opportunities, no money, no land, no work, no electricity, no schooling, no training. Insofar as the land and work on the land were seen in the local way of thinking as the source of almost all necessary resources, and basically the embodiment of fertility and life, it is easy to understand that the environment can be taken to symbolise life in general. However, this does not mean that individuals consider themselves to have the (strategic) capability to rehabilitate these environments – by building dams, or planting trees. Young people do not have these skills, nor the intention to use them; once more it was seen 'not to be worth it'. What was worth doing was to get all one could out of all one had, and then move on to something new; new solutions were needed, a new life, and the city was the ideal embodiment of this new life and new opportunities.

Professional mobilities

Professional mobilities reveal the ingenuity of children who move to places where they can acquire new expertise. In this case, the mobility can be explained by the desire to acquire new professional skills. In this ethnographic study, children's mobilities from Oueme to the forge at Dantopka provide a very good illustration. The children are there – under the supervision of a master – to develop skills in handling metals. On leaving, they have acquired not only French language skills (through a training programme initiated by the NGO, Terre des Hommes Benin, and the Salesian sisters), but also practical skills to get on in day-to-day life.

So the forge becomes a professional area enabling the child to become more autonomous. The child is confronted with new types of everyday relationships, and moves among other people and other languages; to use the frequently-heard expression, 'they learn to understand the world'. The forge does not work according to the model of social reproduction systems (castes and order). While in normal West African life, blacksmithing skills are passed down through the family, in that blacksmiths are a caste, the children working at the forge follow other routes to professional development.

Mobilities towards hubs in the informal economy

One of the categories of mobility brings together many experiences to do with a series of activities which require little in the way of skills, and which develop few skills. This is mobility towards centres of activity in the informal economy. The positions occupied by children and young people are always menial, with unskilled migrants being at the bottom of the ladder, and thus in a situation of considerable vulnerability. Once again the informal nature of the structure governing the exchange of services makes the weakest extremely vulnerable. Naturally, in this case as in others, the main motivation for the migrants – their declared motivation at least – is the acquisition of cash or clothes, a bicycle, or sheet metal.

Here, however, as in the case of agricultural mobilities, young people and children aspire – and some manage – to change their status, their position, from porter to trader, from street vendor to intermediary supplier, from quarryman to intermediary or supplier of cheap, docile labour. The responses and actions of these mobile children and young people are tactical; they hope to progress through the hierarchy of these informal activities, thus reproducing these same systems which generate exploitation. To question these constraining frameworks, to achieve protection and regulation of activities, is beyond the power of the migrants. Faced by the impossibility of putting things right for children, the only solution available to them is to join forces, organise themselves and present their demands. The environment which has produced these situations, namely an economy which cannot feed its population, is barely considered by the NGOs, so it is hardly surprising to find these young people preoccupied by survival, focusing simply on their work. This situation makes it easier to understand the frequent comments about the 'need for endurance', and a 'capacity for suffering'. Added to this, the advancement process reproduces the ideology of seniority, where social age dictates ones social position. You are always someone else's 'junior'. In these mobilities towards economic hubs, two different sub-categories can be identified.

First there are the merchant mobilities towards the markets of Adawlato (known as the Great Market) and Abattoir. These markets play an essential role in merchant exchanges as a result of their geographically central position. In fact they are situated – in West Africa – between Benin, Nigeria and Ivory Coast. Children fulfil several economic functions there, such as working as porters which is 'a service provided solely by women within this market and which consists of carrying baggage for a third party (customers...) on their heads, with a view to receiving payment' (Aniambossou 2008). We can observe that these girl porters depend on the rotating (weekly) pattern of these markets to offer their services. Market areas thus become spaces for economic opportunities, bringing girls flocking to earn a living. These girls are an integral part of the backdrop to the transactions, where they seem to play an indispensable role. These children (boys and girls) come to us from different places, which bears witness to the vigour of this kind of trade.

As ethnographer Maruis (2008) noted in one of his conclusions, the majority of the interviewed porter girls gave economic reasons to explain their movement to Lome; among these are children aged under 12, and the average family size is in the range of six to ten people. It is also interesting to see that the girls have experienced one or two moves within the Vo prefecture, and similarly abroad, particularly to Cotonou and Nigeria. It is easy to see the socialisation mechanisms which have developed, particularly in the way that the older girls take care of them. Finally, in terms of social reproduction, it can be seen that porter girls try to reproduce this commercial system. They wish to (re-)establish themselves as traders, which is evidence of the economic advantage they will draw from being players in the economy.

A second sub-category of mobility involves mobilities towards the quarries in Abeokuta, Nigeria. Like the porter girls and child traders in the markets, children migrate to the quarries in Abeokuta looking for economic opportunities. This form of mobility is ancient and seems to run through the whole history of labour relations between Nigeria and Benin. For more than half a century, children have been setting out from Benin, particularly from the Zou region (Zakpota, Bohion, Djidja, Zogbodomey, Abomey) to go and 'seek their fortune in the quarries of Nigeria'. These journeys have become rites of passage for children, and the smallest details about them are well-known. These mobilities are often supervised under institutional arrangements which have been put in place in Nigeria, such as the notable intervention by Terre des Hommes with its repatriation programme, or the existence of associations for Benin nationals in Nigeria to defend workers' interests.

Mobilities towards these quarries often offer them unquestionable economic opportunities. In fact, these children can earn between 75,000 and 150,000 CFA francs in two years (Feneyrol 2005), or even more than that. In addition to these contractual earnings, it should also be noted that the children are offered opportunities to work for themselves every Saturday. The striking aspect of the quarries is the length of time spent there, which may be more than ten years. Durability is the key to earning substantial sums of money. This is accepted by the children as part and parcel of the system and of their strategies for the accumulation of wealth.

Unlike the forge, the quarries are not necessarily places where specific labour skills can be acquired. Certainly, children learn how to extract sand and stone and to dig trenches. However, this activity cannot of itself be considered a long-term training strategy. When the children leave the quarries, they do not go on to reproduce this model, and tend to throw themselves into other commercial activities instead.

Traditional mobilities

These forms can be seen among certain ethnic groups which have accumulated experience of mobility over the centuries. One example of this form of mobility has been given to us by the Ouatchi. These people belong to the Adja-Ewe ethnic group located in the maritime and Plateau regions. In addition to the Ouatchi, this ethnic group also includes the Mina, Gains, Ana, Ife, Akpossou and Akebou. They are acknowledged as great travellers from time immemorial.

CAUSES AND DECISION-MAKING PROCESS

The causes behind child mobilities are manifold. The ethnographic data which have been collected enable them to be classified into different categories.

1. Looking after their families: As is shown by the ethnographic data (Bonnet 2008; Aniambossou 2008; Rolande 2008), migrant children can find themselves in a variety of family situations: with parents who are poor, ill, separated or divorced; or from single-parent families. Against such a family background, the basic cause of mobility can be found in the desire to look after their families. It is striking to note the force of this social argument, which thus offers evidence of psychological precociousness and an understanding of the social stakes [in families] among the children. This category is certainly linked functionally to mobilities towards economic hubs which can be observed among porter girls, and itinerant or premises-based vendors in Benin and Togo. So it is an issue of helping the family to cope with the burden of financial difficulties and the need to acquire goods, which requires cash.

2. Acquisition of education: Confiage (entrustment) can be used a strategy to deal with the education of children, and it can be a cause of mobility. Education is often very expensive, but this does not always discourage parents from trying to place their children in school. One of the ways in which they get around the problem is to entrust their children to relatives who live in town, which results in their mobility. This is an ancient mechanism for transferring parental responsibility. Once again, in this operation, the mobile child finds himself or herself in a subordinate position in the host family.

3. Discovery of other places: This breaks down the preeminence of economic causes, which seem to dominate the processes behind mobility. This hypothesis has already been outlined

by the Fall and Massart team (2007). The 'other place' is seen by children as somewhere to be conquered. The 'other place' awaiting discovery increases in value as the place of origin, the 'here', is devalued. This comes from children's need for a diversification of their daily experiences, but also from concepts of place and the future; going beyond and discovering outside of one's own limits and village boundaries. This attraction to the 'other place' fascinates children, and sets them on a perpetual movement of discovery.

4. Escaping family tension: The ethnographic data allow us to advance the hypothesis that children's interest in mobility grows in proportion to the degree of social tension within the family structure. As matrimonial conflicts increase – particularly between spouses – so the child feels a more pressing need to engage in mobility or else be exposed to them.

5. Acquisition of professional skills: Under the combined effect of decisions taken by both children and their families, an apprenticeship plan is often worked out. It is absolutely essential for the child to learn a trade, particularly if he or she is outside the reach of formal education. These are the children whom we find, for example, at the Dantokpa forge in Benin.

6. Imitating figures of social success: What do the mobile children bring to their villages? How are they perceived by the immobile children? One of the causes of mobility lies in the tendency to imitate figures of social success within communities. These figures are expressed through the material benefits and ostentation 'offered' to children. These imitation processes are strengthened further if they receive the community's blessing. Immobile children thus become or feel socially inadequate. The figures of social success thus seem to take advantage of this psychological ambivalence which throws immobile children into a two-fold movement of envy and shame.

7. Lack of institutional protection policy: One reason mentioned by the children is to do with the institutional limits on intervention by state structures, from support to devel-

opment. Children have a clear perception of these limits and talk of them as part of the justification of their mobilities.

8. Repressive nature of social spaces: Ethnographic data show that adults do no not allow children space, especially when it comes to their personal development. This certainly results in the nature of the gerontocratic social interactions which govern their relationships. The children thus perceive themselves to be in a place of repression, and seem obliged to fight to get out.

9. Escaping traditional rituals: In the south-east of Togo, traditions continue to carry much weight and children are subjected to ritual and initiatory processes from an early age, being sent to convent schools. To deal with this, children decide to become mobile. In fact, these rituals are expensive and are absolutely necessary to the process of developing the child's mystical and physical personality if they want to integrate into their home environment. Their departure may deprive them of this phase; however, it must be remembered how far mobility is experienced as an initiation, and finally how much this alternative, when combined with non-conformity with local rites, tends to make the place of origin a social dead end for young people, a non-place which they leave.

RESOURCES MOBILISED AND IMPACTS

Accumulation of economic and financial assets

Along the routes of their mobility, children accumulate different kinds of knowledge and skills, for both the workplace and society. Without wishing to engage too far in economism, one could assert, in view of the ethnographic data collected, that the children are accumulating and creating wealth.

This creation and accumulation of wealth can be observed in various series of economic activities within the quarries of Abeokuta, the daily and weekly markets, and the cotton plantations. The resources mobilised are often small in quantity; precarious savings which build up over time, allowing the purchase of a bicycle or clothes, or a contribution to family expenditure.

The data show how girls, by means of their investment in mobility, acquire skills and know-how. Hence, it is possible to observe the progressive acquisition of commercial know-how among the girls who set to work in the markets of Lome and Cotonou. In time, some of them become traders. This is their sole dream, within a context which is dominated by the Nanas Benz, who are the embodiment of social success. This configuration is valid for both premises-based and itinerant children.

Children are confronted by a variety of players driven by differing motivations. This forges their character and develops their relational fibre. At the heart of the mobilities, children manage to build up social capital, as the key to their success. This capital has its roots in many places. It cuts across the children's economic, social, psychological and geographical conditions. Likewise, it is striking how children develop their language capabilities. This proceeds from a desire to be able to communicate with clients. Therefore, they become multi-lingual because of the cultural mixing in which they are centrally involved.

It is striking to note the pendulum movement between the children's forms of skills and knowledge acquisition and their (re-) investment strategies. The children and young people are developing and need to increase their capabilities in finance management. These capabilities take a number of forms, such as: development of savings and financial strategies; early payment towards a bride's trousseau, preparing for marriage; registration for voluntary literacy classes (e.g. Terre des Hommes, Dantokpa market); self-financing of training; and sustaining economic activities by means of savings mechanisms.

Perceptions of the exploitation of children in a state of mobility

Having heard from hundreds of children and young people who have been questioned using different tools, in different geographical areas, and living under different working conditions, we have been struck by this thought: children who have engaged in mobility seem to accept their fate with great dignity and little complaint, even if the suffering they have experienced is known (Behrendt and Mbaye 2008). This state of suffering or of disenchantment, of loss of perspective, is a characteristic of the context in which they live their lives; at least, by moving, they gain a more positive perception of themselves. From the Dantopka forge to the quarries in Abeokuta, via the markets of Lome and Benin, along with other mobility experiences, children seem to bear witness to a conscious and accepted satisfaction with their mobility.

There is no shortage of examples, and these seem to illustrate the fact that these mobility processes are etched into their thought world, and sufferings – be they supposed or real, actual or potential – proceed more from our personal view than their work conditions. What is the explanation for this discrepancy in perceptions? The literature is teeming with negativistic views of child mobility, which are certainly inspired by the categories we use in our evaluations for child protection purposes. However, how often do we take their own points of view into account? Do we know what their own references are with which they value their own position? These are some of the thorny questions which come into play when looking at the complexity of mobility processes. An ideological and political re-evaluation is necessary to get beyond the common opinions which structure the views taken by development agencies.

Indeed, how can the processes of suffering be detached from children's socio-cultural conditions without ending up with a distortion of our knowledge? How can we – in the name of this particularist 'universalism' – not allow children to move and work if we have no answer to their primary living conditions that they left behind? It is certainly here that we need to identify the failings in child protection strategies as implemented by us.

CONCLUSIONS

Three months of ethnographic work in Togo, Benin, Ghana and Nigeria have enabled us to consolidate our hypotheses and political vision regarding the mobility of children and young people in West Africa. A number of key elements merit further organised study.

Child mobilities are complex and cannot simply be reduced to economic push factors. It can be seen that children's mobility practices bear witness to a huge desire to take their future in their own hands. Social pressure and the local ideology of the ideal person combine to encourage the mobility which demonstrates a certain effectiveness, as much at the community level as at the family and individual level. Moreover, the resources which are acquired are nearly always shared between the individual and their family, but also with the rest of the community, which might receive part of them. In addition to this economic motivation, there are a number of factors which contribute to the mobility of children and young people, such as the quest for knowledge, and individualisation strategies through seeking out new horizons. It is striking to see how far these reasons for mobility become interwoven. Factors which explain mobility are not mutually exclusive.

The mobilities seen can astonish one by their extent and diversity. It is known that, historically speaking, these practices have been a reality, so they are therefore present in most local consciousness. Furthermore, West Africa offers huge possibilities to children. One other notable feature connected with the conditions of globalisation, poverty, lack of utopia, individualisation and the consequent breaking-down of the basic institutions of social cohesion (the family, community, school etc.), is the early age at which children embark on their mobility. Moreover, the mobilities observed are just as likely to be national as international. They form part of the region's history.

The historical permanence of mobility and particularly that of children and young people lies at the heart of West African farm production; they are effectively part of the construction of new cultural models (language, clothing, values, relationships, figures of social success).

In fact, mobility is an extremely effective practice for staking their claim to – and therefore assuming a place in – the modern world, for children who have few cultural mediators capable of helping them with this understanding. Certainly, as far as power struggles are concerned, children occupy the menial positions, which are often positions of vulnerability. This is because the processes for the social promotion or integration of mobile children are based on suffering and seniority. However, they are compensated by the social capital they acquire. The economic capital they store up is derisory and almost symbolic, but it plays a part in their survival tactics.

Moreover, a huge gap can be seen between the children's generally positive experiences of mobility and the stigmatisation of these phenomena (particularist universalists) which for many still come down to the notion of slavery. Hence the pressing need to establish a real dialogue between the two visions.

In this ethnographic study, we consider that most mobility behaviours observed are tactical in nature, contrary to other contexts, where people in mobility are organised, stand up for their rights and find them guaranteed by the legal contexts in which they find themselves. Given the children's early entry into mobility, the gerontocratic thread which runs through West African societies, and the ineffective nature of legal structures, mobile children lack the capacity to develop real strategies.

From our point of view, the mobility of children is a phenomenon which deserves to be documented and supervised according to procedures and mechanisms which take their views into account. This is the central message of this exploratory research which deserves to be continued in greater detail.

References

Aniambossou, S. (2008) 'Etude ethnographique des mobilités des enfants et des jeunes en Afrique de l'Ouest. Axes Bénin-Togo-Ghana-Nigeria', Rapport de terrain Bénin et Togo Plan WARO-Tdh.

Behrendt, A. and S. M. Mbaye (2008) 'L'impact psychosocial de la traite sur les enfants dans la région des plateaux et la région Centrale au Togo', Dakar, Sénégal: Plan West Africa Regional Office, AWARE-HIV/AIDS, Family Health International & USAIDS.

Bonnet C. (2008) 'Etude ethnographique des mobilités des enfants et des jeunes en Afriques de l'Ouest. Axes Benin-Togo-Ghana-Nigeria', Rapport de terrain Togo-Benin, Ghana- Nigeria Plan WARO-TDH.

Chronique du CEPED (1998) 'L'immigration ouest africaine en Europe : une dimension politique sans rapport avec son importance démographique', Juillet-Septembre, n° 30.

Dénommée, J. (2007) 'Manuel de systématisation des outils', Plan WARO, Dakar Sénégal.

Fall A. S. and G. Massart (2007) 'Intervention Through Active Listening: Tracing the Lives of West African People', Plan WARO – IFAN, Dakar, Senegal, www.reactions-africa.org.

Feneyrol O. (2005) 'Les petites mains des carrières de pierre. Enquête sur un trafic d'enfants entre le Bénin et le Nigeria', Terres des Hommes.

Imorou Abou Bakari (2008) 'Le coton et la mobilité : les implications d'une culture de rente sur les trajectoires sociales des jeunes et enfants au Nord-Bénin', Plan WARO-Plan UK-Tdh-LASDEL, Dakar, Sénégal.

Maruis, R. (2008) 'Etude ethnographique des mobilités des enfants et des jeunes en Afriques de l'Ouest. Axes Benin-Togo-Ghana-Nigeria', Rapport de terrain Togo, Plan WARO-TDH.

Rolande, D. (2008) 'Etude ethnographique des mobilités des enfants et des jeunes en Afrique de l'Ouest. Axes Bénin-Togo-Ghana-Nigeria', Rapport de terrain Plan WARO-Tdh.

Sabates-Wheeler, R., R. Sabates and A. Castaldo (2005) 'Tackling Poverty-Migration Linkages: Evidence from Ghana and Egypt', DRC working Paper, www.migrationdrc.org/publications/working_papers/WP-T14.pdf .

Notes on Contributors

Mohamed Aderghal is Professor of Higher Education at the Université Mohammed V-Agdal in Rabat. He is a member of the Center for Geographical Studies and Research (CERGEO) and the International Joint Laboratory 'MediTer' (Mediterranean Territories: Environment, Territory and Development at the Institut de recherche pour le développement, France / Université Mohammed V-Agdal). He is also a member of the UNESCO Chair of 'Environmental Management and Sustainable Development'. His scientific interests revolve around the socio-economic changes at the root of territorial dynamics of change. His activities also focus on the study of international migration to and from Morocco.

Lahoucine Amzil is at the Université Mohammed V-Agdal in Rabat. His PhD research focused on the recent transformations in the traditional socio-economic system of the West High Atlas. He was the recipient of a fellowship at the Albert Ludwigs University in Freiburg (Germany) and of a MacArthur fellowship at the International Migration Institute, University of Oxford. Amzil's current research interests focus on migratory processes and rural tourism development, and he also participates in two migration research projects: 'Les migrations des marocains en Andalousie' and 'Nouvelle mobilité autour de la ville de Fès'.

Mohamed Berriane is a Senior Professor at the University Mohammed V - Agdal in Rabat, Director of the Centre for Geographical Research and Study, and Co-Director of the 'Laboratoire Mixte International MediTer' (IRD - France). His research interests include local and regional development issues, and the impact of Moroccans' international emigration on their regions of origin. He has published several articles and books on Moroccan and North-African migration and he has co-edited the *Atlas de la inmigración marroquí en España.* He is a member of the Hassan II Academy of Sciences and Techniques, and a Research Associate at the International Migration Institute, University of Oxford.

Julien Brachet is a researcher at the *Institut de Recherche pour le Développement* (UMR D&S, IRD - Université Paris 1 Panthéon-Sorbonne), and was Visiting Research Fellow at the International Migration Institute (University of Oxford) in 2010. His research investigates patterns of mobility to and through the Central Sahara, in particular in Niger and Chad, where he studies migration networks, transport systems and trade between sub-Saharan and northern Africa.

Stephen Castles is Research Professor of Sociology at the University of Sydney and Honorary Associate of the International Migration Institute at the University of Oxford. He works on international migration dynamics, global governance and migration and development. His recent books include: *The Age of Migration: International Population Movements in the Modern World* (Fourth Edition, with Mark Miller, 2009); and *Migration and Development: Perspectives from the South* (edited with Raúl Delgado Wise, 2008).

Hein de Haas is Co-Director of the International Migration Institute at the University of Oxford. His research focuses on the linkages between migration and broader processes of human development and globalisation, primarily from the perspective of migrant-sending societies. He did extensive fieldwork in the Middle East and North Africa and, particularly, Morocco. He has published on a wide range of issues including migration theory, migration and development, remittances and transnationalism, integration, migration determinants, migration futures and the links between migration and environmental change.

Isaïe Dougnon is Professor of Anthropology at the University of Bamako, Mali, Department of Social Sciences. From 1998 to 2003, Dougnon worked on labour migration from Dogon country to the

Office du Niger (Mali) and to Ghana, about which he published his book *Travail de Blanc, travail de Noir: La migration des paysans dogons vers l'Office du Niger et au Ghana (1910–1980)* (Paris: Khartala, 2007) and several articles. In 2009, he co-edited, with Christophe Daum, *Hommes et Migrations* No. 1279 (May–June 2009), 'L'Afrique en mouvement: un autre regard'. His current research focuses on life cycle, careers and rites, and modern work in Malian society.

Agbada Mangalu Mobhe has a PhD in Demography from the Université Catholique de Louvain (Belgium). He is currently Professor of demography, quantitative methods in social sciences and statistic at the Department of Population Sciences and Development at the University of Kinshasa (Democratic Republic of Congo). His research mainly concerns international migration, remittances and the dynamics between migration and development.

Abdou Ndao is a socio-anthropologist. He works as researcher in several international research and development organisations: UNDP; UNESCO; the Council for the Development of Social Science Research in Africa (CODESRIA); Plan International; the Organization for Economic Cooperation and Development (OECD)/Sahel West African Club; and l'Institut Fondamental d'Afrique Noire at Cheikh Anta Diop University in Dakar. He is currently a lecturer in the Health Reproductive Research Institute at Cheikh Anta Diop University. He specialises in migration issues and qualitative research analysis software.

Tara Polzer Ngwato is a Senior Researcher with the African Centre for Migration & Society at the University of the Witwatersrand in South Africa. She has been conducting research and advocating on migrant and refugee rights in South Africa since 2002. Most recently, she has focused on responses to migration from Zimbabwe, the nature of social cohesion in diverse and mobile urban communities, and early warning indicators for xenophobic violence. Polzer Ngwato holds degrees from Cambridge University and the London School of Economics and Political Science in the UK.

Una Okonkwo Osili is Director of Research at the Center on Philanthropy at Indiana University, a leading academic center dedicated to increasing the understanding of philanthropy and improving its practice worldwide. An internationally recognized expert on philanthropy, Dr Osili frequently speaks across the country on issues related to national and international trends in philanthropy and has been quoted by national news media outlets such as *The New York Times*, the *Chronicle on Philanthropy* and *Nonprofit Times*. She has served as a member of several national and international advisory groups, including the Social Science Research Council, the United Nations Economic Commission for Africa and the United Nations Development Program. In 2006, she received the Stevenson Fellowship from the Nonprofit Academic Centers Council. In 2007, she was appointed as a fellow of the Networks Financial Institute.

Darshan Vigneswaran is a Research Fellow at the Max Planck Institute for the Study of Religious and Ethnic Diversity where he coordinates the Global Cities/ Open Cities project on segregation in the Global South and an international working group on Public Space and Diversity. He is a Senior Researcher at the African Centre for Migration and Society at the University of the Witwatersrand, where he co-coordinates International Policing, Mobility and Crime in South Africa, a two-year initiative funded by the Open Society Foundation. In 2008 he was a British Academy Fellow at the International Migration Institute, University of Oxford. Since completing his doctoral studies at Monash University, Melbourne in 2006, he has authored *Territory, Migration and the Origins of the International System* (2012) and co-edited *Slavery, Migration and Contemporary Bondage in Africa* (2012). Darshan has provided expert consultation for INTERPOL, the EU, UNHCR, Amnesty International and Human Rights Watch and comment for Reuters, the BBC, Al Jazeera, and the New York Times.

Index